D0140799

CASES IN COST MANAGEMENT:

A Strategic Emphasis

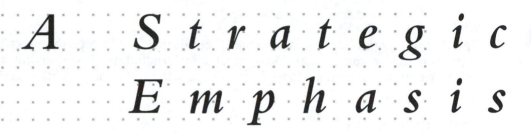

JOHN K. SHANK

The Amos Tuck School of Business
Dartmouth College

SOUTH-WESTERN College Publishing

An International Thomson Publishing Company

Sponsoring Editor: Elizabeth A. Bowers
Production Editor: Peggy A. Williams
Cover Designer: Paul Neff Design
Marketing Manager: Sharon C. Oblinger

Copyright © 1996
by South-Western College Publishing
Cincinnati, Ohio

ALL RIGHTS RESERVED
The text of this publication, or any part thereof, may not be reproduced or transmitted in any form or by any means, electronic or mechanical, including photocopying, recording, storage in an information retrieval system, or otherwise, without the prior written permission of the publisher.

ISBN: 0-538-86045-6

5 6 7 8 9 BN 3 2 1 0 9 8

Printed in the United States of America

I Ⓣ P
International Thomson Publishing
South-Western College Publishing is an ITP Company. The ITP trademark is used under license.

Preface

This set of cases is offered for those instructors who want to augment their managerial accounting courses with a few, several, or many richer, longer "fun" problems. To me, each case is really just a tough, fun, managerial accounting "problem" with specific attention to the business context. Each case includes specific numerical questions to challenge and help develop the students' calculational skill with managerial accounting techniques. Each case also includes broader discussion questions to sharpen the controversial aspects of the calculations and emphasize the managerial issues behind the numbers.

Every one of the cases has been used many times in my courses. Many of the cases have also been used at numerous other schools. The versions presented here have been revised and sharpened based on classroom feedback over the years. Each case in this collection stands the test of time as an excellent classroom vehicle. I hope you will find them as fun to teach as I have.

The book also includes three supplementary readings which I have found to be very useful over the years for use with three particular topics as shown in the Table of Contents.

To make it easier to coordinate the cases with textbook materials, I have cross-referenced the cases with seven leading management accounting texts. This cross-reference appears on the inside of the front cover. While there is certainly some subjectivity in choosing which cases go best with each chapter of the various books, this cross-reference is a starting point for the instructor to decide which cases to use with each topic area.

I have also included recommendations on cases which may satisfy instructor needs for different course structures. These recommendations appear in Exhibit A. This book is intended primarily for use with graduate level courses in managerial accounting. Most of the cases can also be used very successfully in undergraduate courses.

This book can also be used as the basis for an advanced MBA level course in Strategic Cost Management. I teach such a course at the Amos Tuck School. For such a course, I would recommend combining cases with the book, <u>Strategic Cost Management</u> (Shank & Govindarajan, 1993). The cross-reference on the inside front cover identifies the cases which coordinate well with various chapters of that book.

Accompanying this book is an instructor's manual which contains comprehensive teaching commentaries for each of the cases. The manual also includes the course outlines for two MBA courses at the Amos Tuck School (Introduction to Managerial Accounting and Strategic Cost Management) which are based on cases drawn from this collection.

I want to thank my secretary, Susan Schwarz, for her countless hours of work with these cases. Each of the cases has gone through many revisions and edits and has been carefully formatted for electronic access. Also, this book is being assembled electronically for direct transfer to film for the printer, so she has also done all the page formatting and art work. For all practical purposes, she should be the lead author at this point.

John K. Shank
June 26, 1995

EXHIBIT A
Suggested Selections from the Collection

1. **4 cases**   (a small sampling to add a different dimension to a text and problems course)
   4, 5, 7, 22

2. **8 cases**   (a bigger sampling, but still just a sampling)
   4, 5, 7, 9, 15, 22, 23, 27

3. **10 cases**   (1 per week for a trimester term)
   2, 4, 5, 7, 9, 14, 15, 22, 23, 27

4. **15 cases**   (1 per week for a semester)
   2, 4, 5, 7, 9, 14, 15, 19, 22, 23, 26, 27, 28, 30, 32

5. **20 cases**   (a 2 meetings per week trimester course)
   2, 4, 5, 7, 8, 9, 10, 14, 15, 19, 22, 23, 24, 26, 27, 28, 30, 32, 34, 35

6. **30 cases**   (a 2 meetings per week semester course)
   1, 2, 3, 4, 5, 6, 7, 8, 9, 10, 12, 14, 15, 17, 18, 19, 20, 21, 22, 23, 24, 26, 27, 28, 30, 31, 32, 33, 34, 35

Cases in Cost Management: A Strategic Emphasis

TABLE OF CONTENTS

Ajax Petroleum*

This case is set in a small oil refinery owned by a large integrated oil company. The time is 1980 when the "best thinking" in the industry was that oil prices would be well over $50 a barrel by 1990.

Bill MacGregor was still puzzled as he thought about the financial report lying on his desk (see Exhibit 1). The report summarized the key financial statistics for a capital expenditure project which one of MacGregor's subordinates was recommending. MacGregor was the general manager for Ajax Petroleum's Middletown, Ohio, refinery. Although he was a chemical engineer by training, his policy was to rely on the people reporting to him for recommendations about the technical side of the business. He strongly objected to second-guessing his managers on things for which they were responsible.

John Patterson, general superintendent for the catalytic cracking unit ("cat cracker") was pushing strongly for MacGregor's approval of a proposal to install a solvent-decarbonizing unit (SDU) in the refinery at a cost of roughly $30,000,000. The function of an SDU is to clean and purify residual oil so that it can serve as raw material ("feedstock") for the cat cracker. The cat cracker would then convert this feedstock into gasoline. Exhibit 2 is a schematic to help you visualize what goes on in the refinery. "Residual," or "No. 6," oil is one of the outputs when crude oil is refined. However, it represents, literally, what is left after the desirable end products are extracted from the barrel of crude. As the dregs, "resid" is dirty, smelly, and so viscous that it will not even flow at room temperature. It was considered in Ajax to be more a nuisance than anything else. However, there is an established nationwide market for resid, at a low enough price, with uses ranging from heating apartment buildings to generating electricity to asphalt manufacture for highways.

John Patterson was convinced that converting resid into more gasoline was a great idea, particularly since gasoline prices at the refinery were stable at $39.00/bbl. while resid prices were very volatile, having been as low as $18/bbl. in recent weeks. There was sufficient excess capacity at the cat cracker to process the extra feedstock, and no alternative external source of additional feedstock was available.

MacGregor had been intrigued by Patterson's idea because he was no great fan of No. 6 oil either. Because of wide seasonal swings in demand and supply and a relatively thin market, residual prices were notoriously volatile and unpredictable. MacGregor knew that the current price was about $25/bbl., but it had been as low as $18/bbl. and as high as $35/bbl. in recent months. Patterson had also told MacGregor that many of Ajax's competitors already had SDUs in their refineries and that there was always a waiting list for installation of an SDU, so they must be a good investment. MacGregor wasn't particularly impressed by these arguments, however, because he knew that the major oil companies often differed on strategic issues. Just because Ashland and Marathon were de-emphasizing heavy oil (No. 6) to yield more light oil (gasoline) from the barrel of crude did not

* This case was prepared by Professor John K. Shank with the cooperation of a major oil company. All data in the case are generally realistic as of April, 1980, but proprietary information has been disguised.

mean Ajax should automatically follow along. In fact, this might make the heavy-oil business a lot better for the remaining suppliers. MacGregor had heard that Exxon, for one, still considered heavy oil to be a viable item in the product line. Also, MacGregor knew that Ajax's marketing department might not agree with de-emphasizing resid, since there were residual oil sales managers in each sales district and many long-standing customer relationships involved, including many electric utilities in the politically sensitive northeast. MacGregor did know, however, that the additional gasoline could easily be sold now in the wholesale market. Long-run prospects for gasoline demand were less certain.

MacGregor had told Patterson that the key in selling the SDU idea would be return on investment. He told Patterson to work with the economic analysis department to pull together the numbers for the SDU proposal. If it was such a good idea, the numbers would show it and MacGregor would then recommend the project to the corporate capital expenditures committee. The corporate "hurdle rate" for new investment proposals was currently 20%, after taxes. Patterson had eagerly accepted this idea, noting that an acquaintance of his at Ashland Oil had called the SDU in his refinery one of the more profitable investments he had seen in 20 years in the business. When MacGregor received the financial summary report, he was puzzled because the numbers for the SDU project just didn't look that good.

When MacGregor showed the report to Patterson, the latter accused the "bean counters" of trying to scuttle the project with "funny numbers." He took exception to two items in the report, the cost of $29.00/bbl. for fuel gas and the cost of $32.30/bbl for residual oil. He said that fuel gas was really free because there wasn't anything else to do with it except use it as fuel. He argued that since the refinery gets it automatically when a barrel of crude is processed and it has no sales value, it should be considered as free. In fact, he said, fuel gas should show a negative cost since it costs money for equipment to flare it off if it isn't used. He should be encouraged to use it up, he said, to save this cost and to save the hassle with EPA about the air pollution when fuel gas is flared. He was even more unhappy with the reported cost of $32.30/bbl. for resid. He said it was absolutely crazy to show resid at a higher cost than crude itself when, in fact, resid is what's left after you take all the desired products out of the crude. Why should resid show a higher value than raw crude when it was dramatically less desirable to customers? Raw crude itself, although dangerous to handle because of static electricity buildup, is a substitute product for resid in nearly all applications. Patterson had said that he had

never been much interested in cost calculations because he figured that the accountants were accurate, but if this report was an example of how they think, Ajax was in trouble. MacGregor had agreed that Patterson's points seemed to make sense.

MacGregor had subsequently called in Ben Anderson to discuss Patterson's objections to the cost calculations in Anderson's report. Anderson had assured MacGregor that he had no desire to scuttle Patterson's idea. In fact, he said, the analysis in the report was slanted in favor of the proposal and he had even felt guilty about leaning over backward to make the project look good. The problem with the report, he said, was that fuel gas shows an actual cost of $29.00 per equivalent barrel under Ajax' cost accounting system and that this is the cost approved by DOE for determining gasoline "ceiling" prices. However, he said, actual historical cost was not relevant for the proposed new capital investment. Anderson noted that about one-half of the refinery's current fuel needs were being met by fuel gas and the other half by residual oil. The SDU project would not increase the amount of fuel gas generated at the crude still, but it would consume as fuel some of the fuel gas already being generated. The net result for the refinery as a whole would be to increase the consumption of resid used as fuel by an amount equal to the fuel needs of the SDU. Since resid carries a cost of $32.30/bbl. in the accounting records, fuel cost for the SDU project should be $32.30. Anderson called this the "opportunity-cost" concept, as opposed to actual historical cost.

Regarding the question of what No. 6 costs, Anderson said he sympathized with Patterson but that the $32.30 was a factual number. In fact, he said, the refinery *does* produce a set of products at the crude still, *including* residual oil, and these products *must each* carry a share of the costs incurred in producing them. A barrel of residual oil thus costs whatever a barrel of crude oil costs, plus some share of the operating costs at the crude still. These crude-still operating costs, he said, could be allocated based on value of products produced, volume of products produced, total energy value (BTUs) of products produced, or some other basis. But under any allocation scheme, outputs from the crude still will cost more than crude oil. Anderson concluded by saying that with fuel gas and resid at $32.30, the SDU actually would be even less profitable than as shown in Exhibit 1 and that the project just couldn't be justified on economic grounds. But, since most companies use historical costs rather than opportunity costs in their accounting systems, he (Anderson) could "bend" as far as the analysis in the report, as an accommodation to Patterson. The meeting had ended with MacGregor agreeing that Anderson's points seemed to make sense.

MacGregor's background included very little training in cost accounting. He had always considered this area to be a technical specialty for which general managers could hire the expertise they needed. He was, however, feeling very frustrated about which cost numbers to believe for the solvent decarbonizing project. He also felt a little foolish for agreeing with both Patterson and Anderson when they talked to him.

He asked his plant controller, Fred Morton, to have lunch with him one day to look at Ben Anderson's report and comment on John Patterson's objections to it. Morton said the basic issue was what cost to show for No. 6 oil in the calculations. He said that Anderson was correctly using the cost numbers generated by Ajax' cost accounting system. Resid was considered to be one of the joint set of products produced in the refinery and, accordingly, was assigned a cost of $32.30/bbl. (as compared to middle distillate at $32.90 and gasoline at $34.80). He agreed that the *particular* allocation scheme (weight, volume, heat value, etc.) was essentially arbitrary, but he emphasized that charging a share of refining cost to resid makes it more costly.

He said that one way to show significantly lower cost on resid would be to consider it a "by-product" rather than a "joint product." A by-product has the following characteristics:

1. It is not desired output from the production process, it just happens to be created in the process of making the desired products.

2. It is low in sales value relative to the main products.

3. It is produced in relatively small quantities.

A clear example of the distinction between a by-product and a joint product is pigs feet versus bacon to a hog butcher. Morton went on to say that normal cost accounting procedure shows a zero cost for by-products. They are just sold for whatever the market will bring, and the sales revenue is netted back against the costs which must be assigned to the desired products. For the refinery, this would mean allocating the sum of crude cost plus crude-still operating costs minus resid sales revenue to gasoline and middle distillate (jet fuel, diesel fuel, and home heating oil), with resid showing a zero cost for accounting purposes. He noted that several of the major oil companies follow this approach, although several others use the same approach as Ajax.

Under the by-product approach, resid would be valued in the capital expenditure analysis at whatever you could sell it for if you didn't convert it to cracking stock or use it as refinery fuel. With gasoline selling for $39/bbl., he thought resid would average around $20 over its price cycles. However, he added that the long-run average price of resid would certainly be heavily influenced by regulatory pressures to stop utilities from burning resid and by trends in gasoline consumption.

The average price by 1985 could be as low as $17/bbl. or as high as $25/bbl., even if crude prices didn't change. Morton said this is what Anderson termed the opportunity-cost approach, as opposed to the historical-cost approach. He concluded by saying that this same idea applies to the fuel gas item—the reported cost incurred is $29/bbl. and the opportunity cost will average around $20/bbl. (the revenue forgone by not selling a barrel of resid).

MacGregor went back to Anderson the next day and asked him to refigure the SDU project showing both the joint product costing and by-product costing approaches for resid and both recorded cost and opportunity cost approaches for fuel gas. Anderson said that would be no problem and agreed to get the information to MacGregor by the next day. MacGregor wondered how much impact these accounting questions would have on the profitability of the SDU project. He couldn't imagine that bookkeeping issues would be that important to the overall analysis. He was anxious to see Anderson's revised report.

ASSIGNMENT QUESTIONS

1. Using the same format as in Exhibit 1, recalculate the economic return for the project, using both joint product costing ($32.30) and by-product costing for resid and using DOE costing ($29.00) and opportunity costing for fuel gas. All the basic data will be the same as in Exhibit 1 except for the cost of fuel gas and resid.

2. What do you believe is the best accounting method for fuel gas and residual oil? Why? Which set of accounting numbers produces the most meaningful economic return calculations?

3. Is the proposed solvent decarbonizing unit profitable enough to justify the investment? Can you calculate a break-even value for resid? So what?

4. As MacGregor, would you recommend the SDU project to headquarters? What economic analysis would you present to support your recommendation? What qualitative (versus quantitative) factors influence your decision?

EXHIBIT 1
Memorandum

March 17, 1980

TO: W. MacGregor
FROM: B. Anderson, Economic Analyst
RE: The Solvent Decarbonizing Unit Proposal

Here is the information you requested concerning the economics of the SDU project. I have the backup file if you want to dig deeper.

1.	Investment cost	$30,000,000	(delivered and installed)
	Less Investment Tax Credit	3,000,000	(10% of cost)
	Net Investment	$27,000,000	
2.	Annual Operating Costs (three-shift basis)	$3,300,000	(Labor, maintenance, insurance, property taxes, supplies)

<u>*Per barrel of Cracking Stock Produced*</u>

3. Fuel $2.90/bbl.   (See Note 1 below)
4. Feedstock Cost $32.30/bbl.   (See Note 2 below)
5. Value of Cracking Stock Produced $37.50/bbl.   (See Note 3 below)
6. Thruput is 9,000 bbls. per day (assuming an average of 90% utilization of theoretical capacity on a 365-day/year basis). One bbl. of resid will produce one bbl. of cracking stock.
7. Economic life is 20 years. (This is also the depreciable life for tax purposes. The current tax rate is 46%.) Use straight-line depreciation for simplicity and to be conservative.
8. Inflation in costs and prices is ignored. This would tend to offset for a project like this one.

> *Project Profitability*
> Payback = 9.10 years
> Net Present Value (at 20% after taxes) = negative $12.6 million
> Economic Rate of Return = 9%
> Profitability Index = .72
> Return on Capital Employed = 19.8%

Note 1   The SDU runs on fuel gas,[a] to which Ajax currently assigns a cost of $29.00 per equivalent bbl. It takes .10 bbl. of fuel gas to produce a barrel of thruput at the SDU. Thus, fuel gas costs $2.90 per barrel of thruput.

Note 2   Feedstock for the SDU is No. 6 oil. The cost of No. 6 is computed by assigning crude oil cost and crude-still operating costs to the set of outputs at the crude still, based on relative production volumes for each product. With crude running $29.00 average for the refinery, this equates currently to about $32.30/bbl. for resid.

Note 3   Gasoline is currently selling for about $39/bbl. at the refinery. The cost is about $1.50/bbl. at the cat cracker to convert feedstock into gasoline. Thus, the net realizable value of thruput at the SDU which feed the cat cracker is $37.50/bbl. ($39 minus $1.50).

[a] "Fuel gas" is generated at the crude still in a gaseous state as one of the products when a barrel of crude is "cracked." It is not feasible to convert the fuel gas into a salable end product, but it can be used as fuel to power the various production units in the refinery. The DOE-approved guidelines (for measuring the allowable cost of gasoline for price control purposes) charge fuel gas for a proportionate share of the average cost of crude oil but not for any portion of the operating costs of the crude still. Currently, about 5% of the equivalent volumetric production at the crude still is fuel gas. With crude cost at $30.45 for the incremental barrel and $29.00 on average, Ajax followed the DOE-approved approach and costed fuel gas at $29.00 per equivalent barrel.

EXHIBIT 2
A SCHEMATIC OF THE REFINERY TO HELP YOU VISUALIZE WHAT THE "SDU" DOES
AJAX PETROLEUM

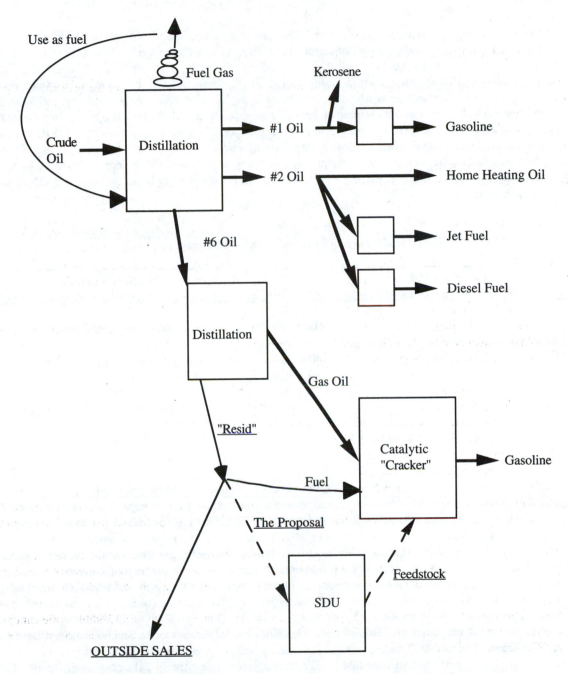

APPENDIX
Some Technical Comments (more than you want to know?) About Oil

Petroleum

    Petroleum is a complex mixture of organic compounds, mainly hydrocarbons, with smaller quantities of other organic compounds containing nitrogen, oxygen, or sulfur. Petroleum is formed over a period of millions of years by the decomposition of marine plants and animals.

    The usual first step in the refining, or processing, of petroleum is separation of the crude oil into fractions on the basis of boiling points. The fractions commonly taken are shown in the table below. The fractions that boil at higher temperatures are made up of molecules with larger numbers of carbon atoms per molecule. The fractions collected in the initial separation may require further processing to yield a usable product. For example, modifications must be made to the straight-run gasoline obtained from fractionation of petroleum to render it suitable for use as a fuel in automobile engines. Similarly, the fuel oil fraction may need additional processing to remove sulfur before it is suitable for use in an electrical power station or a home heating system. At present, the most commercially important single product from petroleum refining is gasoline.

Hydrocarbon Fractions From Petroleum

Fraction	Size Range of Molecules	Boiling-point Range (°C)	Uses
Gas	C_1-C_5	-160 to 30	Gaseous fuel, production of H_2
Straight-run Gasoline	C_5-C_{12}	30 to 200	Motor fuel
Kerosene, Fuel Oil	C_{12}-C_{18}	180 to 400	Diesel fuel, furnace fuel, cracking
Lubricants	C_{16} and up	350 and up	Lubricants
Paraffins	C_{20} and up	Low-melting solids	Candles, matches
Asphalt	C_{36}	Gummy residues	Surfacing roads, fuel

Gasoline

    Gasoline is a mixture of volatile hydrocarbons. Depending on the source of the crude oil, it may contain varying amounts of cyclic alkanes and aromatic hydrocarbons in addition to alkanes. Straight-run gasoline consists mainly of straight-chain hydrocarbons, which in general are not very suitable for use as fuel in an automobile engine. In an automobile engine, a mixture of air and gasoline vapor is ignited by the spark plug at the moment when the gas mixture inside the cylinder has been compressed by the piston. The burning of the gasoline should create a strong, smooth expansion of gas in the cylinder, forcing the piston outward and imparting force along the drive shaft of the engine. If the gas burns too rapidly, the piston receives a single hard slam rather than a strong, smooth push. The result is a "knocking" or pinging sound and the efficiency with which the energy of gasoline combustion is converted to power is reduced.

    Gasolines are rated according to octane number. Gasolines with high octane numbers burn more slowly and smoothly and thus are more effective fuels, especially in engines in which the gas-air mixture is highly compressed. It happens that the more highly branched alkanes have higher octane numbers than the straight-chain compounds. The octane number of gasoline is obtained by comparing its knocking characteristics with those of "isooctane" (2,2,4-trimethylpentane) and heptane. Isooctane is assigned an octane number of 100, whereas heptane is assigned 0. Gasoline with the same knocking characteristics as a mixture of 95 percent isooctane and 5 percent heptane would be rated as 95-octane.

    Because straight-run gasoline contains mostly straight-chain hydrocarbons, it has a low octane number. It is therefore subjected to a process called cracking to convert the straight-chain compounds into more desirable branched-chain molecules. Cracking is also used to convert some of the less volatile kerosene and fuel-oil fractions into compounds with lower molecular weights that are suitable for use as automobile fuel. In the cracking process, the hydrocarbons are mixed with a catalyst and heated to 400-500°C. The catalysts used are naturally occurring clay minerals, or synthetic Al_2O_3-SiO_2 mixtures. In addition to forming molecules more suitable for gasoline, cracking results in the formation of hydrocarbons of lower molecular weight, such as ethylene and propene. These are used in a variety of processes to form plastics and other chemicals.

The octane number of a given blend of hydrocarbons can be improved by adding an antiknock agent, a substance that helps control the burning rate of the gasoline. The most widely used substances for this purpose are tetraethyl lead, $(CH_3CH_2)_4Pb$, and tetramethyl lead, $(CH_3)_4Pb$. The premium gasolines contain 2 or 3 mL of one of these lead compounds per gallon, with a resultant increase of 10 to 15 in octane rating. Although alkyl lead compounds are undoubtedly effective in improving gasoline performance, their use in gasolines has been drastically curtailed because of the environmental hazards associated with lead. This metal is highly toxic, and there is good evidence that the lead released from automobile exhausts is a general health hazard. Although other substances have been tried as antiknock agents in gasolines, none of these has proved to be an effective and inexpensive antiknock agent that is environmentally safe. The 1975 and later model cars are designed to operate with unleaded gasolines. The gasolines blended for these cars are made up of more highly branched components and more aromatic components, because these have relatively high octane ratings.

Allied Stationery Products*

This case is set in the business forms business in 1992 in a company which augments its "commodity" products with value-added distribution and logistics services. The subject is customer profitability analysis using ABC, ABM and SCM.

BACKGROUND

Allied Stationery Products was founded in 1866 in Denver, Colorado as a one-man operation producing note paper and cards for sale in general stores in Denver. By 1992 it had grown to a corporation with annual sales of $900 million.

One division of the company produced specialty paper products, such as writing paper, envelopes, note cards, and greeting cards. Another division manufactured and printed business forms. By 1988, this division was one of the top 6 firms in the U.S. business forms industry.

That year the company expanded into business forms inventory management services. This was an area where Allied believed it could offer value-added management services to differentiate the firm from other business forms manufacturers. The forms manufacturing business was mature by 1988 and all competitors were seeking ways to generate sales growth. Allied embarked on a campaign to enroll its corporate clients in a program which it called "Total Forms Control" (TFC). Allied considered TFC to be a key to future success.

By 1992, sales from TFC were about $60 million and Allied had established a separate company within the business forms division to handle these accounts. The services provided under TFC included warehousing and distribution of forms (including inventory financing) as well as inventory control and forms usage reporting. Allied used a sophisticated computer systems network which enabled them to monitor a client's forms inventory, forms usage, and ordering activities. They provided this information to their clients via comprehensive yet simple to read management reports.

As part of its distribution services, Allied also offered "pick pack" service where trained and experienced workers actually opened full cartons to pick the exact number of forms requested by the clients. Allied's philosophy was that a well run warehousing and distribution network is vital to any forms management program—"we know what you need... the *right* product at the *right* place at the *right* time."

*. This case is adapted by Professor John Shank of the Amos Tuck School, by permission, from earlier versions prepared by Professor Vijay Govindarajan and Jay Weiss (T'93) of the Amos Tuck School, and copyright (1992) by Osceola Institute. This case was made possible with the cooperation of a *Fortune 500* firm. The name of the company and financial data are disguised.

For a small number of clients Allied also offered "desk top delivery," where Allied personnel would distribute the forms to individual offices within the company (forms were usually delivered only to the loading dock). As a comprehensive forms management provider, Allied's product line also had to be comprehensive. Their product line included everything from stock computer printout paper and fax paper to custom designed forms tailored by Allied's team of forms design consultants to meet the exact business needs of the client.

Allied also had the ability to custom design its forms management services to meet the needs of each of its clients. Allied clients ranged from small businesses which desired only basic inventory control, to those who had comprehensive forms management programs. Pricing was handled individually for each account based on what the sales department thought it could charge.

CURRENT COST ACCOUNTING SYSTEM

Allied operated its forms manufacturing and TFC activities as separate profit centers. The transfer of product to TFC was at arm's length with the transfer price set at fair market value.

Allied manufactured business forms in 13 locations. Although the company encouraged internal sourcing for customer orders, TFC salespeople had the option of outsourcing product. The sales force then marked up the cost of product and services by 20%, an average.

Clients who participated in the forms management program kept an inventory of forms at one of Allied's 10 distribution centers. The forms were distributed to the client as they were needed. The client was charged a service fee to cover the cost of warehousing and distribution based on a percentage of the cost of sales of the product for that month, regardless of the specific level of service provided to that client. The standard charges were as follows:

- Warehousing/Distribution, 20.5% of product cost
- Inventory financing, 4.7% of product cost
- Freight to the customer, 7% of product cost

If a TFC client made use of any of the distribution services, they were supposed to be charged a price for the forms which was high enough to allow for an additional 20.5% of product cost to cover warehousing and distribution expenses (everything from storage and requisition handling up to and including desk top delivery), plus 4.7% to cover the cost of capital tied up in inventory, and 7% to cover freight expenses. These percentages were determined based on actual 1990 financial data so that on an aggregate basis, in total, all expenses were covered (see Exhibit 1). As shown in Exhibits 5 and 6, prices for individual accounts could vary from the standard formula.

UNDERSTANDING CUSTOMER PROFITABILITY

With TFC profitability suffering in October 1992, General Manager John Malone began to question the appropriateness of the distribution charges.

"The Business Forms Division used to earn a 20% Return on Investment (ROI). But returns have been dropping for several years. TFC is projected to earn an ROI of only 6% for 1992. Something tells me that we are not managing this business very well! It seems to me that the charge for services needs closer scrutiny. I believe the charges should have nothing to do with the cost of the product. We should just charge our clients for the services they use. It doesn't seem fair that if two clients buy the same amount of product from us, but one keeps a lot of inventory at our distribution center and is constantly requesting small shipments and the other hardly bothers us at all, that they should pay the same service fees."

John looked through his records and found two accounts of similar size, accounts A and B, which were handled by different salespeople. Accounts A and B both had annual sales of $79,320 with the cost of the product being $50,000. Under the current system, these accounts carried the same service charges, but John noticed that these accounts were similar only in the value of the product being sold; they were very different on the level of service they required from Allied.

In the past year, customer A had submitted 364 requisitions for product with a total of 910 lines[1] (all of them "pick-pack") while customer B had submitted 790 requisitions with a total of 2500 lines (all "pick-pack"). Customer A kept an average of 350 cartons of inventory at the distribution center while customer B kept 700 on average. Customer B's average monthly inventory balance was $50,000 ($7,000 of which had been sitting around for a whole year) while that of customer A was only $15,000. Because of the greater activity on customer

---

[1]Whenever a customer requires forms, they submit a requisition for all the different products they need. Each separate product request is a "line." If the request is for whole cartons, it is considered a "carton line." For quantities less than a whole carton, it is considered a "pick-pack line."

B's account, a shipment went out three times a week at an annual freight cost of $7,500 while Customer A required only one shipment a week at an annual freight cost of $2,250. In addition, customer B had requested desk top delivery 26 times during the past year, while customer A did not request desk top delivery at all. John Malone double-checked his records and confirmed that the two accounts had indeed generated identical sales revenues (see Exhibit 2).

With corporate breathing down his neck, John Malone turned to TFC Controller Melissa Dunhill and Director of Operations Tim Cunningham for help. As a first step, they were able to provide John with the following information:

The total expenses for the distribution centers in 1992 were estimated as follows ($'000's):

Rent	$1,424
Depreciation	$208
Utilities	$187
Salaried payroll	$745
Fringe benefits-salaried	$164
Telephone	$96
Security	$3
Taxes/Insurance	$104
Travel/Entertainment	$40
Postage	$56
Hourly payroll - admin	$259
Fringes - hourly admin	$57
Temporary help	$17
Variable warehouse payroll	$1,399
Warehouse fringes	$336
Data processing	$612
Total	$5,707

John said, "How am I going to use this information to solve my problem?" "Well," Tim said, "if we can figure out, without going overboard of course, what exactly goes on in the distribution centers, maybe we can take these financial numbers and assign them to the activities. If we can do that, we'll have a much better idea of what it costs to serve our various clients." Tim knew that two primary activities took place in the distribution centers - the warehousing of forms and the distribution of those forms in response to a customer requisition. He decided to talk to some people in the field to get more specific information.

DISTRIBUTION CENTER: ACTIVITY ANALYSIS

John and Tim visited Allied's Kansas City, MO distribution facility. Site manager Wilbur Smith confirmed, "All we do is store the cartons and process the requisitions. I'll tell you, the amount of warehouse space we need just depends on the number of cartons. It seems like we've got a lot of cartons that just sit here forever. If we got into some flexible lease programs and changed aisle configurations, we could probably adjust our space requirements if the number of cartons we stored was to change. The other thing that really bothers me is that we've got some inventory that's been sitting here forever. What's it to the client? They don't pay for it until they requisition it. Isn't there a way we can make them get this stuff out of here?"

"As far as the administration of the operation goes, everything depends on the number of requisitions. And, on a given requisition, the customer can request as many different items as they like."

The team then interviewed warehouse supervisor, Rick Fosmire, "I don't care if I get a hundred requisitions with one line each or one requisition with a hundred lines on it, my guys still have to go pick a hundred items off the shelves. And those damn "pick-pack" requests. Almost everything is "pick-pack" nowadays. No one seems to order a whole carton of 500 items anymore. Do you know how much more labor it requires to pick through those cartons? And on top of that, this desk top delivery is a real pain for my guys. Sure, we offer the service, but you figure the clients who use it should have to pay something extra. It's not like my guys don't have enough to do."

John and Tim were starting to get a pretty good idea of what goes on in the distribution centers, but there was still one person to talk to. They knew that a lot of money was spent on data processing, mostly labor. They needed to know how those people spent their time.

Hazel Nutley had been a data entry operator at Allied for 17 years. "All I do is key in those requisitions, line by line by line. I've gotten to the point where I know the customers so well that all the order information is easy. The only thing that really matters is how many lines I have to enter."

John and Tim returned to Denver with a better idea of what happens in a distribution center. From what they observed, they broke the distribution center down into 6 primary value-added activities—storage, requisition handling, basic warehouse stock selection, "pick-pack" activity, data entry and desk top delivery. With Melissa's help, they assigned costs to these activities as follows ($'000's). (See Exhibit 3 for calculations):

Storage	$1,550
Requisition Handling	$1,801
Basic Warehouse Stock	
Selection	$761
"Pick-Pack" Activity	$734
Data Entry	$612
Desk top delivery	$250
Total	$5,708

Tim then estimated the following for 1992 based upon historical information and current trends:

- On average, the 10 distribution centers scattered across the country, will have combined inventories of approximately 350,000 cartons (most cartons were of fairly standard size).

- TFC will process about 310,000 requisitions for 1992.

- Each requisition will average 2.5 lines.

- About 90% of the lines will require "pick pack" activity (as opposed to shipping an entire carton).

They were still uncomfortable with the way inventory financing and freight were charged out. John checked with the finance department and learned that Allied obtained financing at the prime rate plus 1%. He thought they could just pass that along.

"Wait a second," Melissa said, "you're probably only going to adjust the charges every 6 months or every year. We better protect ourselves in case our rate changes. Why don't we make it prime + 3.5%?"

"Good thinking."

"Our new computer system is coming on line soon which will track individual freight charges," said Tim, "so, we can just charge the client for what it actually costs us." They all agreed that this sounded fair.

Some things that were said at the distribution center still stuck in Tim's mind. "Don't you think we should do something to get that old inventory moving? What about charging something extra, say 1.5% per month, for anything that's been there over 9 months?"

"Great idea," Melissa said, "this will also help protect us against the loss we often take on old inventory when the clients end up changing their forms. You know we just eat that and never charge them for it."

They were almost finished. "What about desk top delivery?" Tim said. "I think we should charge extra for it, but I don't want this to get too complicated."

John said, "How much extra time does it take your guys on average to run around the client company?"

"I'd say about an hour and a half to two hours."

"Alright. At $15 per hour, that's about $30 each time. Sound fair?"

"Sounds OK to me. Also, that ties pretty well to the $250,000 overall assignment, since we will process somewhere around 8,500 'desk top' requests this year."

"Wait just one second," Melissa said, "There's something I don't quite understand. We are able to provide a great deal of information to our clients, but some require only a minimal amount while others want more sophisticated reporting. We haven't discussed differentiating the charges for that at all."

"That's a good point," John replied, "but you know that generating these reports really doesn't cost us very much extra and that we need to offer these services as a marketing tool in order to win clients. Let's say we still provide a monthly inventory status report free of charge, and we charge $15/month for anyone who wants the other more sophisticated reports."

"I guess that makes sense," Melissa said.

The entire management team, including Doug Kingsley, Chief Financial Officer of the Business Forms Division, felt that there had to be a better way of charging out distribution services and that the solution would help TFC become more profitable. They now had a much better understanding of the drivers of costs involved in distribution services. As the four headed off in Doug's Sedan de Ville for the Bronco's first home game, they tried to figure out how to use this information to find a workable alternative.

SERVICES BASED PRICING (SBP)

"It wouldn't be easy getting the sales force on board with an activity-based pricing program," John said. "Some of them get pretty stuck in their ways and don't like change. Some accounts would see increases because of the additional distribution charges under a Services Based Pricing (SBP) scheme. These salespeople wouldn't be very happy. On the other hand, some salespeople may see their margins increase." Overcoming these organizational problems would be only the tip of the iceberg.

Doug Kingsley, as well as many of the senior managers at corporate, continued to be very concerned with TFC profitability. While everyone thought TFC was making great strides in understanding their cost drivers, they were not convinced that overall profitability would improve without significant changes in the marketing strategy. They were still wondering how to use their new activity based costing (ABC) analysis to improve the profitability of TFC. So they decided to do additional analysis on their customer base.

The accounting department had maintained a database which showed all activity against individual accounts and calculated a contribution from that account. However, they had not yet been able to use this information effectively. TFC management took their data and began to analyze it.

Although TFC maintained 1100 separate accounts, a large portion of the business came from very few accounts. The top 40 accounts represented 48% of the company's net sales (see Exhibit 4).

As a way of understanding customer profitability, TFC management reworked the information in the database as if the accounts had been charged service fees based on actual usage, leaving net sales and product cost the same as before. They recalculated contribution based on these figures. They ranked the accounts according to profit contribution. Exhibit 5 shows the top 20 accounts for the month of August and Exhibit 6 shows the bottom 20.

The team looked at all accounts where the revised contribution was below 20% and determined that if all of these accounts were managed to a 20% contribution, the profit improvement would be $4.3 million annually. The top 40 accounts (ranked by the contribution opportunity if improved to a 20% contribution) represented 70% of the $4.3 million opportunity. Another way of summarizing the range of profitability across the 1,100 customers is shown in Exhibit 7. This was a new way of looking at account management which combined the effects of both volume and contribution margin. Since such a large piece of the opportunity rested with these few accounts, management determined that it might be possible to significantly improve profitability by concentrating on individual account management. The team felt they were on the right track for improving account profitability and wondered what should be the next step. The also wondered what other issues might be important for improving the overall profitability of TFC.

Management called the ABC based pricing system SBP and was seriously considering adopting it for all TFC customers.

ASSIGNMENT QUESTIONS

1. Using the information in the text and in Exhibit 3, calculate "ABC" based services costs for the TFC business.

2. Using your new costing system, calculate distribution services costs for "Customer A" and "Customer B."

3. What inference do you draw about the profitability of these two customers?

4. Should TFC implement the SBP pricing system?

5. What managerial advice do you have for Allied about the Total Forms Control (TFC) business?

EXHIBIT 1
Calculation of Service Fee Charges
(Current Method)
('000's)

1990 Product Sales at Cost	$24,059
1990 Warehousing/Distribution Expense	$4,932
...% of Product Cost	20.5%
1990 Average Inventory Balance	$10,873
1990 Average Cost of Capital	10.4%
Total Cost of Inventory Financing	$1,131
...% Product Cost	4.7%
1990 Total Freight Charges	$1,684
...% Product Cost	7.0%

EXHIBIT 2
Actual Service Fee Charges
(Current Method)

	Customer A	Customer B
Product Cost	$50,000	$50,000
Warehousing/Distribution (20.5%)	$10,250	$10,250
Inventory Financing (4.7%)	$2,350	$2,350
Freight Out (7%)	$3,500	$3,500
Total Service Fees	$16,100	$16,100
Mark-up (20%)	$13,220	$13,220
Net Sales	$79,320	$79,320

EXHIBIT 3
Breakdown of Expenses by Activity
('000's)

	Total Expense		Share of Expense *
Rent	$1,424	x 85%	$1,211
Depreciation	$208	x 85%	$177
Utilities	$187	x 85%	$159
Security	$3		$3
Total Storage Expense			**$1,550**
Rent	$1,424	x 15%	$214
Depreciation	$208	x 15%	$31
Utilities	$187	x 15%	$28
Salaries + Fringes	$909		$909
Telephone	$96		$96
Taxes/Insurance	$104		$104
Travel/Entertainment	$40	x 75%	$30
Postage	$56		$56
Hourly Payroll + Fringes	$316		$316
Temp Help	$17		$17
Total Requisition Handling Expense			**$1,801**
Variable Warehouse Pay + Fringes	$1,735		$1,735
Travel & Entertainment (25%)	$40	x 25%	$10
Total Warehouse Activity			$1,745
Basic Warehouse Stock Selection (44%)			**$761**
"Pick-Pack" Activity (42%)			**$734**
Desk Top Delivery (14%)			**$250**
Total Warehouse Activity			$1,745
Data Processing Expense	**$612**		**$612**

*Some expense items were allocated between activities

EXHIBIT 4
TFC Net Sales, 1991

Annual Sales/Account	No. of Accounts	% of TFC Net Sales
>$300,000	40	48%
>$150,000	53	19%
>$75,000	86	15%
>$30,000	143	11%
>$0	778	7%
Total	1100	100%

EXHIBIT 5
Top 20 TFC Accounts for August, 1992
(Ranked by Contribution $)

Account	Actual Net Sales	Product Cost	ABC Based Service Costs	Revised Contribution
1	76,904	49,620	2,862	24,422
2	130,582	74,396	34,578	21,608
3	72,956	48,216	3,456	21,284
4	64,903	37,981	6,574	20,348
5	45,088	26,098	1,309	17,681
6	104,689	62,340	25,356	16,993
7	52,890	32,083	4,386	16,421
8	38,902	23,087	1,245	14,570
9	87,130	54,923	17,685	14,522
10	67,935	42,012	12,290	13,633
11	58,290	32,074	12,834	13,382
12	84,589	54,023	17,528	13,038
13	36,587	22,657	1,345	12,585
14	47,890	32,545	3,657	11,688
15	56,294	27,801	16,923	11,570
16	61,056	38,924	11,034	11,098
17	56,902	32,789	13,904	10,209
18	45,893	29,570	6,904	9,419
19	62,954	41,034	13,746	8,174
20	26,699	16,830	2,236	7,633
Total	1,279,133	779,003	209,852	290,278

EXHIBIT 6
Bottom 20 TFC Accounts for August, 1992
(Ranked by Contribution $)

Account	Actual Net Sales	Product Cost	ABC Based Service Costs	Contribution
1081	3,657	2,356	2,325	-1,024
1082	38,467	26,301	13,740	-1,574
1083	5,926	3,840	4,214	-2,128
1084	163	89	2,390	-2,316
1085	3,256	2,006	3,590	-2,340
1086	82,086	61,224	23,756	-2,894
1087	29,320	20,647	11,843	-3,170
1088	467	302	4,086	-3,921
1089	17,935	11,087	10,872	-4,024
1090	17,649	12,903	8,903	-4,157
1091	638	420	5,109	-4,891
1092	16,104	9,102	12,134	-5,132
1093	289	178	5,698	-5,587
1094	23,965	17,345	16,523	-9,903
1095	38,065	23,391	27,623	-12,949
1096	32,898	23,054	22,985	-13,141
1097	129,367	73,128	69,527	-13,288
1098	74,569	50,745	45,698	-21,874
1099	88,345	64,930	53,867	-30,452
1100	113,976	82,987	72,589	-41,600
Total	717,142	486,035	417,472	-186,365

EXHIBIT 7
Current Operating Profit for 1992

1.   The most profitable 5% of customers (55) contribute 80%.

2.   The next most profitable 45% of customers (145) contribute 220%.

Profit could be 300% of the current level **if we dropped the remaining 50% of customers (550)**!

3.   48% of customers (528) reduce profit by 140%.

4.   2% of customers (22) reduce profit by 60%.

Arctic Insulation*

This case is set in 1980 in a waste paper converting plant in New York City in a company whose business is tied closely to environmental recycling trends. The subject is product costing and cost control.

Arctic Insulation manufactures material used in home insulation. The company mixes scrap paper and fiber to form the insulation material that is bagged, sold and finally blown into home attics. The company has two methods of obtaining scrap paper. They can buy from the public at nominal rates (through paper drives and individual deliveries to the loading dock) or purchase bulk paper from scrap paper dealers. It is cheaper to buy from the public, but additional labor time is involved in removing the paper, in relatively small amounts, from customer cars and trucks at the loading dock and forming the paper into bales. Direct labor is very expensive with rates at $9.50 per hour in 1979. It was estimated that 2 1/2 bales weighing 300 pounds each are formed per hour by each employee, on average. The process of forming bales is very time consuming because paper must be sorted by type (coated, newsprint, or fine paper), and by color (white, colored), must have any metal removed (staples or grommets), and must be cut to standard sizes. Also, after the bale is formed, it is bound with wire in a baling machine so that it can be stored pending further use. On the other hand, scrap paper can be purchased from paper dealers already sorted and cleaned and cut to standard sizes. The purchased paper is more expensive, but much less labor time is involved because the workers are only required to unload the paper from a truck and bale it. It was estimated that 16 "purchased" bales weighing 300 pounds each are handled per hour by each employee, on average.

Prices in the scrap paper industry are very volatile. Supply and demand factors in large industries regularly cause wide fluctuations in the price per pound for scrap paper. Whenever the price in the scrap paper market drops markedly Arctic cuts the price it offers to the public, thereby reducing the amount supplied, and increases the purchase of bulk paper from dealers. Aggressive scrap paper companies utilize these swings in market price to stock up during price declines for sales in future periods.

Arctic Insulation operates 22 collection and baling depots throughout the New York metropolitan area. These depots feed raw materials into 4 shredding and bagging plants. Arctic is one of two divisions of Recycling Specialists, Inc.; the other division is Scrap Iron and Metal, Inc. In March, 1981, the president of Recycling Specialists was reviewing financial reports for the year ended December 31, 1980 in comparison with 1979. When he came to the report shown below he noted that unit processing costs and also bale volume were increasing.

---

* This case was prepared by Professor John Shank, The Amos Tuck School of Business Administration, Dartmouth College.

Arctic Insulation
Summary Cost Report

	1979		1980	
	$	Cost Per Bale	$	Cost Per Bale
Formed Bales:				
Direct Labor	$4,128,000	$3.84	$3,041,280	$3.84
Depot Overhead	2,765,760	2.57	2,493,850	3.15
Division Overhead	3,384,960	3.15	2,706,740	3.42
Total	$10,278,720	$9.56	$8,241,870	$10.41
Increase - 1980 vs. 1979				$.85
Purchased Bales:				
Direct Labor	$168,000	$.60	$514,800	$.60
Depot Overhead	112,560	.40	422,140	.49
Division Overhead	137,760	.49	458,160	.53
Total	$418,320	$1.49	$1,395,100	$1.62
Increase - 1980 vs. 1979				$.13

He was concerned about the cost control aspects of the increase in per unit costs so he invited the general manager and the cost accountant for the division to his office for an afternoon meeting. In preparation for the meeting, the cost accountant made photocopies of the Supplementary Cost Report (see Exhibit 1). After studying the Summary Cost Report and the Supplementary Cost Report (Table 1 and Exhibit 1), the division general manager was having a difficult time accepting the contention that unit costs had increased. He finally put together his own cost calculations showing that baling costs per unit had in fact declined between 1979 and 1980 (see Exhibit 2). He made photocopies of his calculations to distribute at the meeting.

In 1980, the mix of purchased bales and formed bales changed considerably. Because of a steep decline in the price of bulk scrap paper, the use of purchased bales increased. Formed bales dropped from 78% to 48% of total bales processed. In addition, the total number of bales handled increased approximately 22%. Even though total volume increased, labor costs actually declined in 1980 because of the smaller number of formed bales handled. Costs charged to the collection and baling depots are of three types: first, direct labor (sorting and baling) in the depot; second, overhead charged directly to the depot; and third, an allocated share of general division overhead. Cost of purchased paper is not charged to the depots, but rather is collected at division level and assigned to products at the shredding and bagging plants. The cost accounting department allocates the overhead incurred directly by each depot to the two products

processed (formed bales and purchased bales) within a depot based on the dollars of direct labor for each product. The overhead rate for depot overhead is determined by dividing the total depot overhead by total depot direct labor. The division overhead is allocated to depots based on direct labor dollars. The division overhead rate is equal to the ratio of total division overhead to total direct labor in the entire division, including the four shredding and bagging plants as well as the twenty two collection and baling depots.

The items included in depot overhead are shown in Exhibit 1. The largest item is indirect labor, including salaries for foremen (each forman is in charge of a depot and was paid $22,400 in 1979) and wages of the forklift drivers who deliver bales from the baler to the storage area. These drivers also support the baling operation by refilling the spools of baling wire as they became empty. It was estimated that a driver could handle 7 1/2 bales per hour, on average. The drivers were paid $7.50 per hour in 1979. Depot overhead also includes repairs, supplies, power, payroll taxes, depreciation, insurance and office expenses. Division overhead includes company-wide miscellaneous labor, building repair labor and material, manufacturing administrative salaries and other general costs associated with purchasing, accounting and administration.

During the afternoon meeting, the cost accountant told the president that in 1980, the depot overhead rate had increased from 67% to 82% of direct labor and that the increase in unit cost per bale was, as shown in Table 1, largely attributable to this increase.

Another factor, he said, was a 6% increase in all wages and salaries between 1979 and 1980.

The division manager said that he was certainly not a trained accountant, but that from a common sense point of view it would be very difficult to convince him that cost per unit was <u>increasing</u>, when in fact total costs were <u>decreasing</u> and total output was <u>increasing</u>. He said the problem had to be in the overhead allocation scheme. He said that under the current allocation scheme based on direct labor dollars the formed bales are charged more than a fair share of the overhead. For a correct unit cost determination, he felt that overhead should be allocated on a per bale basis, not as a percentage of direct labor dollars. He gave the president and the cost accountant copies of his schedule (Exhibit 2) in defense of his argument.

The unit costs per bale for formed and purchased bales are used in determining standard costs for the finished product, the bags of insulation. These standard costs, however, are used only sparingly because of the rapidly changing cost conditions in the industry. The company uses standard costs for finished products only as a general guide in measuring the profitability of the bags of insulation sold. Pricing is usually set by competition, but there is some flexibility in product emphasis, particularly over the longer run. When demand for paper and insulation is high, the division operates at capacity. In 1980, operations were at about 80% of capacity.

ASSIGNMENT QUESTIONS

1. Are unit costs per bale rising or falling between 1979 and 1980? Support your answer with the relevant cost calculations.

2. What inferences do you draw regarding the cost control issue which is of concern to the president? How well were costs controlled in 1980?

3. What recommendations would you make regarding the Summary Cost Reports for the collection and baling depots?

4. What other advice do you have for the president?

EXHIBIT 1
Arctic Insulation
Supplementary Cost Report
December 31, 1979 and 1980

	1979		1980	
	$	% of Direct Labor	$	% of Direct Labor
Direct Labor	$4,296,000		$3,556,080	
Depot Overhead				
Indirect Labor	1,875,000		2,019,000	
Repair Labor	101,000		97,000	
Repair Materials	36,000		43,000	
Supplies	53,000		46,000	
Power	55,000		59,000	
Other	758,320		651,990	
Total	2,878,320	67%	2,915,990	82%
Allocated Division Overhead	3,522,720	82%	3,164,900	89%
Total	$10,697,040		$9,636,970	
Formed Bales Processed	1,075,000	(79.3%)	792,000	(48%)
Purchased Bales Processed	280,000	(20.7%)	858,000	(52%)
Total	1,355,000	(100.0%)	1,650,000	(100%)

EXHIBIT 2
Alternative Cost Report as Proposed
By the Division General Manager

	1979		1980	
	$	Cost Per Bale	$	Cost Per Bale
Formed Bales:				
Direct Labor	$4,128,000	$3.84	$3,041,280	$3.84
Depot Overhead	2,283,540	2.12	1,399,675	1.77
Allocated Division Overhead	2,794,780	2.60	1,519,150	1.92
Total	$9,206,320	$8.56	$5,960,105	$7.53
Decrease - 1980 vs. 1979				$1.03
Purchased Bales:				
Direct Labor	$168,000	$.60	$514,800	$.60
Depot Overhead	594,780	2.12	1,516,315	1.77
Division Overhead	727,940	2.60	1,645,750	1.92
Total	$1,490,720	$5.32	$3,676,865	$4.29
Decrease - 1980 vs. 1979				$1.03

Baldwin Bicycle Company*

This case looks at a "private label" opportunity for a small "mid-market" bicycle manufacturer. Analysis of the probelm requires a blending of financial, marketing, and strategic considerations.

In May 1983, Suzanne Leister, marketing vice president of Baldwin Bicycle Company, was mulling over the discussion she had had the previous day with Karl Knott, a buyer from Hi-Valu Stores, Inc. Hi-Valu operated a chain of discount department stores in the Northwest. Hi-Valu's sales volume had grown to the extent that it was beginning to add "house-brand" (also called "private-label") merchandise to the product lines of several of its departments. Mr. Knott, Hi-Valu's buyer for sporting goods, had approached Ms. Leister about the possibility of Baldwin's producing bicycles for Hi-Valu. The bicycles would bear the name "Challenger," which Hi-Valu planned to use for all of its house-brand sporting goods.

Baldwin had been making bicycles for almost 40 years. In 1983, the company's line included 10 models, ranging from a small beginner's model with training wheels to a deluxe 12-speed adult's model. Sales were currently at an annual rate of about $10 million. The company's 1982 financial statements appear in Exhibit 1. Most of Baldwin's sales were through independently owned retailers (toy stores, hardware stores, sporting goods stores) and bicycle shops. Baldwin had never before distributed its products through department store chains of any type. Ms. Leister felt that Baldwin bicycles had the image of being above average in quality and price, but not a "top of the line" product.

Hi-Valu's proposal to Baldwin had features that made it quite different from Baldwin's normal way of doing business. First, it was very important to Hi-Valu to have ready access to a large inventory of bicycles, because Hi-Valu had had great difficulty in predicting bicycle sales, both by store and by month. Hi-Valu wanted to carry these inventories in its regional warehouses, but did not want title on a bicycle to pass from Baldwin to Hi-Valu until the bicycle was shipped from one of its regional warehouses to a specific Hi-Valu store. At that point, Hi-Valu would regard the bicycle as having been purchased from Baldwin, and would pay for it within 30 days. However, Hi-Valu would agree to take title to any bicycle that had been in one of its warehouses for four months, again paying for it within 30 days. Mr. Knott estimated that on average, a bike would remain in a Hi-Valu regional warehouse for two months.

Second, Hi-Valu wanted to sell its Challenger bicycles at lower prices than the name-brand bicycles it carried, and yet still earn approximately the same dollar gross margin on each bicycle sold -- the rationale being that Challenger bike sales would take away from the sales of the name-brand bikes. Thus, Hi-Valu wanted to purchase bikes from Baldwin at lower prices than the wholesale prices of comparable bikes sold through Baldwin's usual channels.

Finally, Hi-Valu wanted the Challenger bike to be somewhat different in appearance from Baldwin's other bikes. While the frame and mechanical components could be the same as used on current Baldwin models, the fenders, seats, and handlebars would need to be somewhat different, and the tires would have to have the name "Challenger" molded into their sidewalls. Also, the bicycles would have to be packed in boxes printed with the Hi-Valu and Challenger names. These requirements were expected by Ms. Leister to increase Baldwin's purchasing, inventorying, and production costs over and above the added costs that would be incurred for a comparable increase in volume for Baldwin's regular products.

* R. N. Anthony and J.S. Reece, <u>Accounting: Text and Cases</u>, Homewood, Ill.: Richard Irwin, Inc., 1983, pp. 742-744. Reproduced by permission of the authors.

EXHIBIT 1
FINANCIAL STATEMENTS
(thousand of dollars)

BALDWIN BICYCLE COMPANY
Balance Sheet
As of December 31, 1982

Assets		Liabilities and Owners Equity	
Cash	$ 342	Accounts payable	$ 512
Accounts receivable	1,359	Accrued expenses	340
Inventories	2,756	Short-term bank loans	2,626
Plant and equipment (net)	3,635	Long-term Note payable	1,512
		Total liabilities	4,990
		Owners' equity	3,102
	$ 8,092		$ 8,092

Income Statement
For the Year Ended December 31, 1982

Sales revenues	$ 10,872
Cost of Goods Sold	8,045
Gross margin	2,827
Selling and Administrative expenses	2,354
Income before taxes	473
Income tax expense	218
Net income	$ 255

On the positive side, Ms. Leister was acutely aware that the "bicycle boom" had flattened out, and this plus a poor economy had caused Baldwin's sales volume to fall the past two years.* As a result, Baldwin currently was operating its plant at about 75 percent of one-shift capacity. Thus, the added volume from Hi-Valu's purchases could possibly be very attractive. If agreement could be reached on prices, Hi-Valu would sign a contract guaranteeing to Baldwin that Hi-Valu would buy its house-brand bicycles only from Baldwin for a three-year period. The contract would then be automatically extended on a year-to-year basis, unless one party gave the other at least three-months' notice that it did not wish to extend the contract.

Suzanne Leister realized she needed to do some preliminary financial analysis of this proposal before having any further discussions with Karl Knott. She had written on a pad the information she had gathered to use in her initial analysis; this information is shown in Exhibit 2.

---

* **Note**: The American bicycle industry had become very volatile in recent years. From 1967 through 1970 sales average about 7 million units a year. By 1973 the total was up to a record 15 million units. By 1975 volume was back down to 7.5 million units. By 1982 volume was back up to 10 million units, still well below the peak years.

EXHIBIT 2
DATA PERTINENT TO HI-VALU PROPOSAL
(Notes taken by Suzanne Leister)

1. **Estimated first-year costs** of producing Challenger bicycles (average unit costs, assuming a constant mix of models):

Materials	$39.80*
Labor	19.60
Overhead (@ 125% of labor)	24.50†
	$83.90

    * Includes items specific to models for Hi-Valu, not used in our standard models.
    † Accountant says about 40 percent of total production overhead cost is variable; 125 percent of DL$ rate is based on volume of 100,000 bicycles per year.

2. **One-time added costs** of preparing drawings and arranging sources for fenders, seats, handlebars, tires, and shipping boxes that differ from those used in our standard models: approximately $5,000.

3. **Unit price and annual volume**: Hi-Valu estimates it will need 25,000 bikes a year and proposes to pay us (based on the assumed mix of models) an average of $92.29 per bike for the first year. Contract to contain an inflation escalation clause such that price will increase in proportion to inflation-caused increases in costs shown in item 1, above; thus, the $92.29 and $83.90 figures are, in effect, "constant-dollar" amounts. Knott intimated that there was very little, if any, negotiating leeway in the $92.29 proposed initial price.

4. **Asset-related costs** (annual variable costs, as percent of dollar value of assets):

Pretax cost of funds (to finance receivables or inventories)	18.0%
Record keeping costs (for receivables or inventories)	1.0
Inventory insurance	0.3
State property tax on inventory	0.7
Inventory-handling labor and equipment	3.0
Pilferage, obsolescence, breakage, etc.	0.5

5. **Assumptions for Challenger-related added inventories** (average over the year):

    Materials: two months' supply.
    Work in process: 1,000 bikes, half completed (but all materials for them issued).
    Finished goods: 500 bikes (awaiting next carload lot shipment to a Hi-Valu warehouse).

6. **Impact on our regular sales**: Some customers comparison shop for bikes, and many of them are likely to recognize a Challenger bike as a good value when compared with a similar bike (either ours or a competitor's) at a higher price in a nonchain toy or bicycle store. In 1982, we sold 98,791 bikes. My best guess is that our sales over the next three years will be about 100,000 bikes a year if we forego the Hi-Valu deal. If we accept it, I think we'll lose about 3,000 units of our regular sales volume a year, since our retail distribution is quite strong in Hi-Valu's market regions. These estimates do not include the possibility that a few of our current dealers might drop our line if they find out we're making bikes for Hi-Valu.

Note: The information about overhead in item 1 above in Exhibit 2 can be used to infer that fixed manufacturing overhead is about $1.5 million per year.

ASSIGNMENT QUESTIONS

1. What is the "relevant" cost of manufacturing a Challenger bike?

2. What is the "relevant" cost (on a per bicycle basis) of carrying the working capital investment involved in the Challenger deal?

3. Should the Challenger deal be charged for the lost sales of bikes through the regular distribution channel ("erosion" or "cannibalization" cost)? If so, what is the "relevant" erosion charge?

4. Can you estimate the incremental return on investment for the Challenger deal?

5. What are the major cash flow implications of the Challenger deal?

6. How would you describe Baldwin's financial situation at the end of 1982?

7. How would you describe Baldwin's strategic position at the end of 1982? Is the Challenger deal a good strategic fit for Baldwin?

Berkshire Threaded Fasteners Company*

This case is set in an "industrial commodities" firm in New England in 1974, as American dominance of world markets was slipping away. The case is about basic cost analysis issues. Or, is it?

In February 1974, Brandon Cook was appointed general manager by Joe Magers, president of Berkshire Threaded Fasteners Company. Cook, age 56, had wide executive experience in manufacturing products similar to those of Berkshire. The appointment of Cook resulted from management problems arising from the death of John Magers, founder and until his death in early 1973, president of the company. Joe Magers had only four years experience with the company and in early 1974 he was 34 years old. His father had hoped to train Joe over a 10-year period, but the father's untimely death had cut this seasoning period short. The younger Magers became president after his father's death, and he had exercised full control until he hired Cook.

Joe Magers knew that he had made several poor decisions during 1973 and that the morale of the organization had suffered, apparently through lack of confidence in him. When he received the income statement for 1973 *(Exhibit 1)*, the loss of over $70,000 during a good business year convinced him that he needed help. He attracted Cook from a competitor by offering a stock option incentive in addition to salary. The arrangement was that Cook, as general manager, would have full authority to execute any changes he desired. In addition, Cook would explain the reasons for his decisions to Magers and thereby train him for successful leadership upon Cook's retirement.

Berkshire Threaded Fasteners Company made only three lines of metal fasteners (nuts and bolts)—the 100 series, the 200 series, and the 300 series. These were sold by the company sales force for use by heavy industrial manufacturers. All of the sales force, on a salary basis, sold all three lines, but in varying proportions. Berkshire sold throughout New England and was one of eight companies with similar products. Several of its competitors were larger and manufactured a larger variety of products. The dominant company was Bosworth Machine Company, which operated a plant in Berkshire's market area. Joe Magers had heard many people describe threaded fasteners as a "commodity" business. But he had also heard a speaker say once that the term is only used by losers in a business.

Price cutting was rare; the only variance from quoted selling prices took the form of cash discounts. Customarily, Bosworth announced prices annually and the other producers followed suit. In the past, attempts at price cutting had followed a consistent pattern: All competitors met the price reduction, and the industry as a whole sold about the same quantity but at the lower prices. Demand was very "inelastic," at least in the short run, for a "derived demand" product like metal fasteners. Eventually Bosworth, with its strong financial position, again stabilized the situation following a general recognition of the failure of price cutting. Furthermore, because sales were to industrial buyers and because the products of different manufacturers were very similar, Berkshire was convinced it could not individually raise prices without suffering substantial volume declines.

---

*This case was adapted by Professor John Shank of the Amos Tuck School from an earlier case written by J.P. Culliton of Harvard Business School.

27

During 1973, Berkshire's share of industry sales was 12% for the 100 series, 8% for the 200 series and 10% for the 300 series. The industry-wide quoted selling prices were $2.45, $2.58 and $2.75 per 100 pieces, respectively.

Upon taking office in February 1974, Cook decided against immediate major changes; he chose instead to analyze 1973 operations and to wait for the results of the first half of 1974. He instructed the accounting department to provide detailed expenses and an earnings statement by product line for 1973 (see Exhibit 2). In addition, he requested an explanation of the nature of the costs including their expected future behavior (see Exhibit 3).

To familiarize Joe Magers with his approach to financial analysis, Cook sent copies of these exhibits to Magers. When they discussed them, Magers stated that he thought the 300 series should be dropped immediately, as it would be impossible to lower expenses on 300s as much as 23 cents per 100 pieces. In addition, he stressed the need for economies on the 200 series line.

Cook relied on the authority arrangement Magers had agreed to earlier and continued production of the three lines. For control purposes, he had the accounting department prepare monthly statements using as standard costs the costs per 100 pieces from the analytical profit and loss statement for 1973 (Exhibit 2). These monthly statements were his basis for making minor marketing and production changes during the spring of 1974. Late in July, 1974, Cook received the six months' statement of cumulative standard costs from the accounting department, including variances of actual costs from standard (see Exhibit 4). They showed that the first half of 1974 was a modestly successful period.

In July 1974, Bosworth announced a price reduction on the 100 series from $2.45 to $2.25 per 100 pieces. This created an immediate pricing problem for its competitors. Cook forecast that if Berkshire held to the $2.45 price during the last six months of 1974, unit sales would be 750,000 100-piece lots. He felt that if the price were dropped to $2.25 per 100 pieces, the six months' volume would be 1,000,000. Cook knew that competing managements anticipated a further decline in activity. He thought a general decline in prices was quite probable.

Cook and Magers discussed the pricing problem. A sales price of $2.25 would be below cost. Magers wanted $2.45 to be continued, since he felt the company could not be profitable while selling a key product line below cost.

ASSIGNMENT QUESTIONS

1. If the company had dropped the 300 series as of January 1, 1974, what effect would that action have had on the profit for the first six months of 1974?

2. In July 1974, should the company have reduced the price of the 100 series from $2.45 to $2.25?

3. Which is Berkshire's most profitable product line?

4. What advice do you have for Mr. Magers?

Exhibit 1
Income Statement - Year Ended December 31, 1973
(000)

Net sales		$10,434
Cost of goods sold		6,511
Gross margin		3,923
Less: Selling expense	$1,839	
General administration	653	
Depreciation	1,359	3,851
Operating income		72
Less: Interest expense		145
Loss before taxes		($73)

Exhibit 2
Analysis of Profit and Loss by Product - Year Ended December 31, 1973

	100 Series		200 Series		300 Series		Total
	$000	per 100	$000	per 100	$000	per 100	$000
Labor	1,293	0.61	610	0.59	688	0.70	2,591
Raw materials	1,340	0.63	774	0.75	795	0.81	2,909
Power	23	0.01	25	0.02	30	0.03	78
Repairs	18	0.01	15	0.01	10	0.01	43
Rent	186	0.09	157	0.15	187	0.19	530
Other factory costs	140	0.07	110	0.11	110	0.11	360
Total	3,000	1.42	1,691	1.63	1,820	1.85	6,511
Selling expense	911	0.43	458	0.44	470	0.48	1,839
General Administration	345	0.16	130	0.13	178	0.18	653
Depreciation	565	0.26	428	0.42	366	0.37	1,359
Interest	52	0.02	40	0.04	53	0.05	145
Total cost	4,873	2.29	2,747	2.66	2,887	2.93	10,507
Sales (net)	5,168	2.42	2,598	2.52	2,668	2.70	10,434
Profit (loss)	$295	0.14	($149)	(0.14)	($219)	(0.23)	($73)
Unit sales (100 pcs)	2,132,191		1,029,654		986,974		
Quoted selling price	$2.45		$2.58		$2.75		

Note: Per unit amounts are rounded here and in Exhibit 4 to simplify the presentation.

Exhibit 3
Accounting Department's Commentary on Costs

Labor: Variable. Union shop at going community rates of $4.20 per hour. (including social security taxes/compensation insurance/fringe benefits). Labor cost includes maintenance, set-up, and inspection as well as direct and indirect production workers.

Raw Materials: Variable. *Exhibit 2* figures are accurate. Includes allowances for normal waste. Purchases are at market prices.

Power: Variable. Rates are fixed. Use varies with activity. Averages per *Exhibit 2* are accurate.

Repairs: Variable. Varies as volume changes within normal operation range. Lower and upper limits are fixed.

General Administrative and Selling Expense: These items are almost nonvariable. They can be changed, of course, by management decision.

Rent: Nonvariable. Lease has 12 years to run. The lease rate, $5 per square foot (net, net, net) per year, is competitive for the area even though the plant is rented from a trust set up for the heirs of John Magers.

Other Factory Costs: This includes building service, property insurance, property taxes, light, heat and factory management. These items are nonvariable.

Depreciation: Nonvariable. Fixed dollar total. The machinery is depreciated over a 20 year life using straight line rates. About half the equipment in use is over ten years old and about half represents equipment purchased in the past ten years. The average age of the equipment is about ten years.

Interest: Nonvariable. Interest expense reflects the annual charge on equipment loans at rates averaging 6%.

Exhibit 4

Profit and Loss by Product (at Standard with Variance) from January 1 to June 30, 1974

	100 Series		200 Series		300 Series		Total		Variance
	Standard per 100 pcs.	Total $ at Standard	Standard per 100 pcs.	Total $ at Standard	Standard per 100 pcs.	Total $ at Standard	Standard $000	Actual $000	Favorable = + Unfavorable = -
Labor	0.61	604	0.59	422	0.70	349	1,375	1,382	-7
Raw materials	0.63	627	0.75	535	0.81	404	1,566	1,543	23
Power	0.01	10	0.02	17	0.03	15	42	42	0
Repairs	0.01	8	0.01	10	0.01	5	23	25	-2
Rent	0.09	88	0.15	109	0.19	95	292	261	31
Other factory costs	0.07	65	0.11	76	0.11	56	197	180	17
Total	1.42	1,402	1.63	1,169	1.85	924	3,495	3,433	62
Selling expense	0.43	426	0.44	317	0.48	239	982	983	-1
General administrative	0.16	161	0.13	90	0.18	90	341	328	13
Depreciation	0.26	264	0.42	296	0.37	186	746	681	65
Interest	0.02	25	0.04	28	0.05	27	80	73	7
Total cost	2.29	2,278	2.67	1,900	2.92	1,466	5,644	5,498	146
Sales (net)	2.42	2,416	2.52	1,797	2.70	1,355	5,568	5,568	0
Profit (loss)	0.13	138	(0.15)	(103)	(0.22)	(111)	(76)	70	146
Unit sales (100 pcs.)		996,859		712,102		501,276			
Quoted selling price		$2.45		$2.58		$2.75			

"Booker Jones"*

This disguised case is set in 1961 in rural Kentucky when a good bourbon whiskey sold for about $5.00 a "fifth" (1/5 gallon bottle) and the Vice President of the United States considered bourbon to be the national beverage.

In August of 1961, Mr. Henry Jones, president of Booker Jones Distillery, Inc. of Turkey Creek, Kentucky sat in his office pondering the results of the previous day's management meeting. A great deal of controversy had arisen over the reported loss of $407,000 for 1961 and how 1961 results should be presented. The company was seeking a $1.5 million term loan from the Ridgeview Bank in Louisville to finance an expansion in production. The bank wanted to see the 6/30/61 financial statements as soon as they were available. The controversy revolved around the accounting treatment of items reported in the "other operating costs" section of the income statement. Mr. Jones felt that a decision had to be reached quickly on these matters since the company had reached a point where additional cash was needed immediately to remain solvent.

COMPANY HISTORY

Booker Jones began distilling whiskey in Turkey Creek, Kentucky in 1880, carrying on a long family tradition of beverage manufacture. He purchased a tract of land on a high knoll adjacent to a small stream fed by a limestone spring and began to distill bourbon whiskey in an old barn behind his home. His business grew to a million-dollar firm by 1911. He attributed this growth to the distinctive, high-quality bourbon whiskey which he produced. The quality of "Booker Jones" bourbon, his only brand, was the result of the unusual iron-free spring water used in the distillation process, and the aging process, which took place in specially prepared fire-charred white oak barrels.

From 1911 to 1933, the years of "Prohibition," Jones' distilling equipment lay dormant, although some of his neighbors remained "professionally active". It was not until late in 1934 that the company renewed operations in a newly constructed building. Sales rose from $500,000 in 1935 to nearly $5 million in 1941, when the plant was converted to defense production of commercial alcohol.

---

* This case is adapted by Professor John Shank of the Amos Tuck School from an earlier case no longer in print which was written by Professor Richard Vancil of the Harvard Business School.

In 1946, Mr. Henry Jones, grandson of Booker, took over as chief operating executive of the company. He doubled sales revenue during the next 10 years. Henry Jones felt that the company had grown because of the stress he placed on marketing one distinctive, high-quality, high-price brand of fine bourbon whiskey. The company's advertising stressed the uniqueness of the cool, bubbling spring water used in the distillation of "Booker Jones" and pointed to its use of "specially prepared and cured fire-charred white oak barrels." This type of promotion had been very effective in establishing a brand image in the consumer's mind that conveyed a concept of full-bodied mellowness, camaraderie, and old-fashioned, backwoods quality.

In 1960, the company produced approximately 1.5% of the whiskey distilled in the United States which made it one of the smaller distillers in the industry. Since the mid-1950s the company's production had been stable. The financial statements for 1960 (Exhibits 1 and 2) were typical of the results for the preceding several years. After the initial surge in demand following World War II, no special effort had been made to gain a larger share of the market. But the company decided in December, 1960 to expand production to try to capture a larger than proportionate share of the increase in whiskey consumption which Mr. Jones was projecting, based on an industry research report. This report showed that the consumption of straight bourbon whiskey had increased (at the expense of blended whiskeys) from 15% of total whiskey consumption in 1947 to nearly 50% in 1959. Based on this report and other industry forecasts, Mr. Jones was projecting a doubling of straight whiskey consumption from 1960 to 1968. In view of this, and because "Booker Jones" was aged for 4 years, he had decided to increase production in 1961 to 63,000 barrels versus 43,000 in 1960.

THE MANUFACTURING PROCESS

Mashing

Hammer mills grind corn, rye and barley malt to a fine meal. The cornmeal plus a little barley malt is cooked in a steel tub, along with the pure, iron-free water that flows from Jones unique limestone springs, .

This mash is cooled before adding rye and the rest of the barley malt. Mashing and fermenting are all natural processes—no chemical additives are used. Although federal law requires that bourbon contain at least 51% corn, the percentage in "Booker Jones" is much higher.

Fermenting

The cooked mash is pumped to a cypress wood fermenting vat. Yeast is added from a private stock which derives from a patented strain perfected in 1942 by Henry Jones' father.

The yeast feeds on fermentable sugars in the converted mash, producing alcohol. Thousands of carbon dioxide bubbles rise vigorously to the surface during the first 24 to 48 hours. Bubbling stops after 72 to 120 hours when fermentation is complete.

Distilling

The fermented mash is pumped into a distillation tower, or "still", where steam separates it from the alcohol and water. As the mash cascades down through the still, steam at the bottom forces the alcohol up through sieve holes. This distills the fermented mash many times as it flows through the still.

The separated alcohol vapors rise to the top, where they condense into a liquid. This "low wine" is drained off and redistilled in a doubler where it is condensed into "high wine," increasing the whiskey's proof and enhancing its flavor. The residue settling at the bottom is called "stillage," which is converted into distillers dried grain (an animal feed supplement). Bourbon is distilled to no more than 160 proof, or 80% alcohol. Jones distills at an even lower proof to retain more of the whiskey's natural, mellow flavor. The high wine, or finished whiskey, is reduced with soft, natural spring water to no more than 100 proof. It is then ready for aging.

Aging

The bitter, colorless liquid produced by distillation is technically whiskey—but it's far from being bourbon.

The final, legally required step in making straight bourbon is aging in new, charred, white oak barrels. Although federal regulations require a two year aging period, Jones ages bourbon for four years to achieve its smooth flavor.

What happens in the barrels to convert raw clear alcohol into golden bourbon is a great mystery—but there is simply no substitute for it. Flash-charring the barrel interiors creates a caramelized layer of wood, through which the whiskey passes back and forth hundreds of times over the years.

During the aging process, the flavors of the char and the barrel are "married" with the whiskey, giving the bourbon its unique taste and rich amber color. To realize the benefit of natural seasonal changes, barrels are stored in an airy hilltop "rack house" until they are fully aged. At just the right moment, the golden contents of the barrels are emptied and filtered to remove any traces of char. The proof is again reduced (to 86 proof) with pure spring water before it is bottled, labeled and shipped.

The cost accumulated in the product prior to its entry into the 50 gallon barrels, including all direct and indirect materials and labor consumed in the production process, was approximately $.52 per gallon. The volume of production had been the same for each of the years 1957-1960 (43,000 barrels), and all costs during this period had been substantially the same as the 1960 costs shown in Exhibit 2.

Since the quality of the aging barrel was so important a factor in determining the ultimate taste and character of the final product, Jones had his 50-gallon barrels manufactured under a unique patented process at a cost of $31.50 per barrel. The barrels could not be reused for aging future batches of bourbon. They were sold to used barrel dealers for $.50 each at the end of the aging period.

The filled barrels were placed in open "ricks" in the rented "rack house," or in that half of the factory building which had been converted into warehousing space. The increased production in 1961 necessitated the leasing of an additional warehouse at an annual rental cost of $100,000. The temperature and humidity of the warehouse space had to be controlled, since the quality of the whiskey could be ruined by aging too fast or too slowly, a process determined by temperature and humidity conditions.

Every 6 months the barrels had to be rotated from a high rick to a lower rick or vice versa (because of uneven temperatures at different locations in the warehouse) and sampled for quality and character up to that point in the aging process. A small amount of liquid was removed from representative barrels at this time and sent to the sampling laboratory for quality inspection by skilled tasters. If the quality of the whiskey was not up to standard, corrective measures were taken, such as adjusting the aging process, to bring it up to standard. At the same time, each barrel was also checked for leaks or seepage and the required repairs were made.

The volume of liquid in a barrel declined substantially during the aging period because of unavoidable evaporation and leakage. A barrel originally filled with 50 gallons of new whiskey would, on average, produce only about 35 gallons of salable 86 proof aged bourbon. The bottling operation was supervised by a government liquor tax agent, since it was at this point that the federal excise tax of about $10.50 per gallon was levied on the whiskey. Once the federal tax was assessed the bourbon was bottled and shipped to wholesalers with the greatest speed possible because of the large amount of cash tied up in taxes on the finished product. During both 1960 and 1961, the company sold 1,500,000 gallons of aged whiskey, equivalent to about 43,000 barrels of original production. Jones held finished goods inventory of about 175,000 gallons as a buffer between production swings and sales swings.

EXCERPTS FROM MANAGEMENT MEETING, AUGUST 3, 1961

Henry Jones: President

Gentlemen, I'm quite concerned about showing a loss of 407,000 in 1961 just when we are trying to obtain a $1.5 million loan to finance our production expansion. We have shown annual profits every year since 1948. Our net sales of $21.0 million this year is the same as last year and yet we incurred a net loss for the year. I think I understand the reason for this, but I'm afraid that the loan officers at the Ridgeview Bank will hesitate in granting us a loan if they question our most recent performance. It might appear that we have lost the ability to operate at a profit.

James Doud: Production Manager

You know as well as I do, Henry, that we increased production by 50% this year, and with this increased production, our costs are bound to increase. You can't produce something for nothing. That's why we showed the loss.

Robert Thompson: Controller

Well, that's not quite so, Jim. Its true that our production costs must rise when production increases, but our inventory account takes care of the increased costs by deferring these product costs until the future period when the product is actually sold. As you can see by looking at our 1961 operating statement, our manufacturing cost charged against sales did not increase in 1961 since the volume of sales was the same in 1961 as in 1960. The increase in production costs has been deferred until future periods, as you can see by looking at the increase in our inventory account of nearly half a million dollars. The real reason for our loss this year was the large increase in "other operating costs" and selling and administrative expenses. Look at "Occupancy Costs" for example. This is really the summation of a group of expense accounts, including building depreciation or rent, heat, light, power, building maintenance labor and supplies, real estate taxes, and insurance. In addition, Warehouse Labor costs also rose substantially. Even Administrative and General expenses went up, due partly to higher interest expense on the additional money we borrowed this year.

Henry Jones

Well, what's your explanation for the large increase in the warehousing costs, Jim?

James Doud

As I said before, Henry, we increased production, and this also means an increase in warehousing costs since the increased production has to be aged for four years. You can't age 50% more whiskey for the same amount of money. We geared up this year to handle 252,000 barrels in inventory instead of 172,000.

Henry Jones

But I thought Bob said that increased production costs were taken care of in the inventory account. Isn't that so, Bob?

Robert Thompson

Well, yes and no, Henry. The inventory account can only be charged with those costs associated with the direct production of whiskey. Our warehousing costs are handling or carrying costs; certainly not production costs.

James Doud

Now just a minute, Bob, I think that some of those costs are just as much production costs as the direct labor and materials going into the distillation of the new whiskey. The manufacturing process doesn't stop with the newly produced whiskey; why it isn't even

marketable in that form. Aging is an absolutely essential part of the manufacturing process. I think the cost of barrels and warehousing should be treated as direct costs of the product.

Henry Jones

Great, Jim! I agree with you that warehousing and aging costs are an absolutely essential ingredient of our final product. We certainly couldn't market the bourbon before it had been aged. I think that all the costs associated with aging the product should be charged to the inventory account. In fact, why not consider all our costs as a cost of the product? Don't you agree, Bob? We would not spend any money anywhere if it weren't for the product.

Robert Thompson

Sure, Henry! Let's capitalize depreciation, interest expense, your salary, the shareholders' dividends, our advertising costs, your secretary's salary—why, let's go ahead and capitalize all our costs! That way we can show a huge inventory balance and small expenses! I'm sure Ridgeview and the IRS would be happy to cooperate with us on it! Why, we'll revolutionize the accounting profession!

Henry Jones

Well, Bob, all joking aside, I'm afraid I really don't see why we couldn't charge all of those costs you mentioned to the inventory account, since it seems to me that they are all necessary ingredients in producing our final product. What distinction do you draw between these so-called "direct" costs you mentioned and the aging costs?

Robert Thompson

By direct costs I mean those costs that are necessary to convert raw materials into the whiskey that goes into the aging barrels. This is our cost of approximately $.52 per gallon and includes the cost of raw materials going into the product such as grain, yeast, and malt; the direct labor necessary to convert these materials into whiskey; and the cost of any other overhead items that are needed to permit the workers to convert grain into whiskey. I don't see how aging costs can be included under this generally accepted accounting definition of the inventory cost of the finished product.

Henry Jones

I think we'd better defer further discussion of this entire subject until our meeting next week. In the meantime I am going to try to get this thing squared away in my own mind. I have never thought that our financial statements told us much that we didn't already know, but now I am beginning to think that they are truly misleading documents!

Well, let's turn next to the question of...

ASSIGNMENT QUESTIONS

1. Calculate the effect on the financial statements in Exhibits 1 and 2 if the accounting system were changed to incorporate the cost of barrels ($31.50 each) into the inventory accounts.

   a. What would pretax profit be in 1961?

   b. If the change were made retroactively as of July 1,1959 (by adding the cost of barrels to all whiskey in inventory), what would be the effect on

      1. The balance sheet at the end of 1960?

      2. The balance sheet at the end of 1961?

      3. The operating statement for 1960?

   The calculations required for question 1 are not massive (it takes more thinking than pencil-pushing). Working those calculations will help solidify your understanding of the relationship between inventory and cost of good sold in a manufacturing company. You'll know you're on the right track if you conclude that the answer to part b(3) is "no effect."

2. Do you believe that Jones went from a profit in 1960 to a loss for 1961, despite the fact that sales were the same and production increased?

3. What method of accounting would you recommend that Jones use in preparing the annual financial statements for submission to Ridgeview Bank and the family shareholders?

4. Based on the accounting method you think best approximates "economic reality," calculate the Return on Equity for the business for 1960. How are they doing? Are they earning their cost of capital?

It is suggested that you spend no more than one half your preparation time on questions one through four.

5. Can you estimate the cash flows for the business for 1961? What about for the 3 year period, 1962, 1963, 1964, combined? (Assume Jones does not change its tax accounting method.) Now, so what?

6. Can you estimate the economic return for the expansion decision?

7. Is the loan to expand production "bankable?" That is, do you believe Ridgeview Bank should be willing to lend Booker Jones the money they need now to complete the four year inventory buildup?

8. What recommendations do you have for Mr. Jones regarding the business problems he faces? (product positioning; production expansion; capital structure; working capital management;...)

Preparation Hint

This is a very rich case which begins with an important question about accounting policy choices for financial reporting. There are many other important issues in the case as well. Don't stop with the accounting policy issues. How many other issues do you see? Do you see why we consider this more a comprehensive business policy case than an accounting case?

EXHIBIT 1
Balance Sheet
(Thousands of Dollars)

| | as of June 30 | |
	1960	1961
Assets		
Current Assets		
Cash	$1,274	$316
Accounts Receivable	1,427	1,831
Inventories:		
Bulk Whiskey in Barrels—Average Cost of $.52 per gallon	4,506	5,030
Bottled and Cased Whiskey—Average Cost of $11.20 per gallon	1,969	1,969
Other Current Assets	942	726
	10,118	9,872
Fixed Assets (Per supporting Schedule A)	1,237	1,394
Total	$11,355	$11,266
Liabilities and Equity		
Current Liabilities		
Short-Term Notes Payable (Ridgeview Bank)	$1,100	$1,500
Accounts Payable	860	419
Other Current Liabilities	609	115
	2,569	2,034
Long-Term Mortgage Notes Payable (5 1/2%)	3,730	4,583
Stockholders' Equity		
Common Stock (closely held)	1,800	1,800
Retained Earnings	3,256	2,849
Total	$11,355	$11,266

SCHEDULE A - Fixed Assets

| | Cost | | Accumulated Depreciation | | Net | |
	1960	1961	1960	1961	1960	1961
Land	70	73			70	73
Building	1,910	2,110	$800	$853	1,110	1,257
Factory Equipment	72	72	26	38	46	34
Warehouse Equipment	35	64	24	34	11	30
					$1,237	$1,394

EXHIBIT 2
Statement of Operations
for the Years Ended June 30, 1960 and 1961
(Thousands of Dollars)

		for the Years Ended June 30		
		1960		1961
Net Sales (to Wholesalers)*			$21,000		$21,000
Cost of Goods Sold					
Federal Excise Taxes ($10.53 per gallon)			15,802		15,802
Cost of Whiskey Sold			1,127		1,127
Production Cost $26.20 per barrel	$1,127			$1,651	
Plus Bulk Whiskey Inventory, July 1					
(172,000 barrels)	4,506			4,506	
Less: Bulk Whiskey Inventory, June 30					
(172,000 and 192,000 barrels)	(4,506)			(5,030)	
Other Operating Costs					
Cost of Barrels Used			1,354		1,984
Occupancy Costs	269			436	
Warehousing Costs	183		452	279	714
Cost of Bottling			229		229
Total Cost of Goods Sold			18,964		19,856
Gross Margin			2,036		1,144
Selling and Advertising Expenses	934			987	
Administrative and General Expenses	350		1,284	564	1,551
Net Profit (Loss) before Tax			752		(407)
Less: Income Tax (39%)			290		--
Net Profit (Loss) after Tax			$462		$(407)

*The Value Chain

Price to Wholesaler	$2.80/fifth
Wholesaler Gross Margin (16%)	.55
Price to Retailer	3.35/fifth
Retailer Gross Margin (33%)	1.65
Price to Consumer	5.00/fifth
(Before State Taxes)	

Boston Creamery, Inc.*

This case deals with the design and use of formal "profit planning and control" systems. It is set in an ice cream company in 1973, a few years before the advent of "designer ice cream."

Frank Roberts, Vice-president for Sales and Marketing of the Ice Cream Division of Boston Creamery, was pleased when he saw the final earnings statement for the division for 1973 (see Exhibit 1). He knew that it had been a good year for ice cream, but he hadn't expected the results to be quite this good.

Only the year before the company had installed a new financial planning and control system. This was the first year that figures comparing budgeted and actual results were available. Jim Peterson, president of the division, had asked Frank to make a short presentation at the next management meeting commenting on the major reasons for the favorable operating income variance of $71,700. Peterson asked him to draft his presentation in the next few days so that the two of them could go over it before the meeting. Peterson said he wanted to illustrate to the management group how an analysis of the profit variance could highlight those areas needing corrective attention as well as those deserving a pat on the back.

THE PROFIT PLAN FOR 1973

Following the four-step approach outlined in the Appendix, the management group of the Ice Cream Division prepared a profit plan for 1973.

Based on an anticipated overall ice cream market of about 11,440,000 gallons in their marketing area and a market share of 50%, forecasted overall gallon sales were 5,720,329 for 1973. Actually, this forecast was the same as the latest estimate of 1972 actual gallon sales. Since the 1973 budget was being done in October of 1972, final figures for 1972 were not yet available. The latest revised estimate of actual gallon volume for 1972 was thus used. Rather than trying to get too sophisticated on the first attempt at budgeting, Mr. Peterson had decided just to go with 1972's estimated volume as 1973's goal or forecast. He felt that there was plenty of time in later years to refine the system by bringing in more formal sales forecasting techniques and concepts.

This same general approach was also followed for variable product standard costs and for fixed costs. Budgeted costs for 1973 were just expected 1972 results, adjusted for a few items which were clearly out of line in 1972.

---

* This case was prepared by Professor John Shank of the Amos Tuck School from an earlier version he wrote at Harvard Business School with the assistance of William J. Rauwerdink, Research Assistant.

Original Profit Plan for 1973

	Standard Contribution Margin/Gallon	Forecasted Gallon Sales	Forecasted Standard Contribution Margin
Vanilla	$.4329	2,409,854	$1,043,200
Chocolate	.4535	2,009,061	911,100
Walnut	.5713	48,883	28,000
Buttercrunch	.4771	262,185	125,000
Cherry Swirl	.5153	204,774	105,500
Strawberry	.4683	628,560	294,400
Pecan Chip	.5359	157,012	84,100
Total	$.4530	5,720,329	$2,591,300

Breakdown of Budgeted Total Expenses

	Variable Costs	Fixed Costs	Total
Manufacturing	$5,888,100	$612,800	$6,500,900
Delivery	187,300	516,300	703,600
Advertising	553,200	--	553,200
Selling	--	368,800	368,800
Administrative	--	448,000	448,000
Total	$6,628,600	$1,945,900	$8,574,500

Recap

Sales	$9,219,900
Variable Cost of Sales	6,628,600
Contribution Margin	2,591,300
Fixed Costs	1,945,900
Income from Operations	$645,400

ACTUAL RESULTS FOR 1973

By the spring of 1973 it had become clear that sales volume for 1973 was going to be higher than forecast. In fact, actual sales for the year totaled over 5,968,000 gallons, an increase of about 248,000 gallons over budget. Market research data indicated that the total ice cream market in their marketing area was 12,180,000 gallons for the year as opposed to the budgeted figure of about 11,440,000 gallons.

A revised profit plan for the year at the actual volume level is shown on the next page.

The fixed costs in the revised profit plan are the same as in the original plan, $1,945,900. The variable costs, however, have been adjusted to reflect the actual volume level of 5,968,000 gallons instead of the forecasted volume of 5,720,000 gallons, thereby eliminating all cost variances due strictly to the difference between planned volume and actual volume.

For costs which are highly volume dependent, variances should be based on a budget which reflects the volume of operation actually attained. Since the level of fixed costs is independent of volume anyway, it is not necessary to adjust the budget for these items for volume differences. The original budget for fixed-cost items is still appropriate.

Assume, for example, that cartons are budgeted at $.04 per gallon. If we forecast volume of 10,000 gallons, the budget allowance for cartons is $400. If we actually sell only 8,000 gallons but use $350 worth of cartons, it is misleading to say that there is a favorable variance of $50 ($350-$400). The variance is clearly unfavorable by $30 ($350-$320). This only shows up if we adjust the budget to the actual volume level:

Carton Allowance	= $.04 per gallon
Forecast Volume	= 10,000 gallons
Carton Budget	= $400
Actual Volume	= 8,000 gallons
Actual Carton Expense	= $350
Variance (Based on Forecast Volume)	= $400 - $350 = $50F
Variance (Based on Actual Volume)	= $320 - $350 = $30U

ANALYSIS OF THE 1973 PROFIT VARIANCE

Exhibit 1 is the earnings statement for the division for the year. The figures for the month of December have been excluded for purposes of this case. Exhibit 2 is the detailed expense breakdown for the manufacturing department. The detailed expense

Revised Profit Plan for 1973
(Budgeted Profit at Actual Volume)

	Standard Contribution Margin/Gallon	Actual Gallon Sales	Standard Contribution Margin
Vanilla	$.4329	2,458,212	$1,064,200
Chocolate	.4535	2,018,525	915,400
Walnut	.5713	50,124	28,600
Buttercrunch	.4771	268,839	128,300
Cherry Swirl	.5153	261,240	134,600
Strawberry	.4683	747,049	349,800
Pecan Chip	.5359	164,377	88,100
Total	$.4539	5,968,366	$2,709,000

Breakdown of Budgeted Total Expenses

	Variable Costs	Fixed Costs	Total
Manufacturing	$6,113,100	$612,800	$6,725,900
Delivery	244,500	516,300	760,800
Advertising	578,700	--	578,700
Selling	--	368,800	368,800
Administrative	--	448,000	448,000
Total	$6,936,300	$1,945,900	$8,882,200

Recap

Sales	$9,645,300
Variable Cost of Sales	6,936,300
Contribution Margin	2,709,000
Fixed Costs	1,945,900
Income from Operations	$763,100

breakdowns for the other departments have been excluded for purposes of this case.

Three days after Jim Peterson asked Frank Roberts to pull together a presentation for the management committee analyzing the profit variance for 1973, Frank came into Jim's office to review his first draft. He showed Jim the following schedule:

Favorable Variance Due to Sales:		
Volume	$117,700F	
Price[a]	12,000F	$129,700F
Unfavorable Variance Due to Operations:		
Manufacturing	$99,000U	
Delivery	54,000F	
Advertising	29,000U	
Selling	6,000F	
Administration	10,000F	58,000U
Net Variance—Favorable		$71,700F

[a]This price variance is the difference between the actual sales value of the gallons actually sold and the standard sales value ($9,657,300 - $9,645,300).

Frank said that he planned to give each member

of the management committee a copy of this schedule and then to comment briefly on each of the items. Jim Peterson said he thought the schedule was okay as far as it went, but that it just didn't highlight things in a manner which indicated what corrective actions should be taken in 1974 or indicated the real causes for the favorable overall variance. Which elements were uncontrollable, for example? He suggested that Frank try to break down the sales volume variance into the part attributable to sales mix, the part attributable to market share shifts, and the part actually attributable to overall volume changes. He also suggested breaking down the unfavorable manufacturing variance to indicate what main corrective actions are called for in 1974. For example, he said, how much of the total was due to price differences versus quantity differences? Since the division was a pure "price taker" for commodities like milk and sugar, he wondered how to best treat the price variances. Finally, he suggested that Frank call on John Vance, the corporate controller, if he needed some help in the mechanics of breaking out these different variances.

As Frank Roberts returned to his office, he considered Jim Peterson's suggestion of getting John Vance involved in revising the variance report. Frank did not want to consult John Vance unless it was absolutely necessary because he thought Vance always went overboard on the technical aspects of any accounting problem. Frank couldn't imagine a quicker way to put people to sleep than to throw one of Vance's number-filled six-page memos at them. Jim Peterson specifically wants a nontechnical presentation, Frank thought to himself, and that rules out John Vance. Besides, he thought, you don't have to be a CPA to focus on the key variance areas from a general management viewpoint.

A telephone call to John Vance asking about any written materials dealing with mix variances and volume variances produced, in the following day's mail, the document shown here as the Appendix. Vance said to see Exhibit A for the variance analysis breakdown. Armed with this document and his common sense, Frank Roberts dug in again to the task of preparing a nontechnical breakdown of the profit variance for the year.

The next day Frank Roberts learned that his counterpart, John Parker, Vice President for Manufacturing and Operations, had seen the draft variance report and was very unhappy about it. Roberts and Parker were the only two vice presidents in the division. Parker had apparently told Jim Peterson that he felt Roberts was "playing games" with the numbers to make himself look good at Parker's expense. Organizationally, Sales, Marketing and Advertising reported to Roberts and Manufacturing, Delivery and Administration to Parker.

ASSIGNMENT QUESTIONS

1. What changes, if any, would you make in the variance analysis schedule proposed by Frank Roberts? Can the suggestions offered by Jim Peterson be incorporated without making the schedule "too technical"?

2. Can you speculate about how John Parker might structure the variance analysis report. For example, Parker felt it was Marketing's responsibility to set prices so as to recover all commodity cost increases.

3. Indicate the corrective actions you would recommend for 1974, based on the profit variance analysis. Also indicate those areas which deserve commendation for 1973 performance.

4. The approach to "profit planning and control" described in the case is still very common in the 1990s. Many people still consider this approach to be "bread and butter" management theory. What do you see as the main weakness in this approach to management? What is your overall assessment of this "management tool," from a contemporary perspective?

EXHIBIT 1
ICE CREAM DIVISION
Earnings Statement
December 31, 1973

| Month | | | Year-to-Date | |
Actual	Flexible Budget		Actual	Flexible Budget
		Sales—Net	$9,657,300	$9,645,300
		Manufacturing Cost (Schedule A-2[a])	6,824,900 *	6,725,900
		Delivery (Schedule A-3)**	706,800	760,800
		Advertising (Schedule A-4)[Note]	607,700	578,700
		Selling (Schedule A-5)	362,800	368,800
		Administrative (Schedule A-6)	438,000	448,000
		Total Expenses	$8,940,200	$8,882,200
		Income from Operations	$717,100	$763,100

Variance Analysis in Exhibit 3.

[a]Schedules A-3 through A-6 have not been included in this case. Schedule A-2 is reproduced as Exhibit 2.
*See Exhibit 3.
Note—In 1973 the company changed from an advertising "budget" of $.06 per gallon sold to a "budget" of 6% of Sales.

EXHIBIT 2
ICE CREAM DIVISION
Schedule A-2
Manufacturing Cost of Goods Sold
December 31, 1973

	Month		Year-to-Date	
Actual	Flexible Budget		Actual	Flexible Budget
Variable Costs				
Dairy Ingredients			$3,679,900	$3,648,500
Milk Price Variance			57,300	--
Sugar			599,900	596,800
Sugar Price Variance			23,400	--
Flavoring (Including Fruits and Nuts)			946,800	982,100
Cartons			567,200	566,900
Plastic Wrap			28,700	29,800
Additives			235,000	251,000
Supplies			31,000	35,000
Miscellaneous			3,000	3,000
Subtotal			$6,172,200	$6,113,100
Fixed Costs				
Labor—Cartonizing and Freezing**			$425,200	$390,800
Labor—Other			41,800	46,000
Repairs			32,200	25,000
Depreciation			81,000	81,000
Electricity and Water			41,500	40,000
Spoilage			31,000	30,000
Subtotal			$652,700	$612,800
Total			$6,824,900	$6,725,900

**The primary reason for the increase in labor for cartonizing and freezing and decrease in delivery cost was a change during the year to a new daily truck loading system:

Before: Every morning, each route sales delivery driver loads the truck from inventory, based on today's sales orders, before leaving the plant. Drivers spend up to 2 hours each day loading the truck before they can begin their sales route.

After: Carton handling workers sort daily production each day onto pallets grouped by delivery truck, based on tomorrow's sales orders. This substitutes lower cost factory labor for higher cost driver labor for loading the trucks and also frees up some driver time each day for more customer contact and point of sale merchandising.

EXHIBIT 3
Analysis of Variance from Forecasted Operating Income

Month	Year to Date
(1) Actual Income from Operations	$717,100
(2) Budgeted Income at Forecasted Volume	645,400
(3) Budgeted Income at Actual Volume	763,100
Variance Due to Sales Volume and Mix [(3) minus (2)]	117,700F
Variance Due to Operations [(1) minus (3)]	46,000U
Total Variance [(1) minus (2)]	$71,700F

APPENDIX

This description of the financial planning and control system is taken from a company operating manual.

The Financial Planning and Control System for the Ice Cream Division

The beginning point in making a profit plan is separating cost into fixed and variable categories. Pure variable costs require an additional amount with each increase in volume. The manager has little control over this type of cost other than to avoid waste. The accountant can easily determine the variable manufacturing cost per unit for any given product or package by using current prices and yields. Variable marketing cost per unit is based on the allowable rate (for example, $.06 per gallon for advertising). Costs that are not pure variable are classified as fixed, but they, too, will vary if significant changes in volume occur. There will be varying degrees of sensitivity to volume changes among these costs, ranging from a point just short of pure variable to an extremely fixed type of expense which has no relationship to volume.

The reason for differentiating between fixed and variable so emphatically is because variable cost spending requires no decision; it is dictated by volume. Fixed costs, on the other hand, require a management judgment and decision to increase or decrease the spending. Sugar is an example of a pure variable cost. Each change in volume will automatically bring a change in the sugar cost; only the yield can be controlled. Route salesmen's salaries would be an example of a fixed cost that is fairly sensitive to volume, but not pure variable. As volume changes, pressure will be felt to increase or decrease this expense, but management must make the decision; the change in cost level is not automatic. Depreciation charges for plant would be an example of a relatively extreme fixed cost. Very large increases in volume can usually be realized before this type of cost is pressured to change.

In both cases of fixed cost, a decision from management is required to increase or decrease the cost. It is this dilemma that management is constantly facing: to withstand the pressure to increase or be ready to decrease when the situation demands it. It would be a mistake to set a standard variable cost for items like route salesmen's salaries or depreciation, based on past performance, because they must constantly be evaluated for better and more efficient methods of doing the task.

Advertising is the only cost element not fitting the explanation of a variable cost given in the first paragraph. Advertising costs are set by management decision rather than being an "automatic" cost item like sugar or packaging. In this sense, advertising is like route salesmen's expense. For our company, however, management has decided that the allowance for advertising expense is equal to $.06 per gallon for the actual number of gallons sold. This management decision, therefore, has transformed advertising into an expense which is treated as variable for profit planning purposes.

Following is an example of the four-step approach to one-year profit planning.

The <u>first step</u> in planning is to develop a unit standard cost for each element of variable cost, by product and package size. Examples of two different packages for one product are shown below. As already pointed out, the accountant can do this by using current prices and yields for material costs and current allowance rates for marketing costs. After the total unit variable cost has been developed, this amount is subtracted from the selling price to arrive at a standard marginal contribution per unit, by product and package type.

APPENDIX - continued
Hypothetical Numbers

STEP 1
VANILLA ICE CREAM

Item	Regular 1-Gallon Paper Container	Premium 1-Gallon Plastic Container
Dairy Ingredients	$.53	$.79
Sugar	.15	.15
Flavor	.10	.12
Production	.10	.16
Warehouse	.06	.08
Transportation	.02	.025
Total Manufacturing	.96	1.325
Advertising	.06	.06
Delivery	.04	.04
Total Marketing	.10	.10
Packaging	.10	.25
Total Variable	1.16	1.675
Selling Price	1.50	2.40
Marginal Contribution per Gallon	.34	.725

Step 2 is perhaps the most critical in making a profit plan, because all plans drive from the anticipated level of sales activity. Much thought should be given in forecasting a realistic sales level and product mix. Consideration should be given to the number of days in a given period, as well as to the number of Fridays and Mondays, as these are two of the heaviest days and will make a difference in the sales forecast.

Other factors that should be considered are:

1	General economic condition of the marketing area
2	Weather
3	Anticipated promotions
4	Competition

STEP 2
VANILLA ICE CREAM SALES FORECAST IN GALLONS

	January	...	December	Total
1 Gallon, Paper	100,000		100,000	1,200,000
1 Gallon, Plastic	50,000		50,000	600,000
2 Gallons, Paper	225,000		225,000	2,700,000
1 Gallon, Premium	120,000		120,000	1,440,000
Total	495,000	...	495,000	5,940,000

Step 3 involves setting fixed-cost budgets based on management's judgment as to the need, in light of the sales forecast. It is here that good planning makes for a profitable operation. The number of routes needed for both winter and summer volume is planned. The level of manufacturing payroll is set. Because this system is based on a one-year time frame, manufacturing labor is considered to be a fixed cost. The level of the manufacturing work force is not really variable until a time frame longer than one year is adopted. Insurance and taxes are budgeted, and so on. After Step 4 has been performed, it may be necessary to return to Step 3 and make adjustments to some of the costs that are discretionary in nature.

APPENDIX - continued
Hypothetical Numbers

STEP 3
BUDGET FOR FIXED EXPENSES

	January	...	December	Total
Manufacturing Expense				
Labor	$7,280	...	$7,920	$88,000
Equipment repair	3,332	...	3,348	40,000
Depreciation	6,668	...	6,652	80,000
Taxes	3,332	...	3,348	40,000
Total	$20,612	...	$21,268	$248,000
Delivery Expense				
Salaries—General	$10,000	...	$10,000	$120,000
Salaries—Drivers	10,668	...	10,652	128,000
Helpers	10,668	...	10,652	128,000
Supplies	668	...	652	8,000
Total	$32,004	...	$31,956	$384,000
Administrative Expense				
Salaries	$5,167	...	$5,163	$62,000
Insurance	1,667	...	1,663	20,000
Taxes	1,667	...	1,663	20,000
Depreciation	833	...	837	10,000
Total	$9,334	...	$9,326	$112,000
Selling Expense				
Repairs	$2,667	...	$2,663	$32,000
Gasoline	5,000	...	5,000	60,000
Salaries	5,000	...	5,000	60,000
Total	$12,667	...	$12,663	$152,000

Step 4 is the profit plan itself. By combining our marginal contribution developed in Step 1 with our sales forecast from Step 2, we arrive at a total marginal contribution by month. Subtracting the fixed cost budgeted in Step 3, we have an operating profit by month. If this profit figure is not sufficient, a new evaluation should be made for Steps 1, 2 and/or 3.

STEP 4
THE PROFIT PLAN

	Standard Marginal Contribution	January Gallons	January $	...	Total Year
1 Gallon, Paper	$.340	100,000	$34,000		$408,000
1 Gallon, Plastic	.305	50,000	15,250		183,000
2 Gallons, Paper	.265	225,000	59,625		715,500
1 Gallon, Premium	.725	120,000	87,000		1,044,000
Total Marginal Contribution	$.3957	495,000	$195,875		$2,350,500
Fixed Cost (See Step 3)					
Manufacturing Expense			$20,612		$248,000
Delivery Expense			32,004		384,000
Administrative Expense			9,334		112,000
Selling Expense			12,667		152,000
Total Fixed			$74,617		$896,000
Operating Profit			$121,258		$1,454,500

Once the plan is completed and the year begins, profit variance is calculated monthly as a "management control" tool. To illustrate the control system, we will take the month of January and assume the level of sales activity for the month to be 520,000 gallons, as shown below. Looking back to our sales forecast (Step 2) we see that 495,000 gallons had been forecasted. When we apply our marginal contribution per unit for each product and package, we find that the 520,000 gallons have produced $6,125 less standard contribution than the 495,000 gallons would have produced at the forecasted mix. So even though there has been a nice increase in sales volume, the mix has been unfavorable. The $6,125 represents the difference between standard profit contribution at forecasted volume and standard profit contribution at actual volume. It is thus due to differences in volume and to differences in average mix. The impact of each of these two factors is also shown in Exhibit A:

APPENDIX - continued
Hypothetical Numbers

EXHIBIT A
JANUARY

	Actual Gallon Sales	Standard Contribution Per Gallon	Total Standard Contribution
1 Gallon, Paper	90,000	$.340	$30,600
1 Gallon, Plastic	95,000	.305	28,975
2 Gallons, Paper	245,000	.265	64,925
1 Gallon, Premium	90,000	.725	65,250
Total	520,000	$.3649	$189,750
Forecasted Standard Contribution (at 495,000 Gallons)			195,875
Variance			6,125U

	Planned	Actual	Difference
Gallons	495,000	520,000	25,000F
Contribution	$195,875	$189,750	$6,125U
Average Std. Contribution	$.3957	$.3649	$.0308U

F, favorable; U, unfavorable.

Variance Due to Volume

25,000 gallonsF X $.3957 = $9,892F

Total variance = $6,125U

Variance Due to Mix

$.0308U X 520,000 gallons = $16,017U

Exhibit B shows a typical departmental budget sheet for the month of January comparing actual costs with budget. A sheet is issued for each department, so the person responsible for a particular area of the business can see the items that are in line and those that need attention. In our example, there is an unfavorable operating variance of $22,750 ($570,537-$593,287). You should note that the budget for variable cost items has been adjusted to reflect actual volume, thereby eliminating cost variances due strictly to the difference between planned and actual volume.

EXHIBIT B
MANUFACTURING COST
January

Month Actual	Month Flexible Budget		Year-to-Date Actual	Year-to-Date Flexible Budget
$312,744	$299,000	Dairy Ingredients		
82,304	78,000	Sugar		
56,290	55,025	Flavorings		
38,770	37,350	Warehouse		
70,300	69,225	Production		
11,514	11,325	Transportation		
$571,922	$549,925	Subtotal—Variable		
7,300	7,280	Labor		
4,065	3,332	Equipment Repair		
6,668	6,668	Depreciation		
3,332	3,332	Taxes		
$21,365	$20,612	Subtotal—Fixed		
$593,287	$570,537	Total		

APPENDIX - continued
Hypothetical Numbers

Since the level of fixed costs is independent of volume anyway, it is not necessary to adjust the budget for these items for volume differences. The original budget for fixed-cost items is still appropriate. The totals for each department are carried forward to an earnings statement, Exhibit C. We have assumed all other departments' actual and budget are in line, so the only operating variance is the one for manufacturing. This variance, added to the sales volume and mix variance of $6,125U, results in an overall variance from the original plan of $28,875U, as shown:

EXHIBIT C
EARNINGS STATEMENT
January

Month			Year-to-Date	
Actual	Flexible Budget		Actual	Flexible Budget
$867,750	$867,750	Total Ice Cream Sales		
$593,287	$570,537	Manufacturing Cost of Goods Sold		
52,804	52,804	Delivery Expense		
31,200	31,200	Advertising Expense		
76,075	76,075	Packaging Expense		
12,667	12,667	Selling Expense		
9,334	9,334	Administrative Expense		
$775,367	$752,617	Total Expense		
$92,383	$115,133	Operating Profit		

Variance Recap

Actual Profit before Taxes	92,383	(1)
Original Profit Plan	121,258	(2)
Revised Profit Plan, Based on Actual Volume	115,133	(3)
Variance Due to Volume and Mix (3-2)	= 115,133 -	121,258 = 6,125U
Variance Due to Operations (1-3)	= 92,383 -	115,133 = 22,750U
Total Variance (1-2)	= 121,258 -	92,383 = 28,875U

Bridgewater Castings, Inc.*

This heavily disguised case is set in the "mature" woodstoves business in 1986. It is not based on The Vermont Castings Company. The issue is product line strategy based on product line profitability.

In early 1986, Tim Morrissey was reviewing the disappointing 1985 results of operations for his company (see Exhibit 1). The business had been founded in 1938 by Tim's grandfather as a modernization of an older iron forge company which Tim's great-great-grandfather had built up over the years since 1902. The company entered the cast iron wood stove business when that market boomed in the early-1970s. By 1977 wood heating stoves was its only product line. The business operated out of leased factory and office space in Bridgewater, Vermont which was owned by a family trust. Business had been very good through 1980, with a strong market for "environmentally sensitive" heat sources in the New England region which the Company served. Stove sales in 1983 were $9 million for 30,000 units. By 1985, however, the wood stove was a "declining" product with more than thirty competitors, a well known manufacturing technology, a shrinking market, heavy price pressure, and intense rivalry. By the mid-1980s, there was a growing sense that wood stoves were an environmental problem (air pollution), more than an environmental solution. Possible EPA legislation was a concern for the industry.

Faced with declining profitability, declining unit sales and substantial excess manufacturing capacity, Bridgewater had introduced a new product line in 1984--a combination wood stove and baking oven. This product required a minor modification of a wood stove, adding a brick-lined baking compartment with a hinged door and a heat gauge. It was targeted at persons who might consider brick oven baking with wood to be an attractive extension of heating with wood. The idea was not original with Bridgewater, but there were no major competitors at the time. The oven added only $10 per unit to material and labor costs and Morrissey priced the "wood oven" at $50 more than the heating stove alone ($350 vs. $300). The product thus generated a $40 higher contribution margin per unit which encouraged Morrissey to try to develop a market for it.

Bridgewater distributed its heating stoves through a network of appliance and furnace dealers in the Northeast who knew the product well and respected its quality and dependability. For wood stoves, the company did some dealer and customer advertising and sales promotion (6% of sales), but its major marketing effort was the dealer sales force--12 field sales representatives divided into two regions. They all traveled extensively, working to maintain dealer relationships and to build end-user awareness and goodwill, as well as writing sales orders.

---

* This case is adapted by Professor John Shank of the Amos Tuck School, with permission, from an earlier case written by Professor Anthony Atkinson of the University of Waterloo.

When wood ovens were added, Morrissey did not expect heavy dealer penetration immediately so he expanded the sales area substantially. Whereas stoves were sold, essentially, only in Northern New York, and the six New England states, he negotiated sales outlets for ovens over the entire Northeast Quadrant, from Maine to Chicago, St. Louis, and Richmond, Virginia. By 1985, he had added six oven field sales reps, an oven sales manager, and also established relationships with a great many independent sales agents across the Eastern U.S. Establishing the wood oven market also turned out to require much heavier investments in advertising, dealer promotion, dealer discounts, and sales incentives. But with steady hard work the business was being established. Bridgewater sold 10,000 ovens in 1984 and 20,000 in 1985 of which 5,000 were sold in the core area. The 1985 figure was fully 80% the number of wood stoves sold. Competition was still minimal, which Morrissey attributed to the uniqueness of the concept and the strong early lead Bridgewater had established with dealers by its concerted marketing program.

Bridgewater was selling only a few stoves through the expanded sales network and marketing program, because Morrissey was reluctant to push the lower margin product through the higher cost marketing network. Freight cost was also a problem when the shipping distance expanded. Both stoves and ovens were bulky and weighed well over 300 pounds each. Thus, they were very expensive to ship. Bridgewater owned a fleet of trucks which had been expanded from 5 to 10 since the addition of wood ovens to the business. Even though the fleet represented about a $2 million investment, shipping full-load orders in company owned trucks was not uneconomic. But more than half of all shipments went out in partial loads using common carriers and contract haulers. Considering traffic management, dispatching, fleet costs, freight bills, packing cost, and rental charges for public warehouse space, total shipping costs were running about 17% of sales in 1985.

When Tim Morrissey saw the operating results for 1985 he walked into the office of his chief accountant, Caroline Cooper, and asked her how much confidence he should place in the split of operations between stoves and ovens. The loss on stoves was not really surprising to him, given the tough market for that product, but he wasn't sure how Cooper had assigned costs and revenues.

Cooper said she was pretty comfortable with the breakdowns. "This really isn't a complex manufacturing operation for either product, as you well know. The sales breakdown is based on actual sales invoices. It's solid! Manufacturing cost is pretty clean also, since direct product costs are over 54% of the total. Material and labor costs come from our average cost records which are fairly accurate, since we keep track of those costs on each batch that runs through the shop. General factory overhead, which we consider fixed, was $2,520,000 last year. Of that, $800,000 was depreciation. Rent is $550,000. Factory support costs are $1,170,000. I consider these three costs pretty much common to all production, so I assign them on the basis of units produced. Variable manufacturing overhead is another $1.1 million which I also assign based on units. You might argue about the overhead allocations a little," she continued, "but not very much. When we made only stoves, there was no product line allocation to worry about. I suppose now you could go to an allocation based on labor, but the difference would not be large. The ovens each take a little more time to manufacture, but we make fewer total ovens." She gave him a summary of manufacturing costs for the year (Exhibit 2) to look at.

Cooper continued explaining, "Allocating non-manufacturing costs is always a lot more subjective, but the way I split them seems very reasonable to me. Stoves generated more total volume in units and dollars, but ovens have been harder to sell and distribute. Stoves really constitute the base business, with ovens as the incremental, new business. After thinking about it for awhile, I decided to charge selling and shipping on the basis of percent of sales dollars across the two products. Then I just split the half million of general expenses equally between the two lines since the sales are about equal. General expenses have not changed much for several years. Since we seem to be in both product lines now for the foreseeable future, and both seem to be generating positive profit contribution, I don't suppose the allocation of SG&A matters much anyway." Morrissey thanked her for the up-date and walked slowly back to his office.

As he studied the results, Morrissey thought to himself:

The numbers really do confirm my intuition. The market for stoves is getting so competitive that we just can't seem to make a profit there in spite of our best efforts. We have tried everything I know and we just keep sliding down further and further. But the crazy wood oven is a real "comer." We've turned the corner there and things should get better and better.

I don't like to admit defeat, but I really think we should start phasing out of stoves altogether. If we couldn't even break-even in 1985, after all our hard work, we aren't ever going to do it. I always remember the article by Peter Drucker in which he said, "If you can't make good profit in a product, get out. Focusing on contribution margin is just a trap that will drag you down.

You are in business for the long run, and in the long run all costs are relevant. If you can't cover them, don't kid yourself." The secret for getting us back "in the black" is to capitalize on our great start in wood ovens and throw all our efforts there, just like we did with stoves ten years ago.

Morrissey called his Sales Vice President, George Murphy, to tell him that he was just about ready to "pull the plug" on stoves. Murphy was aware of the 1985 financial results and was not in love with the stove business. "I wouldn't object to that, Tim, even though it would mean a lot of grief in scaling back operations in the shop and in selling and distribution. Without wood stoves, a lot of people would have to go. But I suppose it's better to save the fast growing half of the business rather than let stoves drag us all down, slowly but surely. Since the selling and shipping budgets are each just about two and a half times what they were when we introduced ovens, there are a lot of fairly new people there. So it's not like we would be laying off twenty-year veterans. We still have a long way to go on ovens, but the trends are all good. I think we could probably sell 30,000 ovens this year if we concentrated on just that one product and held our prices. One "hang up" I still struggle with is that stove orders average ten units while oven orders are only two units on average. We both know that getting orders is what the sales game is all about, but small orders make it harder to amortize the effort. We work a lot harder to sell and distribute an oven outside New England than we do for a stove in New England, but I know we price ovens a lot higher, too. And, we're still learning that business." Murphy paused for a moment and then concluded, "I'm with you Tim, whatever you decide. We've both got a lot of years invested in this place and I'd hate to see it slip away from us."

ASSIGNMENT QUESTIONS

1. a. What is your estimate of the 1983 income statement and balance sheet?

    b. What is your estimate of Return on Assets in 1983? (Assume a 40% tax rate.) How is the company doing in 1983? For simplicity, you may assume that individual price and cost components have not changed between 1983 and 1985.

2. Taking a closer look at cost allocation for manufacturing, selling and shipping expenses, what is your estimate of ovens profit and stoves profit for 1985?

3. What is your estimate of the income statement for 1986 if only ovens were sold (30,000 units)?

4. Should Bridgewater drop the stoves product line?

5. How much does it cost, on average, to ship a stove within the core area? How much does it cost, on average, to ship a stove outside the core area?

6. How much does it cost, on average, to generate a sales order for stoves in the core area (order getting costs)? How much does it cost, on average, to generate a sales order for ovens outside the core area? So what?

7. What is your advice to Tim Morrissey?

EXHIBIT 1
Results of Operations - 1985

	Ovens	Stoves	Total
Sales	$7,000,000.	$7,500,000.	$14,500,000.
Cost of Goods Sold (Exhibit 2)	3,600,000.	4,250,000.	7,850,000.
Gross Margin	3,400,000.	3,250,000.	6,650,000.
Selling Cost	1,500,000.	1,625,000.	3,125,000.
Shipping Cost	1,200,000.	1,300,000.	2,500,000.
Sales Commissions (5%)	350,000.	375,000.	725,000. [1]
General Expenses	245,000.	245,000.	490,000.
Profit Before Taxes	$105,000.	$(295,000.)	$(190,000.)

Note: Cost of Goods Sold equals Manufacturing Cost since there was no change in inventory levels for the year.

[1]For the 5% Sales Commission:

    2% to a Customer Allowances Fund
    3% to Employees (2% to the Sales Rep, 1/2% to the Sales Manager, 1/2% to the Sales VP)

EXHIBIT 2
Manufacturing Costs - 1985

	Ovens		Stoves		Total
	Per Unit	$	Per Unit	$	$
Materials	$45.00	900,000.	$40.00	1,000,000.	1,900,000.
Labor and Benefits ($10/hr.)	55.00	1,100,000.	50.00	1,250,000.	2,350,000.
Variable Overhead	24.00	480,000.	24.00	600,000.	1,080,000.
Fixed Overhead	56.00	1,120,000.	56.00	1,400,000.	2,520,000. [1]
Total	$180.00	$3,600,000.	$170.00	$4,250,000.	$7,850,000.

[1]Fixed Factory Overhead:

Depreciation (15 year lives)	$800,000
Rent (110,000 square feet)	550,000
Factory Support*	1,170,000

*The factory manager estimated that 60 percent of factory support cost is due to ovens, because of the special problems related to the large number of small batch factory orders. Ovens cause special problems in scheduling, set-up, rework, and heat gauge calibration.

Brunswick Plastics*

This case deals with cost analysis for pricing new business in a small injection molding job shop in "the Maritimes" in 1986, a good business year.

In September of 1986 Michael Smith, Division Manager of Brunswick Plastics, faced an important pricing decision on a major new bid opportunity. Michael knew that pricing too high meant losing a bid that would employ currently unused capacity. On the other hand, pricing too low meant losses on the job. In the first two months after Michael arrived in November of 1984, the presses were running only about 40% of available machine hours. The division had recently lost two large contracts and was struggling to find a solid market position. Michael had instituted a policy of "contribution margin pricing" to restore profitability. He reasoned that the fixed costs were already in place and there was heavy excess capacity. Any orders that generated positive contribution would enhance bottom line profits. In two years, machine running time was up to almost 50% of available machine hours and the number of different products manufactured was up from 30 to 50.

THE COMPANY

In addition to the 50 different products BP was selling, it was also typically experimenting in the factory with a few others at any given time. New product introductions seemed to Michael to be a key step in filling up the factory. Smith's best estimate of sales for 1986 was $1,200,000 and he thought BP would again be just above the break even level on profits. An estimated income statement for 1986 is shown in Exhibit 1. The division had 20 full-time employees. Since the factory was not unionized, factory employment fluctuated monthly, based on demand. Factory employment had ranged between 13 and 31 people in the past 2 1/2 years. Through strict attention to quality control, and by aggressively promoting its products, BP had developed a reputation as a reliable supplier of high quality products. In several markets, BP products were specified by major customers and had become the industry standard for quality.

BP sold its products in both domestic and US markets and faced a highly competitive environment. There were many injection molding companies in eastern Canada and the northeastern part of the U.S. As a result, pricing was a key to success, both from the point of view of securing contracts, and from the point of view of profitability.

Manufacturing at BP was done in two different modes. Some of the high volume products were manufactured to stock in long runs to minimize set-up costs and to maintain required inventory levels. However, for most products, production was in response to a specific order.

---

* This case was adapted by Professor John Shank, with permission from the author, from an earlier case written by Professor Anthony Atkinson of the University of Waterloo under a grant from the Society of Management Accountants of Canada.

THE COSTING ENVIRONMENT

There were five major injection molding presses in use at BP. The machines were of varying ages and all experienced frequent down-time because of set-ups, raw material problems, regular repairs, and special repairs related to complex products or new product problems. The factory typically operated 2 shifts a day, 5 days a week, but volume fluctuations also led sometimes to one shift or three shift operations. There were four common stages involved in manufacturing a product: (1) set up of the production machine, (2) the production operation, (3) the assembly operation, and (4) the testing operation. The set up, assembly, and testing operations were labor-intensive. The labor content of the production operation varied widely from product to product.

In injection molding, molten plastic is forced into a mold where it is "cured". The curing process requires cooling the mold, usually with water. Once the product has cured, the mold is opened and the product removed.

Some products were produced in stationary molds that required little manual intervention. Water was passed through these molds during the curing cycle. At the completion of the curing cycle, the molds were opened and the products were ejected automatically. For these products, the direct labor content was minimal and the operation was machine-paced.

Other products were produced in removable molds that required manual intervention. After the molten plastic was injected, these molds were removed from the molding machine and placed into a vat of water for the curing cycle. At the completion of the curing cycle, the molds were opened manually and the product removed. For these products, the direct labor content could be significant since the operation was labor-paced.

The products also varied widely in terms of the assembly and testing time required. On the one hand, the company manufactured pediatric syringes used in the care of premature infants. These syringes required extensive attention to quality control and a considerable amount of manual assembly in a "clean room". On the other hand, the company also manufactured wheel chocks that required only a cursory inspection and no assembly. The other products produced by BP varied between these two extremes.

In addition to the product costing complications caused by the wide mix of manufacturing, assembly, and testing requirements, there were difficulties caused by the machines. Typical of the industry, the machines used at BP differed widely in terms of their reliability and their performance when producing different products. A machine problem meant that the machine would have to be stopped and reset. Because the machine stoppages were highly unpredictable, incorporating a normal or average machine failure cost into the product cost was difficult.

On the other hand, the materials, assembly, and testing costs of most products were well understood since each of these costs could be measured with reasonable accuracy. Materials costs could be estimated by the weight of the final product since the material in most defective products could be reused. The assembly and testing operations involved the use of machines that were both highly reliable and labor-paced.

These difficulties and the costing issues were all on Michael's mind as he considered the milk crate contract.

THE MILK CRATE CONTRACT

Dairies in eastern Canada used plastic crates to ship milk cartons from the dairies to the stores. The annual sales volume of milk crates in the local region was about 300,000 units. Dairies merged their orders for crates through the Dairy Council in order to take maximum advantage of possible quantity discounts. Michael had been asked to submit a bid on an initial order of 150,000 units. It was clear in Michael's mind that a successful initial bid would give BP a competitive advantage in future orders.

Michael felt that the successful bid price for these crates would be "$3.00 plus or minus ten cents." Michael had been approached by the customer several times and felt that BP's reputation for quality would ensure that a $3.00 bid would be successful. As a result, estimating the bid price was not the major issue. The question to be resolved was whether or not, given its cost structure, $3.00 could cover BP's costs of producing this product.

Discussions with Walt Roberts and Larry Bobbit, BP's technical and production supervisors, suggested that the machine cycle time to produce this product would be 50 seconds per unit. The product would be produced in a stationary mold and would be automatically ejected at the rate of one every 50 seconds. As a result, Michael calculated that it would require 2083[1] hours of machine *running* time to fill the order. On the basis of his discussion with Walt Roberts, Michael expected that the rate of defective crates produced by this process would be negligible.

Following discussions with Larry Bobbit, Michael felt that during the machine cycle time the machine operator would have sufficient time to trim the excess plastic (flash) off the previous crate that had been made and stamp that crate with the particular dairy's name.

Based on BP's experience, which was comparable to the industry average, Michael calculated that the molding machine would run for only 60% of the time that it was scheduled for operation. The rest of the time that it was scheduled for operation the machine would be down for repair, set-up, or maintenance.

---

[1] (150000*50)/3600

Consequently, Michael estimated that it would require 3472[2] hours of scheduled machine time to achieve the required 2083 hours of machine operating time. Since the operator would be required for most of the repair time, all the set-up time, and all the maintenance time, an operator would have to be scheduled for each hour of scheduled machine time.

Michael decided that the production of the milk crates could be undertaken on BP's 750 ton injection molder. This would require that some of the production scheduled for that machine be rescheduled to other machines. Because BP currently had excess capacity available on other machines, Michael felt that the new order would not require sacrificing any production of any other products.

The cost of a production mold used to manufacture the milk crates would normally be $90,000. However, the Dairy Council already owned a suitable mold which they had agreed to lend to the successful bidder on the contract.

Each milk crate weighed 1.6 kilograms. Polyethylene would be used to produce the milk crate. The cost of polyethylene was $1.07 per kilogram. Michael felt that plastic trimmed off crates, or plastic in defective crates, could be reprocessed at a minimal cost. Consequently, the cost of raw material per crate was estimated as $1.71.[3]

Since the machine operators were paid $6.00 per hour (including benefits), the labor cost per crate was computed as $0.14.[4]

The materials cost to stamp the crates was estimated as $0.01 per side, yielding a total cost of $0.04 per crate. In addition, a stamping machine costing $5000 would have to be acquired. The life of this simple stamping machine was estimated as 10 years, at least.

The crates did not require packaging for shipping and the Dairy Council paid for shipment. Michael estimated that the labor costs to load the crates on a truck at the factory door would be $0.02 per crate.

As a result of these calculations, Michael believed that the direct variable cost of producing the milk crates would be $1.91 (1.71 + .14 + .04 + .02).

This still left the matter of the overhead associated with producing each milk crate. This issue had been a source of continuing concern to Michael on almost every contract he negotiated. Michael knew that a common "rule of thumb" in his plant was to apply variable overhead to products at a rate of $13 for each machine hour (running time). An industry rule of thumb was to estimate total variable cost as being 1.3 times the direct material and direct labor costs.[5]

Some analysts also advocated looking at fixed, as well as variable, manufacturing overhead.[6] Based on a recent study of BP's costs, the corporate controller estimated that, on average, selling price must equal at least 2.33 times the sum of direct material and direct labor costs in order to earn average industry margins of 6% (pre-tax) when operating at the industry average 90% capacity utilization ratio (scheduled hours). Some comparative data on industry economics is summarized in Exhibit 2.

Michael wondered about the accuracy of any of these approaches in general and, in particular, he wondered if any one was suitable in this situation. Michael looked at the ratio of market price to the sum of direct material and direct labor cost for some of his more popular products and found that this ratio varied from two to seven. As a result, he wondered what, if anything, was the implication of the 2.33 factor.

As a guide to understanding the relationship between direct costs (material and labor) and fixed manufacturing overhead Michael developed the data that appears in EXHIBIT 3. The plant accountant advised Michael that plant fixed manufacturing overhead did not include direct materials, direct labor, variable overhead or plant supervision (about $50,000 per year).

In addition to manufacturing costs, BP was incurring about $220,000 per year in Selling, General and Administrative (S, G &A) expenses.

Michael was not sure how to use Exhibit 3 to help him assign overhead cost to the milk crate order. The results did seem to indicate that overhead was virtually unrelated to the level of output in the factory. The results thus did seem to support his "contribution margin pricing" policy. Michael was still unsure, however, as to how he should approach this large incremental order. He observed to the case writer:

> "If I only knew my cost structure better, I would feel more confident about what I am doing. Right know I feel that I am shooting in the dark."

---

[2](2083/0.6)

[3]1.6*$1.07

[4](50/0.6)*(1/3600)*$6.00

[5]One source of this data was the publication *Financial and Operating Ratios,* published by The Society of the Plastics Industry, Inc. This survey indicated that the total of variable costs was, on average, about 74% of sales for injection molders. Since the sum of direct materials and direct labour costs was, on average, 57% of sales, this implied that total variable costs were, on average, 1.3 times the sum of direct material and direct labour costs (74% = 1.3 x 57%).

[6]See, for example, "Machine-hour costs: processors must know them if they are to survive", in *Plastics Engineering*, October, 1977.

ASSIGNMENT QUESTIONS

1. Based on your interpretation of Exhibit 3, what is your estimate of the change in "PFMOH" cost if the factory were to run one extra batch of 150,000 milk crates?

2. What is your estimate of the incremental cost per unit for one batch of 150,000 milk crates?

3. What does Exhibit 2 suggest would be a "normal" price for milk crates for an "average" job shop? What does this suggest about the $3.00 price which seems to prevail at the time of the case?

4. What is the "strategically relevant" cost per unit for milk crates? (for purposes of deciding whether or not the $3.00 "market price" is profitable, on an ongoing basis)

5. What is your advice to Mr. Smith regarding the milk crate opportunity? Be specific and show the calculations supporting your advice.

6. What overall strategic advice do you have for Mr. Smith? Why isn't the business doing better, given the new "specialties strategy" and good business conditions? Support your answer with relevant cost analysis.

EXHIBIT 1
Estimated Income Statement (1986)

(Given)		
(1/2.33 = 43% of Sales)	Sales	$1,200
(15,000 x $13)	Direct Material plus Direct Labor	(515)
	Variable Overhead	(195) (16% of Sales)
	Contribution Margin (CM)	490
(205 + 220 + 50)	Fixed Overhead	(475)
(Just above break even)	Profit Before Taxes	$15

EXHIBIT 2
Industry Economics

	At "Normal" Capacity (90% Utilization)		At Full Capacity	
	Average	BP	Average	BP
Sales	100%	100%	100%	100%
DM + DL	57	43	57	43
Variable Overhead	17	16	17	16
Fixed Overhead	20	35	18	31.5
Profit Before Taxes	6%	6%	8%	9.5%

When operating near capacity, BP shows up as the High CM/High Fixed Cost/High Profit Player. But note that the profit impact (Profit % of Sales) of BP's apparent strategy only shows up near full capacity. High volume is a key to high profit for BP.

EXHIBIT 3
Cost and Activity Data

Year	Month	Direct Labor Hours (production, assembly, testing)	Indirect Labor Hours (set-up, repair, and maintenance)	Total Machine Hours (running time)	Plant Fixed Manufacturing Overhead (PFMOH)
	January	1679	1305	1885	3536
	February	2298	863	1775	17196
	March	3785	991	1800	13462
	April	2646	1287	1643	4194
	May	2606	1686	1848	15958
1984	June	2661	1505	1274	7644
	July	1670	938	1182	3530
	August	1844	1337	1003	7073
	September	1839	1343	1351	6094
	October	2088	1295	1837	10072
	November	2330	1743	1533	4173
	December	1434	1416	601	6078
	Total	26880	15709	18321	99010
	January	1694	1019	1104	3811
	February	1701	933	1128	4712
	March	2103	1532	917	11325
	April	1756	1192	1211	1161
	May	2184	1276	1249	6572
1985	June	1625	890	829	10063
	July	1775	1256	1278	7621
	August	2007	1728	1095	11028
	September	2094	1337	1824	15198
	October	2178	1503	1788	4690
	November	2992	1868	1471	9484
	December	2079	1751	1313	5615
	Total	24188	16290	15207	91280
	January	2714	1922	1899	18293
	February	2240	1328	1567	15733
	March	2275	1663	1723	39988
1986	April	1737	1157	954	3033
	May	1547	1443	654	9358
	June	1389	1434	634	20166
	July	2394	1948	1735	16308
	August	990	856	1005	14267
	Subtotal*	15286	11751	10171	137146
*Annualized for 1986 (12/8)		~23000	~17500	~15000	~205000

TO EXPLORE THE CAUSAL RELATIONSHIPS REFLECTED HERE, MICHAEL DEVELOPED THE FOLLOWING FOUR LINEAR REGRESSIONS:

		R^2	t-Statistic
1.	(PFMOH) versus Machine Hours (MH): PFMOH = \$3681 + (\$4.86* MH)	0.07	1.48
2.	PFMOH versus Direct Labor Hours (DLH): PFMOH = \$4321 + (\$2.85* DLH)	0.04	1.15
3.	PFMOH versus Indirect Labor Hours (ILH): PFMOH = \$1684 + (\$6.25* ILH)	0.07	1.49
4.	PFMOH versus MH and DLH: PFMOH = -\$79 + (\$2.89* MH) + (\$1.87* DLH)	0.09	0.70/0.81

Buchanan Steel*

This case is set in a modern American steel "finishing mill" in 1979, a good business year. The subject is profit variance analysis for the "TMW" billing program.

Buchanan Steel is the newest mill of Pennsylvania Steel, a major US integrated producer. Buchanan is a small division for the parent company, but it would be a Fortune 300 company if it were separately owned and publicly traded. Buchanan, a finishing mill, buys hot-rolled steel coils (hot bands) from sister divisions and processes them further into cold-rolled and galvanized (zinc-coated) products. It buys already cold-rolled coils to make unikote (galvanized on one side only) products. A schematic representation of mill operations is shown in the Appendix to the case.

Buchanan operates as a separate profit center within Pennsylvania Steel. It pays market-based transfer prices for all purchased coils. Product profitability data (per ton) through six months of 1979 is shown in Exhibit 4.

The Buchanan mill was built in 1965 on a large tract of land which the parent company had acquired for $5 million as a possible site for a new fully integrated mill. Tough times in the steel industry during the 1970s led Pennsylvania Steel to limit its investment there to just the finishing mill.

THE TMW PROGRAM

Until 1970, virtually all steel in the United States was sold by weight. Steel companies established prices per ton which, when multiplied by the actual shipped weight of a particular order, would give the total selling price. In 1970, a theoretical minimum weight (TMW) billing program was initiated by one of Buchanan's competitors as a marketing response to customer complaints regarding the industry-wide practice of rolling orders heavier than the gauge specified by the customer. Due to this additional thickness, a customer specifying a given footage had to accept more weight and thus higher cost than ordered. As long as revenue was based on weight shipped, there was no real incentive at the mill not to "roll the order heavy."

The TMW program was immediately matched by the other major steel companies. It effectively changed the marketing practices of the industry, for the products affected, from selling by the actual tonnage to selling by surface area times desired gauge. Many steel executives complained that TMW was just a "sleazy sales trick" to build volume by cutting prices. Others saw TMW as conceptually correct—why should customers be expected to pay for tonnage they don't want and didn't order?

---

*This case was prepared by Professor John K. Shank of the Amos Tuck School, with the cooperation of a major steel company. It is based on an earlier version written with the assistance of Mr. David Templin. All information in the case has been disguised.

Only the most modern steel finishing mills had accurate footage counters on their processing equipment. For these mills TMW was a feasible calculation. The amount billed on the order is the theoretical weight of the coil, calculated as:

Ordered minimum gauge x actual length x ordered width x standard steel density factor

For example, for a .0280-gauge 48-inch-wide order and a coil 9800 feet long, as measured coming off the finishing unit, the theoretical weight of that order is

(.0280 in.) x (9800 ft.) x (12 in./ft.) x (48 in.) x (.2833 lb./cu. in.) ÷ (2,000 lb./ton) = 22.4 tons

This figure multiplied by the price per ton gives the selling price of the coil.

Most American finishing mills could only <u>estimate</u> footage on each coil, and not necessarily accurately. These mills applied TMW based on their estimate of footage shipped. If their customers had accurate footage counters, there could be discrepancies in the invoices resulting in claims for refunds. Since the mills weren't really sure what footage they were shipping, they had to honor all refund claims.

A few of the smaller, older mills made no pretense of being able to measure the footage shipped. They just negotiated price discounts with their customers, averaging 3 to 4 percent, based on a guess of excess thickness being shipped.

In recent years, the TMW program had been causing progressively larger losses for Buchanan. In July of 1979, Buchanan Steel president Phil Palmintere called a meeting to discuss the problems with the theoretical minimum weight billing program. In attendance were the production control manager Brad Schmidt, the chief metallurgist Al Falenski, the sales manager Max Heilburg, and the controller Andy Birrel.

MR. PALMINTERE: President

I think you all know why we're here. In the last few months we've been taking a bath on our TMW billing program. According to these figures from Andy, we've lost approximately $6.9 million so far this year due to TMW (see Exhibit 1). Furthermore, as Exhibit 2 shows, our "percent giveaway" has been increasing steadily over the last 3 years. Couple this with rising prices for finished steel and the result is the current sorry state of our giveaway losses.

TMW Loss—Revenue or Cost?

MR. HEILBURG: Sales

Andy, just how are you computing the dollar loss due to TMW?

MR. Birrel: Controller

For any particular product, we simply multiply the difference between the actual tons shipped and theoretical tons billed times the corresponding revenue-per-ton figure. The reason is that under normal billing practice we'd charge for the actual tons shipped, while under TMW we're only charging for the theoretical tons shipped. The cost of what we ship is the same either way.

MR. HEILBURG: Sales

I don't think that's the appropriate way to figure the TMW loss, Andy. TMW essentially changed our billing practices from selling by the ton to selling by the foot. The customer stamps parts, say for fender panels, out of the coil. In order to produce the desired number of parts, they want a certain number of feet at a particular gauge. When we roll heavier than the ordered minimum gauge, we're giving the customer something they aren't interested in having and don't want to pay for. The revenue will be the same whether we roll right on the ordered gauge or heavier than the ordered gauge, since the selling price of the coil is calculated using the actual footage and the ordered gauge rather than the actual gauge. What we're losing is the manufacturing cost of the giveaway weight.

MR. FALENSKI: Metallurgy

You know, Max, the more I think about it, the more I think that sales revenue is the relevant measure of our loss. The lineal feet aren't really fixed at all on a given TMW order. Let me give you an example. Suppose a customer orders 5,000 tons of .028 gauge steel with a particular width and finish. That order is based on the customer's calculation of the weight needed to yield the desired lineal footage. In order to yield the desired number of lineal feet of the specified product, we schedule, say, 5,500 tons of, say,

.029 gauge. However, we end up running .030 gauge. We then bill the customer according to the theoretical weight of the actual footage shipped which, as Andy pointed out, is calculated using the ordered gauge. However, if we had "squeezed" that coil tighter to .028 thickness and converted that extra gauge into additional footage, the coil would have a higher selling price. The cost of the coil is whatever it is. The loss is due to producing the coil thicker instead of longer. Lost revenue is thus the proper measure of the profit impact.

MR. SCHMIDT: Production Control

Wait a minute, Al. That customer is only going to buy a given number of lineal feet from us over time in order to stamp out a given number of parts. If we ship longer coils now, they will just cut back on future orders. Over time, we're already collecting all the revenue we're going to get. The problem is the extra weight of the footage that we're selling. Our loss is thus the cost of that extra weight.

MR. BIRREL: Controller

Brad, I think you're being too technical about the amount of footage the customer will take. Generally, they take whatever footage is in the coil we ship. Hell, a lot of the customers don't even have footage counters on their equipment.

MR. SCHMIDT: Production Control

What we're talking about, Andy, is a difference of opinion about the scrap control practices of our customers. I think their controls are pretty tight in the long run and you don't.

Measuring the Cost of Giveaway Tons

MR. HEILBURG: Sales

Even if we go to cost instead of revenue as the relevant loss measure the fixed portion of the cost is irrelevant since it won't actually change. I agree that we should look at cost instead of revenue to measure our loss, but we should only consider the variable costs.

MR. BIRREL: Controller

Ignoring the fixed costs makes sense in short-run analyses, Max, but TMW isn't a short-run problem. We've been in the program for 9 years already, and over that long a time frame nearly all of our costs are variable. Full cost of the giveaway tonnage is the best measure of what we're losing, if we aren't going to use revenue.

MR. HEILBURG: Sales

The question, Andy, is how much are we losing this year? The fixed costs are there regardless of our billing practices. What we're losing this year is only the variable cost of steel.

MR. SCHMIDT: Production Control

Whether we take a long- or short-run view of variable production costs may not make any difference anyway since most of our production costs vary more as a function of lineal footage than tonnage. Under TMW, the lineal footage is given. Therefore, nearly all the production costs are given. The problem is extra thickness, and that additional thickness costs us only the additional material cost. Accordingly, we should be multiplying the difference between actual and theoretical tons by our hot-band costs (raw material) to get our relevant loss, in which case it goes down to about $4.9 million for the first half of 1979.

MR. FALENSKI: Metallurgy

Brad. You're ignoring our yields. For cold-roll and galvanized, the yield is 88%, while it's 87% for Unikote. In other words, we have to buy 1.136 tons of hot band in order to give away 1 ton of cold-roll or galvanized, and we have to buy 1.149 tons of full-finished cold-roll in order to give away 1 ton of Unikote. Taking this into consideration would raise our TMW dollar loss to $5.6 million for the period in question.

MR. BIRREL: Controller

What you guys are suggesting totally undercuts our basic accounting system. The entire steel industry, Buchanan included, measures costs on a per ton rather than a per foot basis. Standard costs per ton are designed to reflect run speed, gauge, and width variations adjusted for actual yields. In other words, all of these other variables are taken into account in computing standard cost per ton for a given product. What we lose from the TMW giveaway therefore includes processing costs as well as material costs.

MR. SCHMIDT: Production Control

Well, Andy, over the 2 to 5% deviations that we're talking about here, I just can't see that the processing costs will change. I still think it's only material cost that changes over this range.

MR. PALMINTERE: President

I'm not sure we've made any progress on the appropriate dollar basis for the giveaway tons, but, any way you slice it, because of TMW our profits are less than they could be and should be. As long as we are stuck with TMW we need to control the negative impact. As I see it, we're giving away an average of 4.02% of our actual tonnage of these products according to the six months figures (Exhibit 1). Al, can you give me some kind of a breakdown of that figure?

Decomposing the "Giveaway" Percentage

MR. FALENSKI: Metallurgy

As a matter of fact, Phil, I just happen to have such a report with me (see Exhibit 3). I used the percent giveaway figures for last March since they were high, although not too far above the year-to-date average. Please bear in mind, however, that these numbers are pretty soft. As the table shows, the four main categories of our TMW loss are incoming raw material, providing practices, operating practices, and reapplications of dispositioned material.

MR. HEILBURG: Sales

Excuse me, Al, but I'm a little vague on some of the terms you're using. Can you fill me in on the meanings of 'providing' and 'operating' practices?

MR. FALENSKI: Metallurgy

Sure thing, Max. First, when we're rolling steel, we aim for a particular gauge. However, the gauge that we finally produce varies around that target gauge. Sometimes it comes out heavier than aimed for, and sometimes lighter. Graphically, we get something like this:

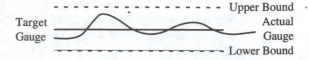

If we aimed for the customer's ordered gauge, some of the steel would come out too thin to be acceptable to the customer. This would lead to an increase in our 'light gauge claims,' which would really hurt our reputation in the market. To avoid this, we aim for a gauge that's sufficiently thicker than the ordered gauge; therefore, the actual gauge is almost always heavier than the ordered gauge, like this:

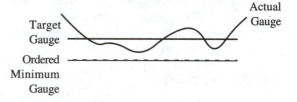

This is the purpose of our providing practices. They show the amount by which we must aim above the ordered minimum gauge to ensure that virtually none of the steel comes out lighter than that gauge.

Our providing practices can be broken down into the part pertaining to the steel and the part pertaining to the zinc-coating process. We not only try to ensure that the steel satisfies minimum thickness requirements, we also want to avoid coating the galvanized products too lightly.

It may interest you to know that the deviation from the ordered minimum gauge that we aim for through our providing practices is significantly smaller than that considered to be acceptable by the American Iron and Steel Institute.

I've compiled some examples of the standard AISI tolerances, the associated percent deviations for various gauges, and the percent anticipated deviations resulting from our providing practices. Please take a minute to look these over.

| | AISI | | Buchanan's Providing |
Gauge (in.)	1/2 AISI Tolerance	Deviation (%)	Practice (%) Deviation
Cold-Roll			
.0168	+.002	11.90	4
.0304	+.003	9.87	3
.0494	+.004	8.11	3
.0786	+.005	6.37	3
Galvanized (including Unikote)			
.0181	+.003	16.57	4
.035	+.004	11.43	3
.054	+.005	9.26	4
.069	+.006	8.70	4
.0876	+.008	9.14	4

Given the percent deviation that's acceptable according to industry standards, it's perhaps less surprising that we're having so much trouble adhering to our strict divisional standards.

The operating practices category is composed of the cold mill, the sheet-temper mill, and zinc coating. To a large extent, the operating practices detail the difference between what we aim for and what we actually produce. As I mentioned before, to ensure that our steel is not thinner than a specified minimum gauge, we aim, via our providing practices, for a slightly heavier gauge. However, as the last illustration shows, the actual gauge we produce varies around our aimed-for gauge. It's this variation that the 'operating practices' illustrate.

The portion of our giveaway coming from incoming raw material exists because whenever we order a hot band from one of our sister divisions, they roll the steel a bit heavier than the specified gauge, much as we do for our TMW customers. However, since the TMW program does not cover hot-rolled steel (hot bands), they bill us for the actual weight shipped rather than the theoretical weight. This category also captures the portion of our giveaway that's due to the 'crown' that's imparted to the hot band when

our sister divisions produce it.

MR. HEILBURG: Sales

Excuse me, Al, but that's another term that I've been meaning to ask you about. Could you briefly explain 'crown' to me?

MR. FALENSKI: Metallurgy

Gladly, Max. Steel producers and steel users would like the finished product to have a 'flat' profile (see diagram A below):

A.

However, because of technical factors in the production process, the strip always comes out with a 'rounded' profile (see diagram B below):

B.

The area outside the desired rectangular shape is called 'crown.'

As I was saying, even for cold-roll and galvanized, where we're doing our own cold reduction, the crown that's imparted to the hot band stays on the steel throughout the finishing process. The greater the crown that our sister divisions send us, the more steel we end up giving away in the form of additional gauge to ensure that it satisfies the minimum-gauge requirements at the edges as well as at the center of the strip.

The cold mill is used to achieve the main portion of the reduction in gauge between the incoming hot band and the desired customer coil. Our percent loss increases whenever the cold mill takes less of a reduction than is being aimed for.

Among other things, the sheet-temper mill is designed to further reduce the gauge of the steel by 1%. However, it often takes as little as a .75% reduction, which explains the sheet-temper portion of our giveaway loss.

Finally, we come to the zinc-coating portion of

our giveaway. Zinc coating increases our percent giveaway whenever we put a thicker coating on the steel than we're aiming for via our providing practices. This can be particularly important since zinc costs us about $750 per ton as compared to $310 per ton for hot bands. We can't really do much better here without spending the money to get better zinc measuring and monitoring equipment.

Does that clear up "crown" and providing practices and operating practices?

MR. HEILBURG: Sales

Yes, Al, but why isn't Unikote affected by our operating practices on the cold mills? (Exhibit 3)

MR. SCHMIDT: Production Control

I think I can answer that one, Max. We're buying full-finished cold roll from our sister divisions in order to make Unikote. Even though our giveaway percent is affected by that steel having passed through both hot and cold mills, it's been through both mills by the time that we get it. Accordingly, we don't know how much is accounted for by each mill. This component of our giveaway instead gets combined as part of incoming raw material.

MR. HEILBURG: Sales

So even though I have to use TMW for my cold-roll customers, we pay for full tonnage on the cold-roll we buy inside the company to make unikote? Sweet deal for our supplier division! Also, while your explaining, what is "reapplications" all about?

MR. FALENSKI: Metallurgy

Let me give you an example from a reapplication that I recently approved. A coil of galvanized with an ordered gauge of .0278 and an actual gauge of .0292 was 'dispositioned' (returned by the customer as unsatisfactory quality). The best 'reapplication' (reuse of the coil on an order requiring lower quality) that we were able to make within a reasonable amount of time was to a .0260-minimum-gauge order. In doing so, we immediately went from a poor 5.04% giveaway to an awful giveaway of 12.3%. Since about 10% of our total tonnage becomes "dispositioned reapps," it all adds up to a pretty big dollar figure. A computer matching model is probably required to do much better on reapplications.

TMW—The Profit Impact

MR. PALMINTERE: President

What I really want to know, Al, is, what's the profit-improvement potential from these factors?

MR. FALENSKI: Metallurgy

Well, Phil, each of the percent giveaway figures multiplied by the appropriate total actual tons gives he tonnage effect of that factor. The tonnage effect multiplied by *some* dollar amount gives us that factor's profit impact. However, *which* dollar figure to use brings us back to where we were earlier in the meeting. What's most appropriate—sales price, full cost, variable cost, raw material cost, or who knows what?

MR. PALMINTERE: President

All right then, Andy, take the results of today's discussion and prepare a schedule for me showing the profit improvement potential for each of the factors we have discussed for the month of March. I'll be expecting it within the week. Good day, gentlemen.

ASSIGNMENT QUESTIONS

1. There is enough information in the case to estimate an income statement for the mill and mill assets for 1979. How is the mill doing? So what?

2. What, in your opinion, is the relevant measure of the profit impact of TMW?

3. Prepare the schedule requested by Mr. Palmintere at the end of the meeting. Consider carefully what format would provide the most useful information about the cost management problems here.

4. What other cost management issues are raised in the case?

5. What advice do you have for Mr. Palmintere?

EXHIBIT 1
Six Months Year to Date, 1979

TMW Categories	Actual Tons Shipped	% Giveaway	Average Selling Price per Ton	Lost Sales Revenue
Unikote	31,211	4.75%	$530	$786,000
Galvanized	153,919	3.20%	$515	$2,537,000
Cold-Rolled	198,728	4.54%	$395	$3,562,000
Total	383,858	4.02%	$446	$6,885,000

EXHIBIT 2

	Unikote*		Galvanized		Cold-Roll	
Year	Actual Tons	Percent Giveaway	Actual Tons	Percent Giveaway	Actual Tons	Percent Giveaway
1976	11,292	2.86	315,937	3.17	227,119	3.22
1977	57,907	3.10	244,089	3.31	247,960	3.50
1978	58,722	3.83	270,297	3.17	279,847	3.68
1/79	4,294	2.17	23,773	2.68	29,759	3.39
2/79	3,128	4.73	18,050	2.92	31,174	3.71
3/79	4,681	4.98	32,473	3.38	40,942	4.68
4/79	4,143	5.24	30,292	3.47	30,999	5.14
5/79	7,084	4.98	26,585	3.41	37,477	4.84
6/79	7,881	5.57	22,746	3.09	28,377	5.40
1979 Year-to-date	31,211	4.75	153,919	3.20	198,728	4.54

*Unikote is steel galvanized on only one side. To produce Unikote, steel is run through the galvanizing bath, which adds coating on both sides, and then immediately run through a machine which strips off the coating from one side. This is clearly a cost ineffective way to produce steel coated on one side only. But Buchanan was experimenting with this product at the urging of Chrysler who wanted to try lighter weight galvanized steel in its cars. If the experiments were successful, Buchanan would spend the millions of dollars necessary to build equipment capable of applying coating to only one side of the sheet.

EXHIBIT 3
Rough Breakdown of TMW Percentage Giveaway
March 1979

	Unikote	Galvanized	Cold-Roll
Providing Practices			
Pickling, Cold Reduction, and Annealing (Including Crown Compensation)	3.05	3.42	3.51
Zinc Coating	.15	.30	---
Incoming Raw Material	1.13	.03	.03
Operating Practices			
Cold Reduction Mill	---	(1.27)*	.65
Sheet-Temper Mill	.20	---	.10
Zinc Coating	.25	.40	---
Reapplications of Dispositioned Orders	.20	.50	.39
Total	4.98	3.38	4.68

*A negative number means more reduction than planned.

EXHIBIT 4
Product Line Profitability - Per Ton

	Unikote	Galvanized	Cold-Roll
Selling Price per Ton (6 months average)	$530	$515	$395
Standard Cost[1]			
Raw Material	471	358	352
Variable Processing	35	41	26
Fixed Processing	24	27	17
Depreciation*	7	5	4
Mill Overhead	10	7	6
Selling & Administration	9	6	5
Total	$556	$444	$410
Mill Profit	$(26)	$71	$(15)
Mill Contribution	$24	$116	$17

[1] The standard costs are for the year 1979, based on current sales/production volume and including an allowance for manufacturing yields and for expected TMW "giveaway."

*25 year life, straight line rate.

Appendix

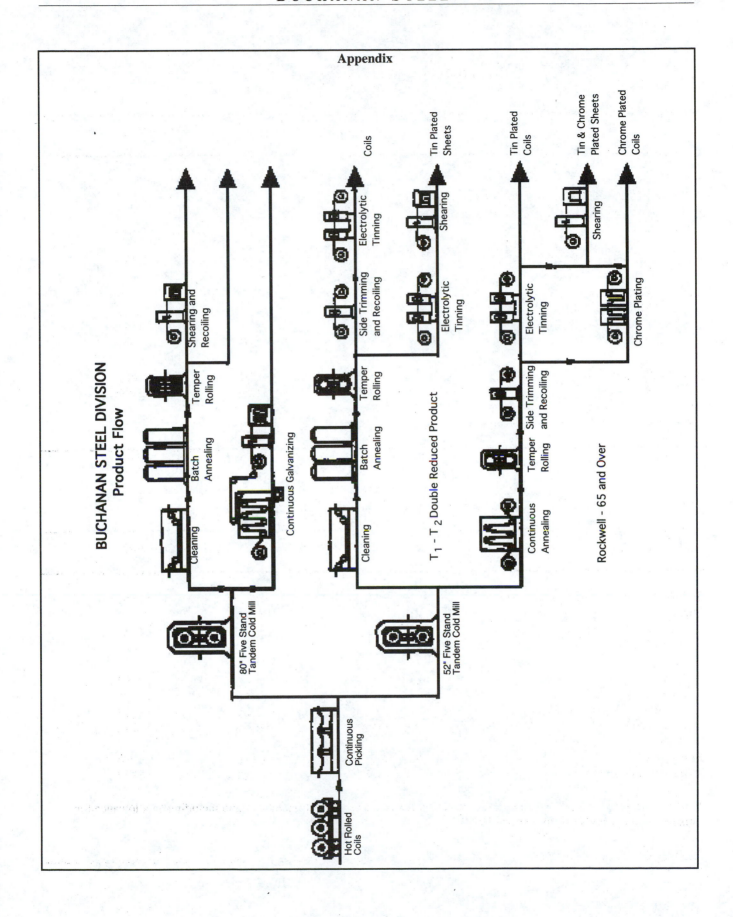

BUCHANAN STEEL DIVISION
Product Flow

California Products Company*

This disguised case is designed to explore issues related to the profit impact of capacity allocation in multi-product firms.

The California Products Company (CPC) was started in 1983 to manufacture and distribute an industrial commodity product (product I) based on a patent owned by the founder. CPC sales volume was disappointing at about 400,000 units that year. From 1983 to 1987, the company produced only product I. Although profits were not high, they were deemed sufficient for a start-up venture by the founder and his investors.

During 1987, the management of the company decided to change from absorption costing to direct costing (variable costing) upon the advice of a consulting firm. Also in 1987 a second product (product J). was introduced to use the excess capacity after filling all the orders for product I. A third product, K, was introduced in 1991 to further utilize excess plant capacity.

From 1988 to 1992, the company generated losses or very small profits each year. The earnings statement for 1992 (see Exhibit 1) showed that the company "broke even" during that year. At the management meeting held shortly after the financial statements for 1992 were released,, optimism was voiced concerning the future profit prospects of the company. The reasons for this optimism were as follows:

1. Products J and K, it was believed, had overcome start-up troubles and had finally found market acceptance.

2. Products J and K are both high-contribution-margin products (see Exhibit 2).

3. During 1992, some overtime had been incurred, which cut into profits. It was anticipated that this would not be repeated next year.

4. The sales force had finally become convinced of the desirability of pushing product K because of its high contribution margin.

Despite this optimism, the earnings statement for 1993 (see Exhibit 1) was anything but encouraging. CPC sustained a loss during this year in spite of a large backlog of unfilled orders. The overtime was not eliminated, although the overall production decreased by 50,000 units (see Exhibit 3).

---

* This case is adapted by Professor John Shank of the Amos Tuck School of Business from an earlier version written by Professor Felix Kollaritsch of the Ohio State University.

The management meeting which followed the release of the 1993 financial statements was very contentious. Everyone accused everyone else of lax management. Without producing any specific evidence, the sales manager accused the production manager of gross inefficiency. Evidence was, however, introduced which indicated that firm orders for products I and J, and even a little K, had to be turned down because production could not supply the products within the normal delivery time.

The production manager accused the sales manager of pushing the wrong product. He pointed out that all the troubles started with the introduction of products J and K. He also accused the controller of misleading reporting by focusing only on contribution margin at the level of individual products. He stated that the contribution margin (see Exhibit 2) was nothing except "fancy data" which misleads everyone. "Nobody gets rich using contribution margin logic," he said.

The controller said that he was comfortable that the variable expenses, shown in Exhibit 2, were correct. He also said that the prices for the products had not been changed for two years and there was little hope of a price increase in the next year either. Thus, contribution margin by product was solid.

Assigning fixed costs to products was a futile exercise in useless information, he said. But, if anyone wanted to try, he said the $800,000 fixed expenses, shown in Exhibits 1 and 2, included $430,000 which was a "joint" fixed cost and $370,000 of "separable" fixed cost attributable to the three products as follows:

Product I	$ 60,000
Product J	200,000
Product K	110,000
	$370,000

The joint fixed cost of $430,000 included:

Manufacturing Expenses	$ 40,000
Selling and General Expenses	70,000
Depreciation (Based on 15 year lives)	
Machine A	100,000
Machine B	20,000
Machine C	200,000
	$430,000

Regardless of how they were classified or allocated, the full amount of $800,000 was incurred if all three products were sold, regardless of sales volume for the products.

Information gathered concerning the production process disclosed that each product had to pass through each of the three machines, and that the three products required different processing times on each machine. The average production capacity of the machines is given in Exhibit 4.

It was estimated that each machine was operated about 1900 hours during a normal year (practical capacity), which takes into consideration maintenance, repairs and set-up. The maximum operations time one could expect from a machine during a given year without incurring unreasonably high additional expenses was about 2,000 hours.

ASSIGNMENT QUESTIONS

1. Can you estimate machine hours for each machine for each product for both 1992 and 1993? What do you infer about how the production manager assigns available machine time?

2. What is the apparent cause of the overall loss for 1993? What is the production "bottleneck?"

3. Would you have recommended a different product mix for the year just ended (1993)? What mix seems best? How do you decide?

4. Can you estimate profit for each of the three products for 1993 under full absorption costing? Is there any managerial relevance to these calculations?

5. What are your recommendations to the president of CPC? Support your recommendations with specific analysis.

EXHIBIT 1
Earnings Statements

	Product I	Product J	Product K	Total
1992				
Sales	$1,479,000	$1,320,000	$284,000	$3,083,000
Variable Costs	1,131,000	960,000	192,000	2,283,000
Contribution Margin	$ 348,000	$ 360,000	$ 92,000	$ 800,000
Fixed Expenses				$ 800,000
Net Profit				$ -0-
1993				
Sales	$1,224,000	$1,056,000	$568,000	$2,848,000
Variable Costs	936,000	768,000	384,000	2,088,000
Contribution Margin	$ 288,000	$ 288,000	$184,000	$ 760,000
Fixed Expenses				$ 800,000
Net Loss				$ (40,000)

EXHIBIT 2
Product Contribution Margins

	Product I	Product J	Product K
Sales Price	$5.10	$6.60	$7.10
Variable Costs[1]			
Materials	$2.00	$3.00	$2.50
Labor (at $12 per hour, including fringes)	1.00	1.20	1.00
Variable Manufacturing Overhead	.30	.40	.30
Sales Commission	.60	.20	1.00
Total	$3.90	$4.80	$4.80
	$1.20	$1.80	$2.30

[1]Includes reasonable allowance for normal overtime and for normal scrap.

EXHIBIT 3
Units Sold and Produced

	1992	1993
Product I	290,000	240,000
Product J	200,000	160,000
Product K	40,000	80,000
Total	530,000	480,000

EXHIBIT 4
Average Product Throughput per Machine Hour
(Units)

	Product I	Product J	Product K
Machine A	312	260	130
Machine B	364	208	156
Machine C	520	312	104

Each machine could work on only one product at a time. Set up time was trivial since each machine was already programmed for all three products.

Chalice Wines*

This case is set in 1993 in California's Sonoma Valley, home of many wine-making millionaires. Here is where they spend their millions, not where they make them.

The Chalice Wine Group's brochures describe its Cimarron winery in the following terms:

<u>Cimmaron, A Place in Time</u>

"A pair of red-tailed hawks hover in the thermal plume rising from the cliffs below the Feather Vineyard. In winter, you hear the muted roar of three creeks cascading down the canyons from the ridges above. Fog nestles like ocean foam over the bay and valleys. The rocky outcrops and dense chaparral of madrone, oak, laurel and aromatic wild sage are the natural home of coyotes, rattlesnakes and mountain lions. The vineyards and winery of Cimmaron are literally carved into the volcanic stone of the mountain—we are here for the long term. A great wine is not a commodity. It must artistically communicate its context, its place and time. We are dedicated to expressing the most beautiful and unique aspects of a place we love. We hope that you will share in our love of this place called Cimmaron as we apply our skills each vintage to create for you a memorable sensory snapshot in a bottle of wine."

The company is somewhat less effusive in describing its financial results in the 1993 Annual Report:

"Notwithstanding our strong fourth quarter, we had a net loss of $700,000 (after tax) for the year, but that is almost $50,000 less than we lost in 1992."

In fact, things have been pretty much downhill, financially, for Chalice since 1990 as the following trend indicates:

	Assets	Sales	Net Earnings
1990	$49 million	$14.2 million	$650,000
1991	$68 million	$15.0 million	$58,000
1992	$70 million	$17.3 million	$(741,000)
1993	$74 million	$18.3 million	$(700,000)

---

* This case was prepared by Craig Scarborough (T'94) under the supervision of Professor John K. Shank, The Amos Tuck School of Business Administration, Dartmouth College. Copyright © 1994.

THE PROJECT

Bill Evanson, President and CEO of Chalice was sharing a bottle of his wine with former colleague Sam Davis. Sam was describing how his just completed first year in the MBA program of a small eastern college had changed his perspective on the wine industry.

"Personally, if a business has no hope of profit then I'm just not interested. But it's not at all clear to me that small wineries are a hopeless cause. I'd hesitate to make that call without understanding what's happening along the entire value chain. Of the retail price somebody pays for a bottle of your wine, where does the money go? How much is profit versus cost for each of the players involved in making the product and delivering it to the consumer? Is there room for a winery to maneuver upstream or downstream in the value chain? And what causes the costs of each stage for each player? If you don't understand the whole picture, then you may misassess the options when you develop strategies to cope with changing business conditions, or even decide to abandon the effort. The value chain concept is a big deal at B-school these days, and I'm sold on it."

Evanson looked intrigued. "That's interesting Sam. I've been thinking along these same lines lately. What does it cost us to make wines the way we do? Many of our specific costs seem to get lost within our accounting system. I suspect we understate some and overstate others. Who is making money in this industry, and how do they do it? This would be great stuff to know. But this is a complex industry—practically every winery has a unique approach, and every wine is different. And Chalice is a particularly complicated company. Would a value chain analysis be meaningful, or even possible for this company in this industry?

Sam Davis grinned and raised his glass. "Why don't we find out, Bill? We can certainly set up the value chain for a particular wine, and hopefully the process will reveal some generalizable insights. I've got the time if you've got the interest. We're drinking one of your wines now, aren't we? Why don't we track this one?

Bill Evanson watched the sun reflect through the delicate flaxen color of the 1991 Cimarron Meritage White in his glass. "OK, hotshot, let's do it! Come to my office next week and I'll show you the numbers we've got."

THE CHALICE WINE GROUP (CWG)

Evanson had not exaggerated when he described Chalice as complicated. The Group owns two vineyards (Chalice and Cimarron) and one-half of a third (Delta). It owns three wineries (Chalice, Cimarron and Alicia) and one-half of a fourth (Opera Valley) which it operates for a management fee on behalf of the joint venture owners. It has a cross-investment with a prominent French wine company for distribution in the US of its French and Chilean wines. CWG also owns a one-half interest in a vineyard in eastern Washington State with plans to build a winery at this site.

Of the four wineries, the flagship is Chalice, founded in 1969. The Opera Valley Joint Venture was established in 1980. Cimarron and Alicia were acquired in 1982 and 1986, respectively. Chalice went public in May of 1984. Until June, 1993 with the initial public offering for Robert Mondavi Winery, Chalice was the only publicly-held company in the United States whose principal business is the production and sale of premium wines. Among the serious patrons of the California wine industry, CWG enjoys a prestigious reputation for producing consistently elegant wines.

Each of its four California wineries is located in a different legally designated viticultural area. Each one is a separate profit center with its own president, typically the winemaker. The Company's wines are sold in specialty wine shops and grocery stores, and selected restaurants, hotels and private clubs across the country and in certain overseas markets. Virtually every distribution channel in the industry is used by CWG in one market or another. It's wines are distributed via direct mail in those states where it is legal and, in limited quantities, "over the counter" at the wineries. Out of state, the company sells through the traditional 3-tier system (maker, distributor, retailer). In Northern California, a wine distributor is used as a broker. In Southern California, CWG owns and operates its own distribution network.

Because of aging, sales in any one year do not match that year's production. Exhibit 1 contains selected industry sales and concentration data for 1991 and 1992. Total production and sales for the company for 1990, 1991 and 1992 are shown in Exhibit 2. Exhibit 3 shows the consolidated financial statements for the company for 1990, 1991, and 1992.

EXHIBIT 1:
California Winery Shipments (000 Cases) *

	1992		1991		
	Cases	% total	Cases	% total	
All California Wineries	160,536	100%	157,734	100%	
E & J Gallo	64,219	40%	66,070	42%	
Heublein Wines	17,139	11%	15,712	10%	(Almaden, Inglenook)
The Wine Group	12,777	8%	9,981	6%	(Franzia, Summit, MD)
Vintners International	8,328	5%	8,549	5%	(Taylor, Paul Masson)
Top 4 Bulk Wineries	*102,463*	*64%*	*100,312*	*63%*	
Sebastiani	4,762	3%	4,749	3%	
Sutter Home	4,760	3%	4,163	3%	
Robert Mondavi	3,950	2%	3,261	2%	
Wine World	3,863	2%	3,285	2%	(Beringer, Napa Ridge)
Glen Ellen	3,778	2%	3,270	2%	
Top 5 Premium Wineries	*21,113*	*12%*	*18,728*	*12%*	
18 Wineries w/ Sales of 100K-250K Cases	2,570	1.60%	2,406	1.53%	
Chalice Wine Group	175	0.11%	138	0.09%	

* estimates from Gomberg, Fredrikson & Associates

EXHIBIT 2:
Wine Production in Case Equivalents

	1992		1991		1990	
By Variety	Cases	% total	Cases	% total	Cases	% total
Chardonnay	141,200	68%	131,600	71%	117,900	71%
Sauvignon Blanc	4,000	2%	4,100	2%	10,100	6%
Pinot Blanc	6,700	3%	2,800	1%	3,100	2%
Other White	5,800	3%	5,600	3%	5,700	4%
Total White	157,700	76%	144,100	77%	136,800	83%
Pinot Noir	26,100	13%	23,100	13%	20,200	12%
Cabernet Sauvignon	16,900	8%	17,600	9%	6,600	4%
Other Red	5,500	3%	1,600	1%	1,600	1%
Total Red	48,500	24%	42,300	23%	28,400	17%
Total	206,200	100%	186,400	100%	165,200	100%

Wine Sales in Cases

	1992		1991		1990	
By Channel						
Independent Distributors						
US	61,100	35%	45,300	33%	42,000	31%
International	9,100	5%	5,600	4%	8,700	7%
	70,200	40%	50,900	37%	50,700	38%
Company Direct						
California Retail	90,200	51%	76,000	55%	71,800	53%
Mailing List	15,300	9%	11,600	8%	12,000	9%
	105,500	60%	87,600	63%	83,800	62%
Total Sales	175,700	100%	138,500	100%	134,500	100%

EXHIBIT 3:
Consolidated Balance Sheets, The Chalice Wine Group, Ltd.
(Thousands)

| | December 31, | | |
	1992	1991	1990
ASSETS			
Cash	$ 74	$ 78	$ 185
Accounts Receivable	3,464	2,650	2,516
Inventories	26,091	24,298	19,601
Other Current	1,007	1,154	89
Investment in French Wine Company	12,524	12,524	3,176
Property, Plant & Equipment, (net)	22,454	22,290	19,582
Goodwill (net)	3,297	3,394	3,492
Other	1,503	1,541	509
Total	$70,414	$67,928	$49,150
LIABILITIES			
S/T Notes & Current Maturities	$15,512	$12,593	$7,906
Accounts Payable & Accruals	3,522	2,236	2,352
Long-term Debt	30,414	31,945	19,658
Other	3,935	4,073	3,643
	53,383	50,847	33,559
SHAREHOLDERS' EQUITY			
Common Stock	16,633	15,942	15,215
Retained Earnings	398	1,139	1,376
	17,031	17,081	16,591
Total	$70,414	$67,928	$49,150

The Chalice Group
Consolidated Income Statements

	1992	1991	1990
Wine Sales	$17,319	$14,951	$14,182
Cost of Sales	11,011	8,096	7,296
Selling, General & Administrative Expenses	4,610	4,119	3,760
Interest Expense	2,757	2,334	1,679
Other Expense (net)	7	239	293
Income Tax	(323)	104	505
Net Earnings	$ (741)	$ 58	$ 650
Net Earnings Per Common Share	(0.19)	0.02	0.18
Stock Price, High	9.75	11.00	11.00
Low	7.00	8.50	7.75

The big picture portrayed in these numbers was certainly not strong. Sam's task was to break the numbers down in order to understand the financial story of one particular wine from one of the particular wineries of the company. Was *it* losing money? If so, where? Was anyone making money on it? How much? How? The inquiry would require tracing the path(s) followed by the 1991 Cimarron Meritage White, from the grape grower all the way through to the final consumer along the Meritage White value chain shown as Exhibit 14.

THE WINERY

"The vineyard would be the logical place to start, but we're here now, so let's start here. It's simple: I need revenues and costs, starting with cost of goods."

Bill Evanson glanced down at his most recent Report to Stockholders. "No problem. Revenues—$17.3 million; cost of goods sold—$11 million."

"It's not that simple, Bill. How much per case of 1991 Cimarron Meritage White?"

"I was kidding. Of course we track all of our wines separately. We sell the Meritage White to our distributors for $76.00/case. As of 12/31/92, the wine carried $52.73 in product costs. Here's the file showing where our numbers come from." Evanson gave Sam a thick file folder from his desk.

The file was thick because of the complex production process. Wine isn't produced in a day or even a month. Some wines are effectively "in production" for years, so the various pools of periodic production costs must be allocated among many different wines from different vintage years. CWG's method was as straightforward as possible, given the complexity of the situation. All of the Cimarron Winery's costs were considered product costs and wound up as Cost of Goods Sold for some particular wine. Grape costs were easy to assign directly to particular wines. Winemaking, bottling and bottle aging costs were collected into pools and allocated equally to specific wines according to the percentage of the total volume processed. Obviously, only wines that were bottled in a year absorbed bottling costs for that year. But all wines held in bulk inventory in a period absorbed their relative proportions of winemaking costs for that period (regardless of what actually happened to the wine) and all wines held in bottled inventory absorbed bottle aging costs. Exhibit 4 shows the yields and the product cost breakdown for the 1991 Meritage White.

EXHIBIT 4
1991 Meritage White Product Costs

Tons Crushed		89.17
Gallons of Juice Fermented		14,713
Gallons Aged		13,984
Gallons of Wine Produced		13,255
Cases Bottled		5,575

Production Cost	Total	Per Case
Grapes	$73,901	$13.26
Winemaking	117,486	21.07
Bottling	93,657	16.80
Bottle Aging	8,937	1.60
Total	$293,981	$52.73

Sam Davis knew that eventually each of the components of product cost would warrant further analysis. But, for the purpose of constructing the first level of the value chain profitability analysis, he decided to accept CWG's numbers. The task now was to derive a per case operating profit for this wine, and the per case Return on Assets (ROA). An estimate of per case SG&A expenses was derived by applying the percentage of CWG's sales revenue generated by Cimarron to the total corporate SG&A., then dividing by Cimarron's case sales for the year. A similar approach could be used to estimate the CWG assets employed specifically by Cimarron Meritage White. In 1992 the Cimarron winery sold 37,205 cases for total revenues of $2.7 million with a cost of sales of $2.1 million, and a depreciable asset base of $4.9 million set on 3 acres. Because its bottling line and crushing/pressing equipment were only in operation during a short period each year, overall utilization of these assets was less than 10% of annual capacity.

The profitability analysis for one case of 1991 Cimarron Meritage White demonstrated the contribution of that wine to the overall financial performance of the Chalice Group *according to the cost accounting methods used by the winery*. As he went about the task of collecting financial data from other links in the value chain, Sam couldn't help thinking about those product costs that were assigned "equally" to the various wines. If no two wines are the same, then why should they absorb production costs at the same rate? How are they different, and is the difference relevant? He made a mental note to revisit this question once the first level value chain was complete.

THE VINEYARD

Cimarron Meritage White is a blend of Sauvignon Blanc and Semillon grapes, neither of which is grown at Cimarron Vineyard. All the grapes for this wine are purchased from Pinnacle Vineyards, CWG's partner in the Opera Valley Joint Venture. The price paid in 1991 for both varieties was $812.36/ton (62.42 tons of Sauvignon Blanc and 26.75 tons of Semillon). Total hauling costs from Opera Valley to the winery in Sonoma Valley amounted to $1,463. A review of price information published by The California Department of Agriculture revealed that the average price paid per ton for grapes grown in that district that year was $562.50 for Sauvignon Blanc, and $350 for Semillon. Had these prices been paid by CWG the total grape cost, including hauling, would have been only $45,937 instead of $73,901. The potential incremental $5 per case profit led Sam to ask, "Bill, why are you spending so much money on grapes?"

"The simple answer, Sam, is you get what you pay for. We don't produce average wines, so we don't buy average grapes. We also consider our contract for these grapes in the context of our long-term relationship with Pinnacle and the Opera Valley Joint Venture which is very important to us. But we have to get our costs down, and you've raised a good point. Actually, we've been looking at a 30 acre vineyard in Sonoma County near Cimarron as a potential alternative source of supply. The price is right: $525,000. That's tempting just as a real estate investment. And the land is clearly capable of producing the quality of grapes we need. But since the vineyard has phylloxera[1], it would have to be cleared and replanted. So it's tough to say if it would represent a significant improvement on our $13.26/case grape cost."

Sam began thinking out loud. "I need accurate revenue, cost, and asset information for a typical vineyard to complete that piece of the value chain, and you need to know if it makes sense for you to develop your own vineyard to provide grapes for the Meritage White. Let's kill two birds with one stone. I know that the University of California Extension Service and the Sonoma County Farm Advisor have done a lot of research on vineyard costs. Let's see what they can tell us."

Exhibits 5 and 6 describe the costs and assets involved in the establishment and operation of a 30 acre vineyard in Sonoma County as of the end in 1992.

EXHIBIT 5
Costs per Acre to Establish and Operate a Vineyard

	Years				
	1	2	3	4	5 & Forward
Yield (tons/acre)			1.5	3.5	6
Total Planting Costs	5,138	2,440			
Total Cultural Costs	609	1,062	1,216	1,317	1,317
Total Harvest Costs @ $120/ton			180	420	720
Total Overhead Costs	622	622	642	698	718
Total Cash Costs	6,369	4,124	2,038	2,435	2,755
Depreciation (see Exhibit 6)				843	843
Total				3,278	$3,598*

*$3,598/Acre = $600/T = $9.59/case [62.5 cases per ton]

With these cost and asset numbers it was possible to complete a profitability analysis for the vineyard (in full production) in terms of each case of 1991 Meritage White sold. Sam assumed revenue for the vineyard would be $812.36/ton, the price paid by Cimarron to Pinnacle Vineyards. This, of course, assumed production of "better than average" grapes.

It should be noted that vineyard profitability is extremely sensitive to fluctuations in grape prices. A ten year history of the weighted average market price paid in California for five leading varieties is shown in Exhibit 7. The Sonoma County average prices are always higher than the state average. The 1992 Sonoma County premium is shown in parentheses for each variety.

---

[1]Phylloxera is a plant louse that attacks the roots of grapevines, decreasing yields and eventually killing the vine. Currently a serious problem in California, the only solution for an infected vineyard is to replant on resistant rootstock.

EXHIBIT 6:
Assets Required to Establish and Operate a 30 Acre Vineyard

Investment		Purchase Price (new)	Useful Life	Salvage Value	Annual Depreciation
Land (30 plantable acres)		525,000			
Vineyard Establishment (A)		339,374	22	0%	15,426
Reservoir		30,000	30	0%	1,000
Buildings		15,750	30	10%	473
Drip Irrigation System		52,400	25	10%	1,886
Frost Protection System		40,300	25	10%	1,451
Shop Tools		10,000	15	10%	600
Pruning Equipment		1,200	10	10%	108
ATV, 4wd		6,500	5	10%	1,170
Tractor		29,900	15	10%	1,794
Duster		3,035	10	10%	273
Mower	(B)	5,500	10	10%	495
Orchard Sprayer		4,560	10	10%	410
Weed Sprayer		2,000	10	10%	180
Pickup Truck		16,500	7	10%	2,121
Total Investment, with new Equip.		1,082,019			27,388
*Allowance for Used Equipment		(24,598)			(2,110)
Total Investment, 30 Acre Vineyard		$1,057,421			$25,278

A) "Vineyard Establishment" is the accumulated cash costs for 1st 3 years, net of revenue earned in year 3 using the price paid by Cimarron in 1991 as a proxy value for each ton produced.

B) Last 6 items can be purchased used @ an average of 60% of new cost. Allowance is made above (*).

EXHIBIT 7
History of California Grape Prices Per Ton

Variety (*)	1983	1984	1985	1986	1987	1988	1989	1990	1991	1992
Chardonnay (18%)	$980	$998	$904	$856	$922	$1,122	$1,225	$1,128	$1,122	$1,038
Cabernet (32%)	$467	$527	$533	$550	$631	$822	$1,032	$977	$918	$872
Zinfandel (56%)	$269	$253	$269	$340	$480	$817	$546	$391	$363	$434
Sauvignon Blanc (35%)	$487	$486	$441	$401	$414	$474	$571	$518	$541	$552
Semillon (73%)	$215	$260	$210	$245	$254	$289	$311	$310	$328	$360

* The percentages in parentheses represent the premiums paid to Sonoma County growers over the state averages in 1992.

Although grape cost of $9.59 per case for this vineyard represented an improvement over the $12.99 (13.26 - $.27 freight) the winery was paying now, was it a compelling argument for CWG to change it's make/buy policy on grapes for this wine? Bill Evanson was pensive.

"How should we look at this? I suppose we could plant about half the vineyard to supply the Meritage White at cost, and the rest to another variety to sell elsewhere. That would lower our product costs at the winery, and possibly generate an interesting grape business on the side, provided we can predict what the market will want in future years. In light of our current financial situation, it would be a tricky proposition to present to the Board! The fact is that grape &

wine production is a capital intensive proposition, and the returns just aren't overwhelming. What do the numbers look like downstream in the value chain?"

THE DISTRIBUTOR

Stellar Wines is a typical East Coast wine distributor. Stellar's financial statements for 1991 and 1992 are shown in Exhibit 8. In 1992 the company sold 225,000 cases of wine, roughly 50% imported and 50% domestic.

Stellar's product cost for Cimarron Meritage White includes $2.25/case to cover freight from California and state excise tax of $1.56/case. On all premium wines, Stellar's planned gross margin percentage was 25%. Operating expenses per case do not vary significantly among the various wines that Stellar sells. From this information and the financial statements, Sam determined the operating profit and ROA per case of Meritage White sold by the distributor.

EXHIBIT 8
Stellar Wines Financial Statements
(in Thousands)

Balance Sheets

	December 31,	
	1992	1991
ASSETS		
Cash	$ 24	$ 9
Accounts Receivable	2,273	1,806
Inventory	6,500	6,592
Equipment (net)	108	105
Other	333	312
Total	$9,238	$8,824
LIABILITIES		
Note Payable, Bank	$4,953	$4,794
Accounts Payable & Accruals	1,735	1,544
STOCKHOLDERS' EQUITY		
Common Stock	10	9
Retained Earnings	2,540	2,477
	2,550	2,486
Total	$9,238	$8,824

Income Statements

	Year Ended December 31,	
	1992	1991
Sales	$17,078	$15,389
Cost of Goods Sold	12,771	11,313
Operating Expenses	3,394	3,187
Interest Expense	425	507
Net Income Before Tax	$488	$381

A wine distributor sells wine to both "on-premise" accounts (restaurants, bars, hotels) and "off-premise" accounts (grocery stores, liquor stores, wine shops). The profitability of wine sales in on-premise businesses varies considerably with the type of business and the wine pricing philosophy. Some restaurants mark up a bottle of wine 50 cents, others mark it up 250%. "Typical profitability" is a more meaningful concept when applied to off-premise wine sales. Since most of CWG's off-premise wine sales occur in relatively small premium wine shops, it was decided that this type of business should provide the final piece of the value chain.

THE RETAILER

Riverside Wine Company is one of Stellar's best customers. As grocery chains and discount clubs have gained market share, many small premium wine shops have been driven out of business. However, at the top end of the business there remains a demand for service and selection that is difficult to provide in a high volume setting. Exhibit 9 contains selected financial information for Riverside for 1992. As with the distributor, a case is a case. So one way of assigning operating expenses and assets among the cases sold is equal weight. Other approaches are, of course, possible. Sam computed the operating profit and ROA for the retailer as he had for the other players.

EXHIBIT 9
Riverside Wine Company, 1992

Total Sales	$1,889,916	
Cost of Goods Sold	$1,412,000	
Operating Costs	$438,134	
Profit (before tax)	$39,782	
Cases Sold	14,776	
Total Assets	$719,261	($235,333 of inventory)

OVERALL VALUE CHAIN

With this last piece of the value chain in place, Sam and Bill stepped back to consider what the numbers meant, and what were the strategic implications for Chalice. Remembering the original question, "Can this be a good business?", Sam put the profitability figures for the four participants in this value chain together to determine the overall profit margin and the overall return on assets for the industry on every case of 1991 Cimarron Meritage White sold to consumers in retail wine shops.

"Oh well," sighed Evanson, "at least it *is* a beautiful way of life!".

"Yes, but these numbers don't necessarily prove that it can't be profitable. Obviously, some parts are more profitable than others. But this is only the story as told by your cost accounting methods. Are you confident that those methods provide accurate measures of your costs for individual wines? I have some doubts."

"So do I. But the methods are fairly standard for the industry, and the auditors are satisfied. I told you at the outset, every wine is a complex product in the context of a complex product mix. Maybe it is too complex for truly accurate cost accounting."

"Maybe, maybe not. But it's worth a try. The trick is to get your production costs out of the periods in which they happen and into the activities that cause them. Then the activity based costs can be allocated according to the participation of particular wines in each activity. Under the periodic system, a year old wine that sleeps through the following harvest in a barrel still absorbs some of the new costs of crushing, pressing and fermenting. That can't be right. Let's take another look at the breakdown of the product costs for the Meritage White."

WINERY COSTS REVISITED

Sam knew the production cost of $52.73/case from Exhibit 4 was a very crude aggregate average cost. Upon careful reflection, he concluded that the winemaking process can be viewed as involving three distinct stages:

> Stage 1 (crushing, pressing and fermenting)
> Stage 2 (fining, filtering, bulk aging)
> Stage 3 (preparation for bottling)

But at CWG, all wines shared equally in the allocation of all winemaking cost, based on processing volumes. The 1991 Meritage White was made (crushed, pressed, & fermented) in the fourth quarter of 1991. It was bulk aged for 9 months in 1992, and was prepared for bottling in the fourth quarter of 1992. Yet this wine's allocation of winemaking cost was a simple 7% of the 1991 total and 6% of the 1992 total, based on its share of total volume processed in each year. The allocation of $21.07 per case missed all the refinement which an ABC analysis could bring. After a careful review of all cost categories and a careful analysis of activities, Sam prepared Exhibit 10 showing a breakdown of winemaking cost, by stages, for 1991 and 1992, with usage data for the 1991 Meritage White. Based on this exhibit, Sam recalculated winemaking cost for the 1991 Meritage White to be $?.

EXHIBIT 10
Winemaking Cost—ABC Approach*

	1991		1992	
Stage 1	$285,000	(1)	$268,000	
Stage 2	571,000		559,000	(2)
Stage 3	57,000		56,000	
TOTAL	$913,000		$883,000	

*The 1991 Meritage White vintage represented 18% of the wine made in 1991, 15% of stage 2 costs in 1992, and 28% of the wine prepared for bottling in 1992.

(1) Including $12,700 of barrel depreciation, because some white wines are barrel fermented.
(2) Including $154,900 of barrel depreciation.

Sam also discovered that the $16.80 per case for bottling was a very simple overall average allocation. He found, for example, that the cost of wooden shipping boxes was allocated across all wines bottled even though Meritage White was shipped in much cheaper corrugated cartons. Meritage White also used cheaper than average bottles and labels. Exhibit 11 shows a comparison of the average approach and the ABC approach to bottling cost.

EXHIBIT 11
Bottling Cost—Per Case

Cost Category	Average Cost	ABC Cost for Meritage White
Labor	1.16	.75
Supplies	.07	.07
Bottles	6.43	5.00
Corks	2.39	2.39
Capsules	1.19	1.19
Labels	1.99	1.50
Wooden Boxes	.55	0
Taxes	3.02	3.02
TOTAL	16.80	13.92

Third, Sam discovered that barrel depreciation was a very complex issue, involving French oak barrels that had risen in cost from $362 in 1988 to $650 in 1993. White wines are both fermented (three months) and aged in barrels whereas red wines are fermented in tanks. But, red wines are aged 2 years in the barrels versus only nine months for white whites. Yet all barrels at the Cimarron winery are just depreciated, straight-line, over four years , with barrel depreciation as one line item in winemaking cost. Of the $21.07 winemaking cost for the 1991 Meritage White, $4.03 (19%) was for barrel depreciation. Sam had no intuition about how a more accurate ABC assignment of barrel depreciation would affect the $4.03 number. Exhibit 12 was constructed to estimate actual consumption of barrel cost, using estimated market values and the actual barrel usage plan for the 1991 Meritage White.

EXHIBIT 12

	French Oak Barrels						American Oak Barrels	
Year Purchased	1988	1989	1990	1991	1992	1993	All years	
Cost new	$362	$418	$515	$539	$608	$650	$250	
Declining Value								
After 1 year	209	257	269	304	325		125	(50% of cost of new barrel)
After 2 years	129	135	152	163	?		63	(25% of cost of new barrel)
After 3 years	67	76	81	?	?		32	(12.5% of cost of new barrel)
After 4 years	40	40	40	40	40		20	($40 imported/$20 domestic)

	French Oak	
	Depreciation in 1991	Depreciation in 1992
1989 barrels	59 (135-76)	36 (76-40)
1990 barrels	117 (269-152)	71 (152-81)
1991 barrels	235 (539-304)	141 (304-163)

Fermentation and aging plan for 1991 Meritage White (all French Oak)

Ferment in 25% new barrels, 25% one year old, and 50% two years old. Age in the newest barrels used for fermenting.

Ferment: 92   barrels from 1991   Aging: 92   barrels from 1991
(3 months) 92   barrels from 1990   (9 months)   92   barrels from 1990
             184 barrels from 1989   49 barrels from 1989
Total   368 barrels*   233 barrels*

14,713 gallons ÷ 40 gals/bbl = 368 barrels   *13,984 gallons ÷ 60 gals/bbl = 233 barrels
((The barrel is only 2/3 filled for fermentation)

Barrel Depreciation (French Oak) For The 1991 Meritage White

Ferment		Age	
92 x $235 x 1/4 year =	$5405	92 x $141 x 3/4 year =	$9729
92 x $117 x 1/4 year =	$2691	92 x $71 x 3/4 year =	$4899
184 x $59 x 1/4 year =	$2714	49 x $36 x 3/4 year =	$1323

Total = $26,761 ($4.80 per case)

As the cost of French Oak barrels had risen 80% in 5 years, Cimarron had decided they needed to at least experiment with American Oak barrels which had stayed at about $250 throughout. But the winemakers felt sure that French oak imparted better taste to the wine. Sam prepared the following summary table comparing barrel depreciation cost for various costing options:

Barrel Depreciation Cost Per Case	
(1991 Meritage White)	
Average costing	$4.03
ABC approach (3 stage costing)	?
"Declining value" depreciation with actual barrel usage:	
French Oak barrels	$4.80
Domestic Oak barrels	?
Replacement cost depeciation	?

Based on his revised calculations, Sam now estimated the product cost of the 1991 Meritage White, for strategic assessment purposes, as ? per case. He adjusted the overall value chain accordingly.

LYFORD WINERY

As one example of a very different approach to the value chain, Sam was aware of Lyford Winery which had been founded in Sonoma County in 1981. It was constructed as a state of the art winemaking showplace with no expense spared in either the production of the wines or in the effort to build the brand in the marketplace. After the untimely death of the founder, the company was sold to a consortium of several other winery properties which ultimately failed. The winery was sold out of bankruptcy to another California wine company. The brand name was sold to a French company. Wine for the brand was sourced from the bulk wine market. Processing services were purchased from custom suppliers under the direction of the original winemaker who was retained by the French company.

Exhibit 13 gives the per case cost structure for one of Lyford's more recent releases, a 1991 Meritage White. The wine was a blend of three different varieties, each purchased on the bulk market. The final blend was 85% Sauvignon Blanc, 13% Semillon, and 2% White Muscat.

EXHIBIT 13:
1991 Lyford Meritage White
Product Costs per Case

Bulk Wine Cost	$ 9.26
Bottling	2.28
Corks	2.37
Capsules	1.16
Labels	0.70
Bottles	4.60
Lyford Overhead & Supplies	2.02
Wine Tax	3.02
Total	$25.41

The product costs shown in this exhibit tell nearly the entire story of this wine. The "winery" has virtually no capital assets beyond leased office and warehouse space and working capital (assume 30% of sales). All of the services required to bring the product from the bulk wine market to distribution can be purchased either from wineries with surplus capacity or from custom winemaking operations. An allocation of marketing expenses added only about $1.09 to the per case cost of the wine. Leased space and equipment added about another $5 per case.

Lyford sold the wine to wholesale distributors for $45.00 per case, with a target retail price of $7.50 per bottle.*

* Lyford Winery—The Value Chain		
Sales	45	
Costs	?	
Margin	?	
Assets	?	
ROA	?	
Price to Distributor		45.00
+ Freight & Taxes		+ 3.81
Delivered		= 48.81
Price to Retailer (÷ .75)		= 65.00
Price to Consumer (÷ .75)		= 86.67
		=~ 7.22/Bottle (~$7.50 with sales tax)

Sam knew the Chalice winemakers would totally reject this "bogus" approach to "winemaking." But <u>somebody</u> was buying the wines and apparently enjoying them. Sam had to admit that even he thought the 1991 Lyford Meritage White showed very well in tastings. Could Chalice learn anything from the Lyford story?

ASSIGNMENT QUESTIONS

1. First fill in all the relevant calculations discussed in the case but left blank.
2. Then pull together an overall value chain for the project using the format shown here (Exhibit 14).
3. What business issues are raised by the case?
4. What inferences for CWG do you draw from the Lyford wines value chain?
5. What advice do you have for Sam Davis and Bill Evanson regarding the 1991 Cimarron Meritage White? For the CWG business as a whole?

EXHIBIT 14
The Value Chain—1991 Cimarron Meritage White
(per case)

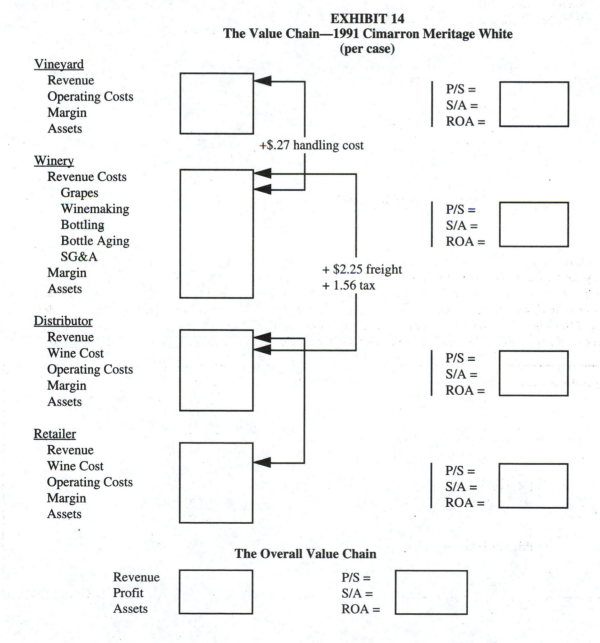

Chaparral Beef*

This case is set in a large feedlot ranch for beef cattle in Colorado in 1991. The ranch has made a profit in only five of the past ten year. The issue is cost analysis for profit improvement, using SCM themes.

It was a hot June afternoon when Junior Wells pulled his Ford pick up into the Chaparral Ranch near Greeley, Colorado. He had been on the road for three days, returning from his first year at a prestigious eastern business school. Junior had been unable to find an exciting summer job and he was unwilling to take a "me too, cookie cutter" job. As always, he could rely on his father's feedlot for summer employment. Junior was not looking forward to spending a hot summer riding pens and feeding cattle, tasks he despised. Like most people in his generation from farm backgrounds, Junior had little or no interest in pursuing an agricultural career.

As he entered his father's office he noticed large piles of feed slips, cost reports, financial statements, and industry periodicals. Junior's father was on the phone negotiating calf prices with a stocker in Wyoming, "Buddy I know you have fine Angus cattle, I just can't pay you more than the market rate for calves that will only bring me market averages when I sell them." Buddy Guy, the rancher, had sold calves to Chaparral for ten years on a spot basis. Although both Guy and Wells had reduced shipping and selling costs through their relationship, neither had explored a long term pricing agreement. Fred dealt with about ten ranchers on a similar basis.

After getting off the phone, Fred began discussing Junior's trip and his first year at business school. Then the phone rang again, "Howdy, Johnny." Johnny Winter, a local cattle buyer for the Monfort Packing plant, was calling to schedule a time to look at five pens of cattle that Fred had recently announced were ready to ship. "Yeah, seven thirty should be fine, but I need to finish by eleven so that I can get over to the sale barn to see how the feeders are selling." Fred's Wednesday schedule was now packed.

No sooner had Junior and Fred resumed their conversation when the phone rang again, "Yes, this is Fred. A water line broke this morning, and we need it fixed by tomorrow for a pen of cattle coming in from California. Can you do it." Fred had spent a good part of his day dealing with a broken water line instead of going to a local seminar on intensive feeding practices. Fred, instead, sent his cattle operations manager, Lonnie Mack, to attend the presentation.

---

* This case was written by Shaun Andrikopoulos (T'92) under the supervision of Prof. John Shank of the Amos Tuck School.

"I can't believe how much time you spend on the phone, dad. I've been here forty five minutes and haven't spoken to you for ten."

"I know, I just can't keep my head above water long enough to spend any time reviewing my monthly cattle performance," Fred continued, "I know I spend 40% of my time dealing with these damned cutthroat buyers. I spend another 20% of my time buying calves and fussing with the stocker farms, like Buddy's."

"By the way, how is Buddy doing?" asked Junior.

"The drought hit him hard, but his cattle are top notch. I'm almost positive that his steers outperform the rest of my animals, I just don't have time to go through my slaughter receipts to verify that they are doing better. Buddy keeps bugging me about paying him a premium. I guess I just can't look into everything! I know how he feels because I'm sick and tired of bickering with the packers over the quality of my cattle. The buyers all know that my cattle are better than most, but all I get is spot price plus whatever I can "negotiate" out of Johnny or the buyers I deal with from the other packers. Besides, Monfort is only two miles down the road. I know they save a hell of a lot on shrinkage and shipping compared to when Excell buys from us." [Excell Beef is located in Sterling, Colorado, 50 miles away]

CHAPARRAL OPERATIONS

The Wells feedlot has an annual capacity of about 60,000 head. With an average holding period of 196 days, this would be about 32,000 head at any one time. Well is currently holding around 28,000 cattle, 18,000 of which are finish ration cattle. On average, the cattle are switched from low to high ration after about 88 days (at a weight of about 1000 pounds).

Pens - Most "efficient" feeder ranchers maintain pens of about 300 cattle. Studies have determined that pens should be designed to provide 160 sq. ft./head for sleeping, standing, and exercising. Cattle require 24 inches of bunk space per head when feeding. Each pen is about 49,000 square feet (650' x 75').

Pens are cleaned every six weeks. Maintaining clean pens, especially in wet months, is essential in preventing respiratory and other disease problems. A full time crew of two men clean the pens while the cattle are in them. Manure is collected, loaded on spreader trucks, and spread on nearby farm land for fertilizer. The cleaning crew is also responsible for emptying and washing feed bunks in each pen.

Feeding - Like most large commercial feedlots, Fred Wells feeds his animals once a day. Feeding occurs all day because cattle are awake during daylight hours and prefer to eat when it is light. Cattle fed in the morning will tend to "rush" the feed bunks because they are hungry. In Summer months, cattle tend to eat only in the morning and in the evening, when the temperatures are below 80 degrees.

Every day, "pen riders" ride the pens to monitor feed consumption patterns. Excess feed in the bunks prior to feeding indicates that the animals are being overfed. Empty bunks indicate underfeeding. A "left over" estimate is made by the riders and is entered into a computer which helps the feedmill operators calculate the daily ration for each pen. Feed that is left in the bunks overnight usually goes to waste because it loses its flavor and aroma. In the Summer, left over feed mildews in the bunks and creates additional respiratory problems in the herd. In Winter months, left over feed is inedible because it freezes solid in the bunk.

Feed drivers start their 9 hour shift before the sun begins to heat the day. Each truck requires one operator. On-board scales must be calibrated each day on each truck. After calibration, the trucks are loaded with feed ration and additives and are weighed prior to mixing. It takes about 2 minutes to load each truck. Although the ration has been pre-mixed, additives must be mixed into the main ration. On board mixers are operated for about 4 minutes while the truck sits idle.

After mixing, the feed is driven to the pens. On average, a round trip takes about 14 minutes and is about 3+ miles in length. The trucks drive alongside the feed bunks and deliver even amounts of feed from a mechanized conveyor which unloads from the bottom of the truck's hopper. "High ration" cattle are fed first, "low ration" cattle second, and hospital pens and special pens third. At the end of each day the trucks are cleaned and then serviced by the full-time mechanic.

Feed rations are carefully calculated for each group of cattle (starter, intermediate, and finish) based on their growing cycle requirements, consumption patterns, and the nutritional value of the feed. Two full time feedmill operators calculate the feed rations each day. The mill operators are accountable for every pound of feed. Rations are recalculated each day. The operators process, blend, and load each truck. Weekly samples are submitted to a professional laboratory for complete nutritional analysis.

The Feed Operations Manager is responsible for supervising the feedmill operators, monitoring waste in the feed bunks on a daily basis, and handling all purchases, shipping, and inventory management.

Starter and intermediate cattle consume an average of 19.2 pounds of ration per day (Lo ration), while finish cattle average 31 pounds per day (Hi ration). Animals coming from stocker operations usually weigh around 750 pounds when they enter the lot, and are slaughtered at about 1300 pounds. Weanling calves that enter the feedlot directly from cow-calf operations could also be purchased. They weigh about 500 pounds and are slaughtered at about 1050 pounds. Wells is not currently using weanling calves.

Equipment - Feedlots utilize hopper trucks that are loaded from an overhead grain conveyer. Fred Wells uses 340 cu. ft. trucks that cost around $40,000 and haul 10,000 pounds of feed per load. On larger operations, where reliability is important, trucks are sold after five years for around $15,000 to smaller farmers who use the trucks for another ten to fifteen years. Maintenance costs average $4,000/year and fuel costs average $12,000/year for each truck.

Wells currently owns and operates three feed trucks. One of his trucks recently passed 150,000 miles and is approaching its fifth anniversary at Chaparral. Another truck is two years old and the third is three years old. Because cattle often rush the bunks when feed is delivered, it is not feasible to only partially fill a pen on a given trip. Each trip must serve an integer number of pens. Currently, Wells has 38 pens of 260 head each on Lo ration (2 pens per trip) and 56 pens of 320 head on Hi ration (1 pen per trip).

Milling equipment is expensive and requires considerable maintenance. Although each feed truck is fitted with a feed scale, a large in-ground truck scale is required to weigh incoming and outgoing cattle. Additional buildings are required for administrative tasks, hospital, and equipment repair. Exhibit 1 shows detailed investment data for equipment items.

Labor - A large feedlot operation employs between 12 and 15 people per shift. Labor is one of the largest cost elements in the feedlot operation, and it is difficult to attract and retain enough skilled and hardworking ranch hands. Because regularity in feeding time is important, reliable and consistent help is essential.

Lonnie Mack, the full-time Cattle Manager, supervises and monitors all the activities related to cattle operations. He is responsible for the health of the herd, shipping, and processing of all animals. Lonnie relies on his pen riders to monitor the health and activity of the cattle every day in every pen. Pen riders are experienced cattlemen who are trained to identify illnesses and other operational problems as they occur. Identifying and treating sick animals in a timely manner prevents the spread of disease, limits death loss, and reduces the overall stress of the animals. During ration changes or extreme weather changes cattle will often bloat. Bloat victims will often die it not treated with 24 hours. For this reason, every animal must be viewed each day. Pen riders will also identify ration problems as they occur by observing fecal matter and animal activity.

The ranch also employs a full-time vet technician. Although the 'vet tech' is not a Doctor of Veterinary Medicine (DVM), he is trained and experienced in treating most health problems at the feedlot. A consulting veterinarian usually visits feedlots twice monthly to treat difficult cases and to identify or warn of health problems that have regional implications.

Administrative Office - The office is staffed by a full time secretary/receptionist who is responsible for greeting visitors and answering calls from buyers, sellers, feed suppliers, and whoever else. Well's receptionist also assists with some computer work.

A full time personnel manager is responsible for maintaining employment records, health insurance and benefits records, monitoring OSHA requirements, and tracking vacations and shift requirements. The personnel manager also serves as a public relations contact.

A full-time accountant is responsible for general accounting, tracking all feed costs, rations, animal costs, and receipts. The accountant spends 50% of her time entering and tracking daily feed slips that are provided by each driver. Commercial feedlots track every ration individually. Drivers manually record one ration slip for each truck load of feed and one ration slip for each pen that is fed. The accountant utilizes a part time assistant to help enter and track all feed slips in the computer.

Fred Wells is responsible for the entire operation. As noted earlier, about 40% and 20% of his time is spent selling and purchasing cattle, respectively. The remainder of his time is consumed making investment and other operational decisions. He also tries to track the feed performance of his cattle every day.

Pen Formation - One major challenge facing the ranch all the time is forming pens of cattle that are of similar age, overall size, and weight. Preferably, the cattle in a pen should also have the same genetic characteristics. The more uniform the pen, the more efficiently the cattle will convert at the packing plant.

Many operators use "order buyers" to supply them with animals of similar makeup. Order buyers travel to cow/calf and stocker operations to purchase herds that will be formed into uniform pens of feeder cattle. These buyers also purchase weekly at regional auctions to form groups of similar cattle which are then delivered to feedlots. Cattle coming directly from the ranch are the most fresh. Animals sold at auction are exposed to more disease and shipping stress, and may come from unknown producers. Using an order buyer saves the general manager considerable time in forming pens.

Junior's Proposal. After a week of riding pens and feeding cattle, Junior began to miss the challenges of his first year MBA program. He began to think of better ways for his father to run the business. He thought to himself, "this place hasn't changed a bit since I was in high school ten years ago. I just can't believe there isn't a more effective way to run a ranch like this."

After feeding the last pen of steers, washing his feed truck, and turning in his ration slips it was 7:30 in the evening. Fred and Junior hopped in the pickup for a hot two mile ride home. Junior made dad a proposition. "Dad, if you let me spend the rest of the summer as a consultant on the business issues for the ranch, I'll bet you I can save you $10 a year for every dollar you are paying me. If not, I will owe you the summer wages.

Fred thought for a few seconds, smiled and said "its a deal." He was worried because declining cattle prices meant ranchers would hold onto their cattle longer. As the national cattle inventory was increasing, buyers would have more purchasing power in the weeks to come. The longer term result would be fewer cattle put into feedlots which would ultimately reduce supply and begin the next upward cycle in prices. In the short run, he was particularly concerned over what price his next sale of 1500 heifers would bring, so he told Junior, "Let's start now. How can you get me higher prices for the next sale?"

Junior rose to the challenge. "One of the things we studied in school this year was the way many suppliers and customers have set up supply linkages to take advantage of quality improvements, scheduling efficiencies, and reduction of marketing costs and purchasing costs. Basically, these guys enter into agreements to act as sole suppliers or customers with a special pricing agreement between the two parties. I'm not sure this concept could ever work in our situation, but it may be something to look into."

"Come on Junior, you know I could never get in bed with Monfort or Excell. Those guys would steal me blind if I let 'em. Anyway, I wouldn't be able to price shop between packers. Everyone wants my cattle and I know that I can always do a little better if I play those guys off against each other."

"Yeah, but that's what every feedlot operator thinks," contended Junior. "If you really do have better cattle, don't you think you could command a better price, on average, if the packers paid only for what they got."

"I'm not sure I follow you son?"

"Well, it seems to me that if you sold you cattle exclusively to Monfort you could work out an arrangement where you got paid a percentage premium above average spot price if your cattle graded out better than the weekly averages."

"Doubtful. The packers already know the price they pay for cattle takes into account an 'average' quality of the carcass grade. Paying more for a better quality carcass would only increase their costs. Anyway, most of those buyers know a good pen when they see one and are willing to settle for a higher price when the quality is there."

"Well, couldn't the arrangement stipulate that for those cattle you sold that were below average grade you would be assessed a penalty. You know that the grading is objective. Those U.S.D.A. inspectors don't like the packers any more than you do."

Fred paused a moment, "You know Junior, I could save a lot of time if I didn't have to deal with those damned buyers every day. I could see where this arrangement could eliminate the need for those guys to come out here and shoot the bull for three hours while we argue about prices."

"That's right dad. Because Monfort would be paying only for what they get, they wouldn't have any uncertainty about the animals they have purchased. Its a kind of ... quality control mechanism!"

"I would love to be able to look into my operation more, I just haven't had the time. Although I have just installed a new computer, and upgraded my scales, I haven't had time to see how my cattle are really converting. I can't even take a day off to go to a presentation on intensive feeding techniques. I know that there are better ways to run this business, I just don't have time to really look into any of them."

Fred Talks to Monfort. "Yes, this is Fred Wells. I'd like to speak to Kenny Monfort." "I'm sorry Mr. Monfort is out of the office at the moment. May I take a message?" "Sure, tell him that I called and that I would like to visit with him as soon as possible," Fred replied.

Kenny reached Fred that afternoon after two tries on the phone. "Howdy Fred, what can I help you with?" The two exchanged pleasantries and got down to business.

"My son has recently returned from business school and has some interesting ideas about how I can improve the business. I realize that you were recently bought out by ConAgra so I'm not sure how much discretion you have over these issues, but I'll give it a whirl."

"Well, I'm still the boss here. What do you have?" Kenny replied.

"My son and I have discussed the possibility of entering into an exclusive sales agreement with you, something they call a 'supplier/buyer' linkage."

"Yeah, since ConAgra bought us out I've been reading up on how to improve my quality. This seems to be a recurring theme," Kenny seemed interested. "But I'm not sure it could work in this industry. Everyone has pretty much the same cattle. You know that."

"Junior and I talked about this. I know that when you buy animals that are over finished or inconsistent they don't grade as well, and they certainly don't yield as well as consistently finished animals. Suppose that I could supply you with consistently finished cattle that yield grade well. You already provide me with the grade results for all of my animals anyway, so I know that it is possible to track my animals through your plant."

"Yes, that's correct."

"If we could agree on a premium that could be paid for each of my animals that yield grade better than average, and a discount for each of my animals that grade below average, we could get rid of the guess work your buyers go through each time they bid on a pen of my animals."

"Sure, but what base price would we use? You know that price discovery in this business is slim at best," Kenny warned.

"Well, I haven't really thought about it, but I'm sure we could work it out. Are you interested in exploring this further?"

"I'd be glad to. I just don't want you to get your hopes up. I'll have to run this past the guys in Omaha." Kenny continued, "Let's get together tomorrow at seven thirty in the morning over coffee."

"Sounds good, I'll meet you at Maxine's Kitchen for breakfast."

"See you there."

Fred and Kenny met several times to discuss their linkage proposal before Kenny presented it to headquarters. In his presentation Kenny emphasized that his Selling and Administrative expenses will be reduced by the agreement. He also emphasized that overall processing costs would be reduced if Wells can in-fact produce consistent, high quality animals. Surprisingly, headquarters was very positive about the plan and gave Kenny full go ahead to experiment with the linkage.

The Wells-Monfort agreement stipulates that Wells will ship cattle, sight unseen, with one week notice to Monfort. Monfort, in turn, will pay Wells an average weekly spot rate for his cattle. After the cattle are slaughtered and carcasses graded, Wells will be paid an 8% to 10% premium (or discount) for his cattle, based on how they compare to all of the cattle slaughtered in Monfort plants during the same week.

Although Fred was still a little apprehensive about having to turn away buyers from Excell and IBP who compete with Monfort for his cattle, he believed that the agreement would have long-term benefits. Fred enjoyed calling the Excell and IBP buyer's offices to inform them that they need no longer call on him.

Fred realized his time savings immediately. Monfort would ultimately pay Wells exactly what his cows were worth. This might be more or less than current prices, depending on who was "winning" the negotiations now. The linkage would only increase overall returns over time if it produced better beef.

The Extension Service Presentation. Fred soon began catching up on the pile of conversion performance reports that had accumulated on his desk. Fred also began to look into some of the latest management practices he had read about. He began to push some ideas at Junior for him to analyze using his high priced Ivy League ideas. Fred ran down Lonnie in the hospital pens. "Hey Lonnie do you have a few minutes to talk to Junior and me about the intensive feeding presentation you went to a couple of weeks ago?"

"Sure, we can talk now. I was impressed by the guys that spoke. They had a lot of interesting feeding techniques to talk about." Lonnie continued, "But I'm just not sure how cost effective these techniques will be in the real world. One researcher showed us how feeding Lo ration cattle twice a day and Hi ration cattle three time a day might improve conversion by three to five percent. But that ain't much. I've got the data in my notes."

"Besides, our trucks hardly ever stop running now and we only feed the cattle once a day. If we fed two or three times a day we would have to buy more trucks. Besides the cost, I'm not ready to deal with the labor problems. There's no way that a four percent increase in conversion would offset those costs."

"What else did they talk about?" Junior said.

"A few guys have been experimenting with pens of 600 cattle. They call 'em 'Superpens.' According to these guys, you can build a more efficient pen system if you go to larger pens. I can see how it would make it easier on the pen riders to have a better look at the cattle each day, but it seems that the pens would have to be huge in order for this system to work. At 24 inches of bunk space per head, a pen would have to be 1200 feet long." Lonnie frowned, showing his skepticism of academia.

"Think I could have a look at your notes Lonnie?"

"Sure, I don't really need 'em. The stuff is pretty farfetched."

Junior discovered that recent research shows that cattle convert better when they are fed close to their natural digestive cycle. Lo ration cattle (the first 88 days of feeding) are fed a high roughage (60% roughage 40%

protein) diet which becomes more protein rich over time. These cattle digest on a 12 hour cycle. Hi ration cattle (the last 112 days of feeding) are fed a 92% protein diet which they digest on an 8 hour cycle.

Cattle, like people, digest more efficiently if they are fed on a regular schedule. The researcher's test site feeds Lo ration cattle twice a day, and Hi ration cattle three times a day. Each feeding is administered within five minutes of the prescribed time each day. Because the researcher feeds more frequently, the cattle do not "rush" the pens to feed. As a result they eat at a slower rate and are able to consume more per day than if they eat only once.

Ration adjustments also turn out to be easier with the smaller, more frequent feedings. As a result the researcher has reduced the overall ration requirement by 1% because of left-over savings. Also, the intensive feeding schedule has resulted in 4% improved conversion efficiency. Because the animals don't rush the bunks during feeding, it is common to observe 1/3 of the cattle sleeping, 1/3 of the cattle standing, and 1/3 of the cattle coming to the feed bunks.

The "Superpen" Innovation. One large operator (100,000 head capacity), Elvin Bishop, has created 32 "Superpens" that house about 600 cattle each. Because Superpens are larger, they are easier for pen riders to monitor than smaller pen combinations with the same capacity. Pen riders can spend more time observing cattle in super pens and less time moving between pens. Increased observation time allows the riders to identify up to 50% more bloat cases and respiratory problems than before. This has resulted in a decrease in mortality rates of up to 50% for Bishop's operation.

Superpens have also resulted in reduced administrative costs. Because each driver completes a slip for each pen fed, the total number of slips that need processing is cut in half. Similarly Bishop, the General Manager, has reduced the amount of time he spends managing individual pens by a similar ratio. Superpens also cut in half the required interactions with cattle buyers.

The primary challenge facing Bishop with his Superpen is to identify 600 similar cattle for each pen. Previously he was able to fill two pens which could differ. For example one pen could be filled with shorter, lighter Angus cattle and another pen could be formed with larger cross-bred cattle. Because Bishop must form larger uniform pens, he relies on order buyers to supply him with calves of similar weight and genetic and geographic backgrounds.

A "Big" Truck. Bishop also uses a "Big" truck to feed his cattle. He claims that he has saved some operation expense with the new truck system, but he hasn't had a chance to look at the long-term benefits of using the truck. The "Big" truck has an operating capacity of 810 cu. ft. and costs around $103,000. The 24,000 pound capacity trucks operate similarly to the smaller trucks but they require about 25% more fuel.

Fred asked Junior to look into a new "Big" truck for the ranch. Junior wasn't sure it would make economic sense to spend $103,000 on a single truck. He realized that the value of the large truck at the end of five years would not be appreciably more than that of a small track. The secondary market for used trucks consisted entirely of small operators who would not be interested in the excess capacity of the "Big" truck.

Fred also asked Junior to investigate the Superpen and Intensive feeding practices to see if they really were cost effective. Junior had his hands full for the Summer as an MBA analyst, but at least it was more interesting than shoveling manure. As the summer progressed, he was often struck by the similarity in the two jobs.

ASSIGNMENT QUESTIONS

1) Using the information in the accompanying industry note and in the case, lay out the economics of the beef value chain from the cow/calf ranch to the supermarket. From this value chain perspective, evaluate the advantages and disadvantages of the Wells-Monfort linkage.

2) Does a larger truck make sense for Wells given his new, enlightened view on management? Is one "Big" truck sufficient to meet the needs of the Chaparral ranch?

3) If you were Junior Wells and you started your analysis of "Superpens" by just analyzing Chaparral's finish-ration cattle, how would you approach the analysis? Would this innovation make sense if the pens cost him $10,000 each to upgrade?

4) If Wells decides to implement intensive feeding, how much will his costs increase if he feeds his animals with the same frequency as the Researcher? Coupled with a 4% improvement in conversion, what is the net impact on Wells' bottom line? Does it make more sense for Wells to use 4% improvement in conversion to reduce the holding period per cow by 4% or to increase the selling weight by 4%?

5) Where would you focus your future management efforts if you were Fred Wells?

6) Assuming that the conversion rates do not change (pounds of feed per pound of weight gain), does it make more sense for Wells to purchase 500 pound animals directly from Cow/Calf operators, or 750 pound animals from Stocker operators? The 500 pound animals will finish at 1050. Assume that both calves will gain weight at the same rate per day and the total ration cost won't change (9.2 ration pounds per pound of weight gain x 500 pounds gained = 4,600 pounds of ration per calf. Assume that a 500 pound animal costs the feedlot $5.00/cwt. more than a 750 pounds animal because the extra 250 pounds is not viewed as equally high quality meat.

Exhibit 1
Financial Information for the Ranch

Feeder Operation

Capacity	60,000	head
Feedlot Utilization	69%	
Head per year (range = 32,000 to 50,000)	41,400	average
Average In-Weight	750	
Desired Finished Weight	1300	
Avg. Daily Gain	2.8	pounds
Holding Period	196	days
Net Gain	550	pounds
Feed Conversion Factor (lbs. per lb of gain)	9.2	
Feed Required Per Head	5060	pounds
Ration Cost/Ton	$118.21	
Market Steers - selling price per cwt.	$74.01	

Fixed Investment for the Ranch:		Annual Fixed Costs:	Per Year
Inventories	$ 17,728,774	Depreciation	$ 268,537
Pens and Equipment	810,198	Interest	298,287
Water and Equipment	130,824	Property Taxes	15,939
Milling Equipment	784,944	Insurance	13,662
Feed Storage Facilities	140,346	Repair/maintenance	34,155
Feed Trucks	135,000	Management (3)	90,000
Manure Equipment	17,802	Administrative Salary (4)	80,000
Transportation Equipment	36,432	Part Time Office Help	10,800
Repair Facilities	42,228	Labor:	
Land	199,134	Drivers (4)	80,000
Office	52,164	Pen riders (5)	100,000
Scales	67,068	Mill operators (3)	60,000
Total	**$ 20,144,914**	Hospital vet tech. (2)	46,000
		Pen Cleaners (2)	36,000
		Mechanic (1)	19,000
		Total	**$ 1,152,380**

Variable Costs:	Per Head	Per Year
Feed	$ 299.07	$ 12,381,552
Mortality loss (1.5%)	14.43	597,483
Veterinary and Medical Supplies	5.89	243,639
Gas and Oil	1.16	47,817
Electricity	2.04	84,249
Natural Gas	1.21	50,094
Telephone	.22	9,108
Shipping	13.00	538,200
Other	.99	40,986
Total	**$ 338.00**	**$ 13,993,128**

Profitability:	Per Year	Per Head	Per cwt
Revenues	$ 39,832,182	$ 962.13	$ 74.01
Purchase Price	23,638,365	570.98	43.92
Variable Costs	13,993,128	338.00	26.00
Fixed Costs	1,152,380	27.84	2.14
Net Profit	**$ 1,048,309**	**$ 25.32**	**$ 1.95**

DairyPak—A "Value Chain" Perspective on Product Line Strategy *

This case is set in 1988 in a consumer goods packaging division of a major forest products company. The product is the polyethylene coated paper carton for milk or orange juice.

Earle Bensing has some very tough decisions to make in the Summer of 1988. As Vice President for the Dairy-Pak Division of Champion International he faces:

- Declining market share in the growing "branded juice" segment of the domestic paperboard carton market.
- A technologically outmoded manufacturing system in terms of the expanding markets.
- A very limited output capability which has not grown in 10 years.
- A dramatically expanding international market which the corporation has seen as fraught with more problems than opportunities.

The capital spending and strategic positioning decisions he must make in 1988 will shape the future of the DairyPak division for many years to come.

I. LIQUID PACKAGING AND THE PURE-PAK CARTON

Millions of Americans, Europeans, Asians and South Americans start their day with milk or juice poured from a paperboard carton. Worldwide, paperboard is still the dominant form of milk and juice packaging today. But the industry has changed dramatically since the "gabled top" Pure-Pak carton rose to prominence in the 1950s.

The Plastic Substitute. Polyethylene replaced parafin to coat paperboard in 1961. It didn't take long after that before someone in the oil industry thought of making plastic cartons instead of plastic coating for paper cartons. Shell Chemical and Hoover International (now Johnson Controls) changed the liquid packaging industry overnight in 1965 when they combined to introduce the plastic resin pellet and the "blow molding" machine to manufacture plastic jugs. The blow molding machine was, and still is, so easy to use that paper packaging dropped from 82% of the milk market in 1971 to 37% in 1985.

But the interesting story here is that although plastic captured 100% of the gallon size carton market, it has not eliminated the other sizes of paper carton as many had predicted it would. Plastic is more economical when resin prices are low. When the price rises, paper looks good. Guessing future levels of ethylene gas prices (the basic driver of polyethylene price) is a notoriously difficult task.

---

* This case was written by Professor John Shank of the Amos Tuck School with the assistance of Mr. David Anthony, T'89.

And the dairy owner also has important non-financial reasons for staying with the paper carton. First, the dairy does not want to be at the mercy of oil companies. By using dual suppliers—paper and plastic—the dairy creates a hedge against volatile input prices. Also, as new uses of the plastic resin are created (industrial and consumer uses of plastic containers), the input price will not go lower since the plastic is just a by-product of ethylene gas. Second, the dairy believes that paper is the best product nutritionally. University studies have shown that paper protects milk vitamins and flavor much better than translucent plastic. Also, recent legislation prohibiting the dumping of plastic in Suffolk County on Long Island has created doubt about the long run viability of plastic.

The Competitors. Exhibit 1 is a global overview of the paperboard packaging business. There are five players in the domestic Pure-Pak industry -- International Paper, Champion, Potlatch, Westvaco and Weyerhaeuser. All of these companies are vertically integrated producers of the carton all the way back to the wood chip. Also, because of the scale and integration economies of these firms, new vertically integrated entrants are effectively shut out. In fact, because of the scale economies in producing a Pure-Pak carton, it is more likely that a small current player would drop out of the industry -- as Georgia Pacific did in 1981 or as Weyco did in the Eastern U.S. in 1982.

International Paper is the industry leader. IP is considered to be the low cost producer, achieving significant economies with a large and diverse extruding and converting capacity. IP is also the technological leader, with significant investment in aseptic (germ free) packaging and rotogravure printing (state-of-the-art technology). IP has continued to expand capacity, aggressively growing in the non-dairy segments by emphasizing their aseptic, hot fill, and other extended life packages, and aggressively pursuing their own off-shore converting operations (e.g. Korea and Japan). Along with these strategies, IP continues to price aggressively. But often IP is considered an unreliable supplier domestically because of their willingness to leave a customer when necessary to grow their off-shore converting operations.

Champion is currently a strong number 2, with more domestic volume than the other three players combined (see Exhibit 1).

Potlatch, Westvaco, and Weyerhaeuser all rank in a third tier of competition. All three face difficulties related to quality and inefficient scale. Weyerhaeuser and Potlatch have responded by looking increasingly to export markets while trying to maintain selected domestic niches. Westvaco is holding on to its domestic niche. Exhibits 1

and 2 summarize the estimated competitive situation for 1988.

Outside of the U.S. there are three major manufacturers supplying Pure-Pak cartons:

Enso-Gutzeit - Finland - They profess to be the World's No. 1 exporter and the World's second largest producer of liquid packaging board-- 342,000 tons of liquid packaging and fast-food board was supplied during 1987.

Billerud - Sweden - Paperboard production of 224,000 tons in 1988. This corresponds to a world market share of 14 percent. Most of the production is exported. TetraPak is the largest single customer.

CIP - Montreal, Canada - Three plants (Quebec, Ontario, and Alberta) convert CIP's polycoated stock into cartons for milk and juice. Its plants have a capacity of only 34,000 tons per year.

The Pure-Pak Customers. There are four groups of customers who form, fill, and seal Pure-Pak cartons. Champion's position in these four segments is summarized in Exhibit 3.

Domestic dairies. In 1976 there were approximately 10,000 dairies across the U.S., processing and distributing milk and juice. Fewer than 1,000 dairies survive in 1988, but dairies are still the largest purchaser of paperboard cartons in the U.S. Today, a typical dairy is a large regional packager of many private brands of milk and juice. The dairy's product is usually considered a commodity -- no ability to achieve a price premium for the brand name. Industry-wide, dairy profit margins are quite slim. Overall, the profits come from the very high turnover rates from being the sole supplier in a region. Overall, this segment has declined 3% per year over the last five years, but now has stabilized.

Differentiated juicers. The second largest segment is the high quality, differentiated juice packager -- basically Seagrams (Tropicana), Coca Cola (Minute Maid) and Procter and Gamble (Citrus Hill). This segment was created in the 50's by Tropicana. Coca Cola entered in the 1960's using its Minute Maid brand name. Procter and Gamble entered in the 1980's with a new brand name (Citrus Hill). In the past five years, chilled juice sales have increased more than 82 percent, compared with 17 percent for the whole juice industry. In 1988, it is estimated that chilled will outsell concentrate for the first time, buoyed by America's craving for convenience. This is the fastest growing segment in liquid packaging today (approximately 10% a year). The segment is extremely competitive as one would guess from the three key players, giants in consumer products: "An orange juice war is intensifying as major players try to squeeze bigger shares" (Wall Street Journal, 4/27/88). The big three juice processors represent over 50% of the ready-to-serve orange juice market -- clearly, a great opportunity for the paperboard industry.

The big three customers want high impact graphics to market the juice, a technologically advanced carton that retains essentials oils, like limonen-d in orange juice, and a carton that will hold the juice over 50 days (versus 14 days for milk). This customer is willing to pay for the differentiated carton.

1988 Domestic Share Of Market for Ready to Serve Orange Juice		Orange Juice Manufacturers' Use of Paperboard Cartons	
		1980	1987
Tropicana	27.3%	11,000 tons	15,000
Minute Maid	17.7%	7,000	10,000
Citrus Hill	9.1%	0	7,000
Dairies	45.9%	18,000	15,000
Total	100%	36,000	47,000

"Special uses." The third segment for polyethylene coated board includes "ovenable board" (frozen food dishes or microwave dishes) and Pure-Pak cartons used to hold such non-liquid items as nails or mothballs. This market has grown slowly. Overall volume and volume per customer are still low. Overall this is only 4% of Champion's volume.

The International Market

U.S. Folding Carton Stock Export for Liquid Packaging by Destination (000 tons)

	1985	1986	1987
Far East	214	233	248
Europe	50	56	59
Australia	30	35	36
Africa	30	28	35
Canada	9	17	33
S. America	30	29	29
C. America	13	8	14
Caribbean	3	5	7
Middle East	2	10	6
Other	14	11	14
Total	395	432	481
Uncoated Rolls	94	103	116
Coated Rolls	272	313	336
Converted Cartons	29	16	29

Export. The fourth group of customers for the Pure-Pak carton is the export market. Worldwide production of Pure-Pak cartons was estimated to be slightly over 1,600,000 tons in 1987 with only 1/3 (562,000) of that used in the United States. The international market has grown by over 16 percent in the last 3 years alone, with consumption increasing by over 100% in some countries as shown in the accompanying table.

II. CHAMPION DAIRYPAK - THE EVOLUTION OF A "HARVEST" STRATEGY

DairyPak began operation in Cleveland, Ohio with 12 employees in December, 1947, as one of the original licensees of the Pure-Pak technology. By 1950, DairyPak shipped 540 million cartons - over $5 million worth - and the company needed another plant to meet the growing demand. Expansion included converting plants built in Athens, Georgia, in 1951; Clinton, Iowa in 1952; Fort Worth, Texas in 1954; and Morristown, New Jersey in 1958. These five similar converting plants remain intact today as Champion's milk and juice carton converters.

Since the early 60's, Champion has produced about 250,000 tons of polyethylene coated board annually. Until 1980, virtually all these tons were converted by the 5 DairyPak plants and sold to dairies. The primary goal of Champion was to be the low cost producer in a commodity market.

The intrusion of plastic containers in the 1960s dramatically affected the paperboard carton industry and Champion's perspective on DairyPak. Champion watched to see what the dairy industry would do. A consulting study by Booz, Allen Hamilton in 1968 which circulated throughout the industry suggested that by the mid-80's not a single paperboard carton would be sold. Champion's reaction was to watch and wait. While Champion watched and waited, the paper carton did not die, but the Champion infrastructure began to get old and technologically outdated. In fact, since a new machine to produce the raw paperboard was built in 1965, very few capital improvements were implemented or considered until the summer of 1988. Of Champion's 33 converting machines, 29 were installed before 1963.

The Situation in 1988. In the early 80's, the explosion of the juice market created new opportunities for the Pure-Pak Carton - opportunities for which Champion was unprepared.

The following shows the changing markets for Champion:

| | Domestic Consumption of Pure-Pak Cartons (000) | | | Champion's Domestic Pure-Pak Cartons | | | |
| | 1980 | 1987 | | 1980 | | 1987 | |
	Tons	Tons	% change	Tons	% Share	Tons	% Share
Dairy	506	374	-26%	200	39	150	40
Non Dairy*	66	120	+82%	30	46	30	25
Total	572	494	-14%	230	40	180	36

Champion's Paperboard Production

	1980 Tons	1987 Tons
Dairy	200	150
Non Dairy*	30	30
Ovenable	0	10
Domestic Coated	9	2
Domestic Uncoated	10	10
Export Coated	11	32
Export Uncoated	0	12
Total	260	246

*Represents juice processors and special end uses of paperboard.

This data clearly indicates that Champion has successfully retained share in the declining market segment while losing almost half its share in the fastest growing segment. Why?

The Cost Structure—A Process Flow Perspective. On way to understand Champion's DairyPak position today is to study the process flow from wood chips all the way to Pure-Pak cartons.

The trees which become chips are a combination of southern pine and hardwood species. The two chip inputs are mixed with cooking and bleaching chemicals to produce pulp. The Canton Mill has paper processing capacity of 1550 tons per day, but only 1400 tons of pulping capacity. Therefore 150 tons of processed pulp are purchased on the open market at $700/ton (the in-house pulp costs $278/ton.). The paper processing capacity of the mill is divided into 850 tons of envelope paper and 700 tons of paperboard.

The purchased pulp and slush pulp (in-house) are mixed in the paper machine where the pulp is dried to make uncoated paperboard. The paper machine stage adds approximately $105 per ton of cost to the pulp.

The uncoated rolls (weighing about one ton each) are then shuttled to the nearby Waynesville, NC extruding plant at a cost of $3 per ton. Polyethylene is applied to both sides of the board at a cost of $94 per ton. From Waynesville, the rolls of coated board travel either to Champion's five converting plants at an average freight cost of $35 per ton, or are sold to export. Canton also sells some uncoated board each year to other converters for other carton applications (see Exhibit 4).

The 5 DairyPak locations pay a fixed transfer price of $680 per ton for the coated board, which includes freight. In the first stage of the converting operation, rolls of coated board are spliced together to form a long, continuous web. Next, each particular dairy's name, logo, and design are printed on one side using flexographic printing which is essentially a 1960's technology. The total cost of the conversion operation is $231 per ton, plus $10 per ton for freight to the end customers. Industry averages show that one ton of board equals 14,400 one-half gallon cartons and the individual carton price is between $.06 and .08 depending on the volume. Average price to a customer for 1/2 gallon cartons is $936 per ton. The half gallon size is not the most profitable item, but represents over 50% of sales. This process flow is the same for both milk and juice cartons since Champion does not distinguish the two.

At the juice processor or dairy, the rolls of flat cartons move along the sealing machines where their polyethylene coating is heated by a gas flame. Each carton is folded and conveyed through "ironing" rolls where it emerges joined together, or "side seamed." Filler machines then form and seal the bottom, fill the carton with liquid, and seal the gabled top. The cycle is complete when dairies and juice processors deliver their product to stores and supermarkets where consumers choose the paper carton over the plastic jug.

A small dairy will usually pay $.08 per 1/2 gallon carton since it cannot achieve volume discounts. The milk purchased from dairy farmers will cost $.75 per half gallon. The pasteurizing process will cost $.06 per half gallon and the distribution and shrinkage will add another $.06. The small dairy can sell a half gallon of unbranded milk for an average of $1.04. When a small dairy produces orange juice, the costs are similar except that oranges cost $.80 per half gallon. The price to supermarkets is $1.20 per half gallon, delivered.

Minute Maid, a large branded juice processor has very different economics. The 1/2 gallon carton will usually only cost $.06 because of volume discounts. The oranges themselves will only be $.64 per half gallon, again because of the tremendous volume. Converting, distribution and shrinkage will total $.11. One major cost a branded juice processor adds is national selling and advertising which averages 25% of the $1.42 wholesale price to supermarkets.

A large New Hampshire supermarket serving a population base of 50,000 sells regional dairy milk for $1.16, Tropicana orange juice for $2.26 (cost of $1.79), Minute Maid for $1.89, and local dairy orange juice for $1.50. This large supermarket sells 1,700 paper half gallons of milk and 7,000 plastic gallons of milk per week. On the orange juice side, 170 half gallons of Tropicana, 170 half gallons of Minute Maid and Citrus Hill together, and 280 half gallons of dairy orange juice are sold each week.

If Champion's accounting system were to separate a 1/2 gallon milk carton from a 1/2 gallon orange juice carton, there would certainly be differences in costs. The following table identifies the process differences between the two segments. Costing these process differences is beyond the scope of this case.

DIFFERENCES BETWEEN MILK AND ORANGE JUICE CARTONS

	Champion Milk Board	Ideal Orange Juice Board
Converting Plant	Faster-Speeds Shorter Runs Lower Print Quality Higher Services Costs	Slower Speeds Longer Runs (lower Setup/Ton) Higher Print Quality & Cost More customer support More Sales Time Per Ton Sold

Extruding Plant	Lighter Coat, "Profile" Coating
	Standard Approach for
	  most customers.
		Heavier Coat, "Flat" Coating
		Differing requirements for different
		  customers - no "standard" approach.

The Paperboard Machine	Production Focus "Get out the tons" Faster Speeds (Lower Printability) Not as Strong as O.J. (shorter shelf life)	Higher "Z" Strength Board Twice as much wet strength Resins (vs. milk) Slower Speeds (Higher Printability) Stronger than Milk (longer shelf life)
Pulping	The envelope paper machine receives pulp requirements first; Milk board last. Result is more variation for milk board.	Standard pulp mixture that would never change.

Champion Strategy Today. Given the cost structure and changing environment already outlined, Champion still believes that the domestic dairy market will continue to be the principal area of profits, even with the contraction due to plastic. Champion will attempt to defend its dominant position, but cannot expect improvement in current volume unless one of the major competitors (IP, Westvaco, Weyerhaeuser or Potlatch) leaves the business. For example, in 1982 Weyerhaeuser exited the paperboard carton industry in the East when their paper mill in North Carolina was converted from board to disposable diapers. It is estimated that Champion picked up 30,000 to 40,000 tons a year of Weyerhaeuser's old business.

Overall, Champion recognizes its strengths as:

- Large and efficient board machine
- Efficient and geographically well-located extrusion facility
- 5 competitive and strategically located carton converting plants
- Successful ovenable board converting plant (in the Midwest)
- Very successful position in the dairy market east of the Rockies
- Excellent service reputation among domestic dairies
- Knowledgeable operating people throughout the system

But Champion also recognizes its weaknesses:

- Limited extrusion capacity
- Lack rotogravure printing
- Champion has been unable to respond efficiently to the diverse needs of the non-dairy segment
- Although tremendous progress has been made, there are still nagging problems with the quality of the board (see Exhibit 5)
- Lack roll wrapping and labeling capability of competitors at the extruding plant
- Reputation of uncertain commitment in export markets

Given the above, the Champion strategy has been, and still is, to be the low cost producer in the commodity dairy segment, to try to make inroads in the differentiated juice segment, to cautiously upgrade its infrastructure but not to invest in latest printing and roll-wrapping equipment, and to view export and special end-use segments as ancillary (no need for major commitments).

III. THE SUMMER OF 1988

Where to compete and how much to invest are the two difficult questions Earle Bensing faces.

The first proposal he is considering is to renovate the paperboard machine at a total cost of $43,000,000. Phase I of this proposal will cost $16,000,000 to rebuild the "wet end" of the machine and will result in improved internal strength of the board (stronger cartons and improved printability). Phase II will cost another $27,000,000 at the "dry end" of the machine (improved smoothness for better print quality).

A second proposal is to add a third extruder at the Waynesville, NC plant. A "state of the art" extruder costs approximately $17,000,000 and would allow Champion to compete in multilayered polymer coating applications. The newly emerging packages in the juice industry require multiple plastic resins and foils to extend shelf life and to hold difficult liquids. The new extruder would be dedicated to expanding Champion's product line to serve customers with complex co-extrusion needs.

A third proposal Bensing is considering is to add roll wrapping equipment at the Waynesville location. Currently, coated rolls are shipped overseas unsealed, exposed while they are handled in transit and while laying in a cargo hold. This leads to both sanitary and aesthetic problems, since moisture and bacteria can attack the board. State of the art roll wrapping equipment would cost $1,750,000 for the initial capital outlay, 1 operator for the machine at $30,000 a year, and $2.50 per one ton roll in material expense. Champion could not charge customers more for wrapped rolls.

The fourth potential area for investment is adding rotogravure printing. Currently DairyPak uses flexography which prints from plates made of rubber. This method is very popular because it is inexpensive. After the initial capital expense of $1.5 million, the plates are about $150 apiece and six are needed for a six color process. The quality is not as good as with offset or rotogravure printing, but high quality printing has never been required in the dairy segment of the business.

In rotogravure (or intaglio) printing, the plate cylinder itself is machined and coated to receive the printing image photographically. The portions of the cylinder's surface which will print are etched as microscopic, cup-like cells while the non-printing areas remain untouched. Rotogravure gives an extremely accurate and high quality finish--but it is expensive. The initial capital expense is similar to flexography (approximately $1.5 million) but one cylinder costs $2,500. With a six color process, $15,000 must be spent for only one run. And once that run is complete, those cylinders will probably never be used again. These investment opportunities are summarized here:

**Resource Allocation Options
1988**

1. Rebuild the paperboard machine:

Phase I—Rebuild "wet end"	$16 million
Phase II—Rebuild "dry end"	$27 million

2. Add a third extruder at Waynesville $17 million

3. Add roll wrapping equipment:

Capital Cost		$1.75 million
Operating Costs:	Labor	$30,000/ year
	Materials	$2.50/one ton roll

4. Add rotogravure printing as an option for customers:

Capital Cost	$1.5 million
Operating Costs	$15,000 per run

5. Do we need additional investments if we want to be a board supplier to Tropicana?

WHERE SHOULD CHAMPION INVEST INCREMENTAL CAPITAL AND OPERATING DOLLARS?

Not only does Bensing face investment decisions, he also has to decide who will get the limited amount of board that Champion produces each year. Will it be the dairies, whose total market has been declining 3% a year but who have always been the main customer of DairyPak; will it be the big juice manufacturers (Coca Cola, or Procter & Gamble) -- whose market is growing at 10% and who will pay top dollar for board, but who demand a consistent quality that Champion has been unable to produce; or will it be the export market -- which is growing rapidly each year, and where a top price is possible because of a favorable currency situation, but where Champion has never tried to compete aggressively, either as a board supplier or a converter.

The marketing of paperboard cartons to the juice industry offers tremendous potential. Although the New York area makes up only 7% of U.S. population, New Yorkers consume 14% of the orange juice sold. If the big three's expansion is successful outside New York and New England, quality carton volume could explode. This is a great opportunity for Champion, if it were ready to compete in that market.

The opportunity is definitely there for DairyPak. But does Earle Bensing have the right information to make his decisions? Is there an accurate picture of the costs and value created at the paper machine, the extruding plant and the converting plants? Is there enough information concerning the competitors and the marketplace? Overall, does Mr. Bensing have the financial tools to evaluate the investment and marketing options open to him?

ASSIGNMENT QUESTIONS

1) Can you construct a "value chain" (see Exhibit 6) of costs and profits from the pulp mill all the way through to the supermarket for milk, for dairy orange juice, and for Minute Maid orange juice? Present all the calculations on the basis of one ton of board. Use the format outlined in Exhibit 7.

2) What insights for the business does the "value chain" provide? For example, of the total profit earned per ton of board, how much is earned by the supermarket, by the processor, and by Champion? (Use a format like Exhibit 8). So what?

3) When asset data (as shown here) is included, what inferences do you draw about ROA for Champion, the dairy, the juice processor and the retailer? (Use a format like Exhibit 9):

Assets in the Process Flow

Assets	Current Market Value ($)	Per Ton of Board
Pulp Mill	400,000,000	$1,600
Paper Machine	300,000,000	1,200
Extruder	42,000,000	190
Converting Plants	141,000,000	830
Juice Processor	55,000,000	2,890
Small Dairy	2,100,000	5,400
Supermarket—space and display cases (dairy section)	103,500	1,800

4) Note that unless a major expansion were undertaken, Champion's output is limited to about 250,000 tons per year of coated board. Which segment[s] do you believe should be targeted?

EXHIBIT 1

ALL PACKAGING INDUSTRY

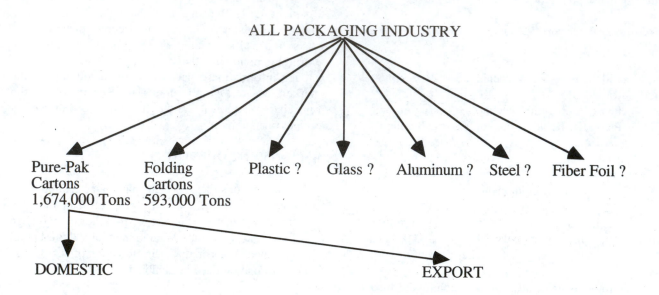

	Tons (000)	Market Share		Tons (000)	Market Share
IP	230	41%	Eso, Finland	342	31%
Champion	202	36%	Billerud	224	20%
W-H	55	10%	I - P	180	16%
Potlatch	50	10%	Potlatch	160	15%
Westvaco	25	3%	W-H	60	5%
	562 Tons	100%	Champion	44	4%
			CIP, Canada	102	9%
				1,112 Tons	100%

WORLDWIDE

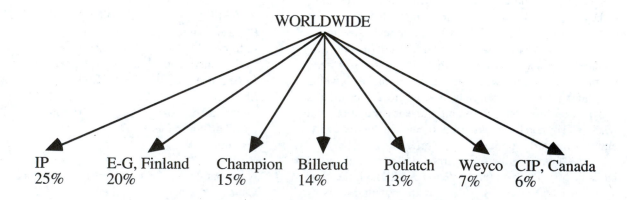

EXHIBIT 2

DOMESTIC COMPETITOR REVIEW - 1986

Company	Extruders	Folding Carton Capacity (000 annual tons). Liquid Packaging is one use for folding carton stock	Liquid Packaging Domestic	Export	Pure-Pak Converting Locations	
International Paper	4 - Pine Bluff, AR 1 - Raleigh, NC 2 - Mobile, AL 1 - Texarkana, TX	709	230	180	Atlanta, GA Bastrop, LA Framingham, MA Kalamazoo, MI	Kansas City, KA Philadelphia, PA Turlock, CA
Champion	2 - Waynesville, NC	250	202	44	Athens, GA Clinton, IA Ft. Worth, TX	Morristown, NJ Olmsted Falls, OH
Potlatch	2 - Lewiston, ID	300	50	160	Ft. Wayne, IN Pomona, CA Sikeston, MO	
Weyerhaeuser	2 - Longview, WA	193	55	60	Los Angeles, CA Vancouver, WA	
Westvaco	1 - Covington, VA 2 - Laurel, MD	147	25	-	Richmond, VA	

EXHIBIT 3
Market Segments for Pure-Pak
1987

U.S. DAIRIES	BRANDED JUICERS		EXPORT
(Milk and OJ)	Minute Maid and Citrus Hill	Tropicana	
Historically, Champion has emphasized this segment (about 150,000 tons in 1988)	Relatively Minor Volume (about 2,000 tons)	Zero Volume	32,000 Tons (Coated) 12,000 Tons (uncoated)
Our tons shrinking 3% per year since 1980	Flat since 1980	Lost this business for quality reasons in 1981	Champion's "swing" market
Overall market has been shrinking about 3% per year since 1980	Overall market growing at 10%; potential to grow faster (growth in ready-to-serve; greater market penetration in Mid-west)		Overall Market growing at more than 10% per year
We have maintained market share (40%) in this declining segment	Are we the "backup" supplier in this segment?		Champion has not been willing to commit here for the long run

WHICH MARKET SEGMENTS SHOULD CHAMPION EMPHASIZE IN THE FUTURE?

EXHIBIT 4

CHAMPION DAIRYPAK SYSTEM-SELECTED SEGMENTS

| | Paper Mill | | Waynesville Extruding Plant | | | | Converting Plants | |
| | Uncoated Board Sales | | Coated Sales to DP | | Coated Sales to Export | | DairyPak Sales | |
	1980	1987	1980	1987	1980	1987	1980	1987
Net Revenue/Ton	$448	$530	$497	$663	$517	$577	$697	$994
Cost/Ton	$365	$471 [1]	$444	$540	$444	$540 [2]	$671	$992
Profit Before Tax/Ton	$83	$59	$53	$123	$67	$37	$26	$2
Tons (000)	10	22	230	180	11	32	230	180

(1)	Pulp Cost	$319	424
	Machine Cost	105	
	Freight to Customer	47	
		$471	

(2)	Mill Cost	$424
	Freight to Extruder	3
	Extruder Cost	94
	Freight to Customer	19
		$540

EXHIBIT 5

Champion
Champion International Corporation

To: Canton Mill, Manufacturing Office   Date: May 19, 1988

From: DairyPak Customer Services   Subject: Board Surface Quality

In our constant effort to improve the print quality of our finished product, one fact is obvious: no matter how good the quality of our inks, plates, artwork, machines and people, we cannot accomplish the high degree of printing excellence we are striving for when our board surface is covered with dimples and pot holes.

The finer the settings on our presses , the more these surface imperfections show up. Please note the enclosed samples. What you see here is the rule, not the exception.

We would greatly appreciate your help in working with whomever necessary to find a way to supply us with a smooth printing surface with which to work. If we may be of assistance please don't hesitate to call.

As always, your comments and/or suggestions are welcome.

cc: Joe Deal, Jr.
         Robert Ray
         Charlie Ward
         Ed Fritch

EXHIBIT 6
Process Flow Value Chain

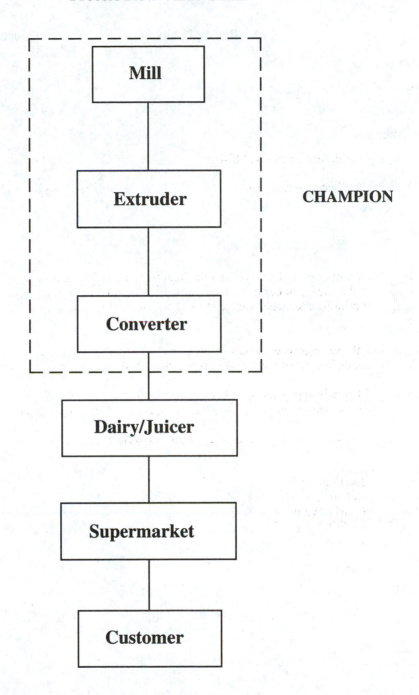

Can we calculate COSTS, REVENUES, ASSETS at each "value activity"?

EXHIBIT 7
A Process Flow Value Chain

	Regional Dairy		Branded OJ		Export
	Milk	OJ	MM/CH	Tropicana	
Per Carton					
Consumer Pays	1.16	1.50	1.89		
Store Margin					
Store Pays					
Dairy/Juicer Margin					
Processor Cost					
Carton Cost					
Per Ton					
Price to Processor					
Converter Margin					
Freight to Processor					
Converter Cost					
Price to Converter					
Extruder Margin					
Freight to Converter					
Extruder cost					
Price to Extruder					
Mill Margin					
Freight to Extruder	3	3	3		
Mill Cost - Pulp*	319	319	319		
Other	105	105	105		

*(~14/15.5 x $278 + ~1.5/15.5 x $700 = $319)

EXHIBIT 8
Margins Per Ton of Board

	REGIONAL DAIRY		BRANDED OJ
	Milk	OJ	
Store			
Dairy/Juicer			
Converter			
Extruder			
Mill			
	_____	_____	_____
Total	_____	_____	_____
CHAMPION %	?		

EXHIBIT 9
Return on Assets Per Ton of Board

	REGIONAL DAIRY						BRANDED OJ		
	MILK			OJ					
	Margin	Assets	ROA	Margin	Assets	ROA	Margin	Assets	ROA
Store									
Dairy/ Juicer									
Converter									
Extruder									
Mill									
Total	____	____	____	____	____	____	____	____	____

Note on Value Chain Analysis*

(For use with DairyPak case.)

One of the major themes in strategic cost management (SCM) concerns the focus of cost management efforts. Stated in question form: How do we organize our thinking about cost management? In the SCM framework, managing costs effectively requires a broad focus, external to the firm. Porter (1985) has called this the "value chain". The "value chain" for any firm in any business is the linked set of value creating activities all the way from basic raw material sources (starting ultimately with the periodic table of the elements) through to component suppliers, to the ultimate end-use product delivered into the final consumers' hands, and, in today's world, perhaps through recycling to the beginning of a new value chain cycle. This focus is <u>external</u> to the firm, seeing each firm in the context of the overall chain of value-creating activities of which it is only a part, from basic raw material components to end-use consumers.

In contrast, conventional management accounting, as explained in leading text books, adopts a focus which is largely <u>internal</u> to the firm - <u>its</u> purchases, <u>its</u> processes, <u>its</u> functions, <u>its</u> products and <u>its</u> customers. Another way of saying this is that management accounting takes a "value-added" perspective, starting with payments to suppliers (purchases), and stopping with charges to customers (sales). The key theme is to maximize the difference —*i.e., the value-added*— between purchases and sales. Simply put, the strategic insights yielded by the value chain analysis are much *different from—and are superior to*—those suggested by the value-added analysis.

This chapter is organized as follows. In the first section, we define the value chain concept, contrast it with the value-added notion, and highlight the strategic power of value chain analysis. We then discuss the methodology for constructing and using a value chain. In the final section, we discuss two real world examples to illustrate the power of the value chain perspective. The first example contrasts the value chains of AT&T, NYNEX, and IBM in the telecommunications industry. The second example is drawn from the airline industry; here, we not only discuss value chain of a major trunk airline but we also contrast the value chains of United Airlines and People Express (in its heyday).

---

* This note was prepared as a basis for class discussion by Professor John K. Shank.

THE VALUE CHAIN CONCEPT

According to Porter (1980), a business unit can develop a sustainable competitive advantage either based on cost or based on differentiation or based on both, as shown in the table below.

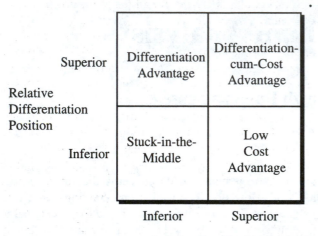

The cost advantage and differentiation advantage are briefly described below.

Low cost: The primary focus of this strategy is to achieve low cost relative to competitors. Cost leadership can be achieved through such approaches as:

1) Economies of scale in production;
2) Experience curve effects;
3) Tight cost control; and
4) Cost minimization in areas such as R&D, service, sales force, or advertising.

Examples of firms following this strategy include: Texas Instruments in consumer electronics, Emerson Electric in electric motors, Hyundai in automobiles, Briggs and Stratton in gasoline engines, Black and Decker in machine tools, Commodore in business machines, K Mart in retailing, BIC in pens, and Timex in wrist watches.

Differentiation: The primary focus of this strategy is to differentiate the product offering of the business unit, creating something that is perceived by customers as being unique. Approaches to product differentiation include: brand loyalty (Coca Cola in soft drinks), superior customer service (IBM in computers), dealer network (Caterpillar Tractors in construction equipment), product design and product features (Hewlett-Packard in electronics), and/or technology (Coleman in camping equipment). Other examples of firms following a differentiation strategy include: Mercedes in automobiles, Stouffer's in frozen foods, Neiman-Marcus in retailing, Cross in pens, and Rolex in wrist watches.

Whether or not a firm can develop and sustain differentiation or cost advantage or differentiation-cum-cost advantage (as the Japanese have demonstrated) depends fundamentally on how the firm manages its value chain relative to the value chains of its competitors. Both intuitively and theoretically, competitive advantage in the market place ultimately derives from "providing better customer value for equivalent cost" (i.e., differentiation) or "equivalent customer value for a lower cost" (i.e., low cost). Thus, value chain analysis is essential to determine exactly where in the chain customer value can be enhanced or costs lowered. Ignoring linkages upstream from the firm as well as downstream is just too restrictive a perspective.

Dangers of Ignoring Value Chain Linkages

The value chain framework is a method for breaking down the chain - from basic raw materials to end-use customers - into strategically relevant activities in order to understand the behavior of costs and the sources of differentiation. We are aware of no firms which span the entire value chain in which they operate.

A firm such as Chevron in petroleum spans wide segments of the value chain in which it operates, from oil exploration to service stations, but it does not span the entire chain. Fifty percent of the crude oil it refines comes from other producers, and more than one third of the oil it refines is sold through other retail outlets. Also, Chevron is not in the auto business at all, the major user of gasoline. More narrowly, a firm such as Maxus Energy is only in the oil exploration and production business. The Limited Stores have "downstream" presence in retail outlets but own no manufacturing facilities. Reebok is a famous shoe brand, but the firm owns very few retail outlets. Reebok does, however, own its factories.

To recapitulate, a firm is typically only a part of the larger set of activities in the value delivery system. Since no two firms of which we are aware, even in the same industry, compete in exactly the same set of markets with exactly the same set of suppliers, the overall value chain for each firm is unique.

Suppliers not only produce and deliver inputs used in a firm's value activities, but they importantly influence the firm's cost/differentiation position. For example, developments by steel "mini-mills" lowered the operating costs of wire products users who are the customers of the customers of the mini mill - 2 stages down the value chain. Similarly, customer's actions can have a significant impact on the firm's value activities. For example, when printing press manufacturers create a new press of "3 meters" width, the profitability of paper mills is affected, because paper machine widths must match some multiple of printing press width. Mill profit is affected by customer actions even though the paper mill is 2 stages upstream from the printer who is a customer of the press manufacturer! As we will discuss more fully below, gaining and sustaining a competitive advantage

requires that a firm understand the entire value delivery system, not just the portion of the value chain in which it participates. Suppliers and customers and suppliers' suppliers and customers' customers have profit margins that are important to identify in understanding a firm's cost/differentiation positioning, since the end-use customers ultimately pay for all the profit margins along the entire value chain.

Exhibit 1a presents a conceptual value chain for the paper industry. The distinct value activities, such as timber, logging, pulp mills, paper mills, and conversion plants, are the building blocks by which this industry creates a product valuable to buyers.

It is possible to quantify the economic value created at each stage by identifying the costs, revenues, and assets for each activity. What we argue is that every firm in Exhibit 1a -- A, B, C, D, E, F, and G -- must

EXHIBIT 1a
Value Chain in the Paper Products Industry

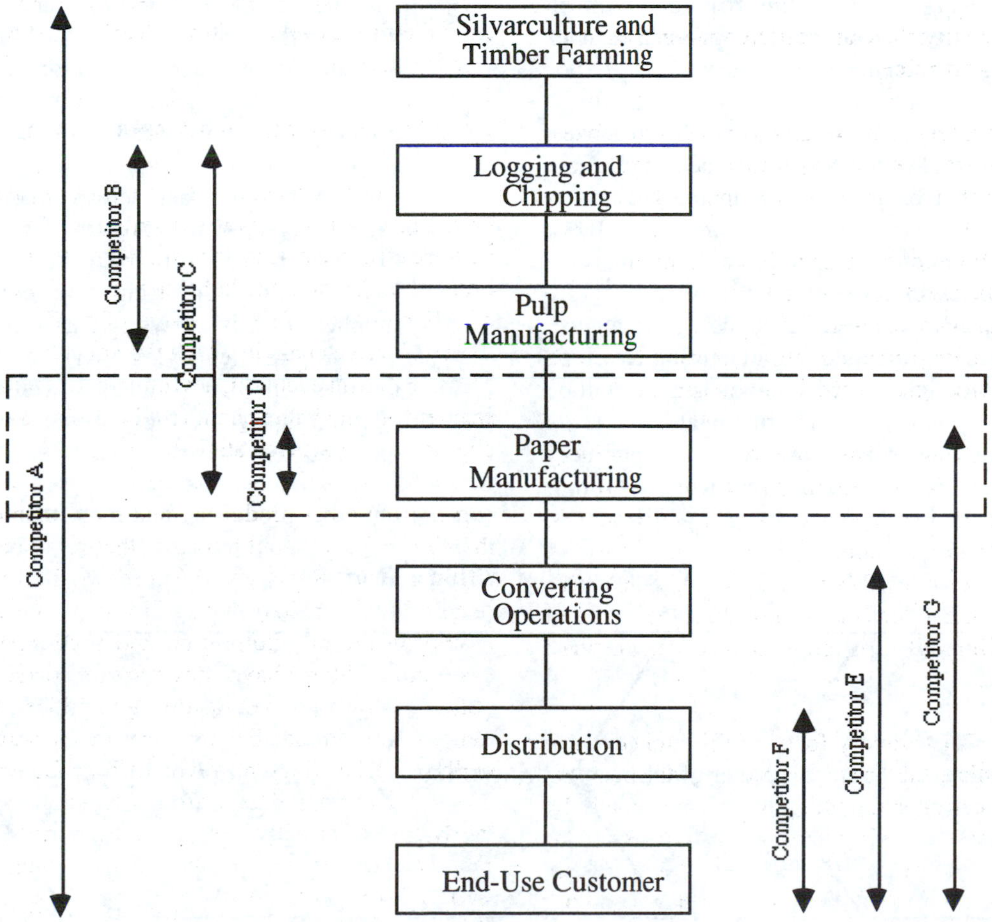

construct a value chain for the total paper industry, breaking the total value in the chain into its fundamental sources of economic value. Such an analysis has potential strategic implications for *every* competitor in this industry.

For instance, consider three firms in the paper products industry. Weyerhaeuser participates in most parts of the value chain, with the exception of logging. James River has very limited timberlands but participates in the remainder of the value chain. Finally, TetraPak does not own trees, or pulp mills, or paper mills but makes cartons from paperboard purchased on the market. We argue that every one of these three firms can benefit by constructing the entire value chain -- even though they do not participate in every stage of the chain.

Value Chain Insights for Different Competitors

- If competitor A (a fully integrated company) calculates the Return on Assets (ROAs) at each stage of the chain by adjusting all transfer prices to competitive market levels, it could highlight potential areas where the firm could more economically buy from the outside instead of "making" (strategic choice of make or buy). For example, most of the "fully integrated" forest product companies (examples: Weyerhaeuser, International Paper) still use independent loggers to cut their trees on the way to their mills.

- With a complete value chain, competitors B, C, D, E, F, and G might be able to identify possibilities to forward or backward integrate into areas which can enhance their performance. Westvaco has stopped manufacturing envelope paper although it still owns a large envelope converter. Champion International has sold its envelope converting business but still produces envelope paper. Both choices, although apparently inconsistent, could be plausible given the specific strategies of Westvaco and Champion.

- Each value activity has a set of unique cost drivers that explain variations in costs in that activity [Shank, 1989]. Thus, each value activity has its unique sources of competitive advantage. Companies are likely to face a different set of competitors at each stage -- some of these competitors would be fully integrated companies and some of them would be more narrowly focused specialists. For instance, firm D in Exhibit 1a faces competition from firms A, C, and G in the paper mill stage. Yet, firms A, C, and G bring very different competitive advantage to this stage of the value chain vis-a-vis firm D. It is possible for firm D to compete effectively with firms A, C, and G only by understanding the total value chain and the cost drivers that regulate each activity. For example if "scope" (vertical integration) is a key structural driver of paper mill cost, Firm A has a significant advantage and Firm D a significant disadvantage in this marketplace.

- Since each firm illustrated in Exhibit 1a is both a buyer and a seller somewhere within the chain, calculating the profit (and ROA) earned at each stage can help in understanding the relative power of buyers versus sellers at that stage. For example, comparing the returns for firm E versus firm F can help identify the relative power within the chain of the converting stage for which E is a supplier but F is a buyer. This then could help the firms in identifying ways to exploit their linkages with their suppliers as well as with their customers to reduce costs or enhance differentiation or both.

EXHIBIT 1b
Value Activities Within a Firm

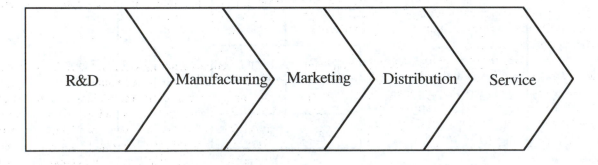

R&D   Manufacturing   Marketing   Distribution   Service

Parenthetically, we might note that the concept of value chain we have described so far includes but goes beyond the traditional view that a firm's value chain represents the collection of activities that the firm performs in the different functional areas. This traditional view is diagramatically represented below as Exhibit 1b:

What we argue is that a firm's value chain is embedded in a larger system which includes suppliers' and customers' value chains. A firm can enhance its profitability not only by understanding its own value chain -- from design to distribution -- but also by understanding how the firm's value activities fit into suppliers' and customers' value chains.

Value Chain Versus Value-Added

The value chain concept can be contrasted with the internal focus that is typically adopted in management accounting. Management accounting usually takes a "value-added" perspective, as noted earlier. From a strategic perspective, unlike the value-added concept, the value chain concept highlights four profit improvement areas:

1)   Linkages with suppliers;
2)   Linkages with customers;
3)   Process linkages within the value chain of a business unit; and
4)   Linkages across business unit value chains within the firm.

Linkages With Suppliers. Value-added concept starts too late. That is to say, starting cost analysis with purchases misses all the opportunities for exploiting linkages with the firm's suppliers. The word "exploit" does not imply that the relationship with the supplier is a zero sum game. Quite the contrary, it implies that the link should be managed so that both the firm and its supplier can benefit. Such opportunities can be dramatically important to a firm. In Chapter 1, we presented an example from the American automobile industry that demonstrated the strategic benefits in explicitly considering supplier linkages.

We present below another example which illustrates how beneficial linkages with suppliers (i.e., linkages with suppliers that are managed in such a way that all parties benefit) can be tracked more accurately with value chain analysis than with value-added analysis.

When bulk chocolate began to be delivered in liquid form in tank cars instead of ten pound molded bars, an industrial chocolate firm (i.e., the supplier) eliminated the cost of molding bars and packing them and a confectionery producer saved the cost of unpacking and melting (Porter, 1985).

Linkages With Customers. In addition to starting too late, value-added analysis has another major flaw; it stops too soon. Stopping cost analysis at sales misses all the opportunities for exploiting linkages with the firm's customers. Customer linkages can be just as important as supplier linkages. Here again, we contend that the relationship with the customer need not be a zero sum game, but one in which both parties can gain.

There are many examples where the linkage between a firm and its customer is designed to be mutually beneficial and where the relationship with the customer is viewed not as a zero-sum game but as a mutually beneficial one.

Some container producers have constructed manufacturing facilities next to beer breweries and deliver the containers through overhead conveyers directly onto the customers' assembly line. This results in significant cost reductions for both the container producers and their customers by expediting the transport of empty containers which are bulky and heavy (Hergert & Morris, 1989).

The value chain framework highlights how a firm's products fit into the buyer's value chain. For instance, under this framework, it is readily apparent what percentage the firm's product costs are in the customer's total costs. The fact that paper constitutes over 40% of the total costs of a magazine is very useful in encouraging the paper mill and the publisher to work together in cost reduction activities. The San Francisco Chronicle adopted Just-in-Time for paper delivery to its printing plant, a program only possible with close supplier cooperation. Since the value-added concept ignores activities after the product leaves the firm, it often does not highlight the degree of buyer power.

Process Linkages Within The Value Chain of a Business Unit. Unlike the value added concept, value chain analysis explicitly recognizes the fact that the individual value activities within a firm are not independent but rather are interdependent. For instance, at McDonalds, the timing of promotional campaigns (one value activity) significantly influences capacity utilization in "production" (another value activity). These linked activities must be coordinated if the full effect of the promotion is to be realized. As another example, Japanese VCR producers were able to reduce prices from $1,300 in 1977 to $298 by 1984 by emphasizing the impact of an early step in the chain (product design) on a later step (production) by drastically reducing the number of parts in VCRs (Hergert & Morris, 1989).

  Conventional management accounting approaches tend to emphasize "across-the-board" cost reductions. However, by recognizing interlinkages, the value chain analysis admits to the possibility that deliberately increasing costs in one value activity can bring about a reduction in total costs. The expense incurred by Proctor and Gamble to place its order entry computers directly in Wal-Mart stores significantly reduces overall order entry and processing costs for both firms.

  Linkages Across Business Unit Value Chains Within the Firm. In sharp contrast to the value added notion, the value chain analysis also recognizes the profit potential accruing from exploiting linkages among value activities across business units. For example, within Procter & Gamble, the cost position of the disposable diaper business unit is enhanced by its ability to share in distribution with other business units whose products (such as soaps and paper towels) also go through supermarkets.

VALUE CHAIN METHODOLOGY

  The methodology for constructing and using a value chain involves the following steps:

1. Identify the industry's value chain and assign costs, revenues, and assets to value activities.
2. Diagnose the cost drivers regulating each value activity.
3. Develop sustainable competitive advantage, either through controlling cost drivers better than competitors or by reconfiguring the value chain.

  These steps are considered in greater detail in the following sections.

Identify The Value Chain

  Competitive advantage cannot be meaningfully examined at the level of the industry as a whole. The value chain disaggregates the industry into its distinct strategic activities. Therefore, the starting point for cost analysis is to define an industry's value chain and assign costs, revenues, and assets to value activities. These activities are the building blocks by which firms in the industry create a product valuable to buyers. Activities should be isolated and separated if:

a. They represent a significant percentage of operating costs; or
b. The cost behavior of the activities (or the cost drivers) is different; or
c. They are performed by competitors in different ways; or
d. They have a high potential of being able to create differentiation.

  Each value activity incurs costs, generates revenues, and ties up assets in the process. After identifying the value chain, one must assign operating costs, revenues, and assets to individual value activities. For intermediate value activities, revenues should be assigned by *adjusting internal transfer prices to competitive market prices*. With this information, it should be possible to calculate Return on Assets for each value activity.

Diagnose Cost Drivers

  The next step is to identify the cost drivers that explain variations in costs in each value activity. Building on the concepts introduced in Chapter 1, in conventional management accounting, cost is a function, primarily, of only one cost driver, output volume. Cost concepts related to output volume permeate the thinking and the writing about cost: fixed versus variable cost, average cost versus marginal cost, cost-volume-profit analysis, break even analysis, flexible budgets, and contribution margin, to name a few. In the value chain framework, output volume <u>per se</u> is seen to capture very little of the richness of cost "behavior"; rather, multiple cost drivers are usually at work. Further, cost drivers differ across value activities.

  Porter [1985] presents one attempt to create a comprehensive list of cost drivers, but his attempt is more important than his particular list. In the strategic management literature better lists exist [Riley, 1987]. Following Riley, the cost drivers are broken into two categories.

1. Structural cost drivers; and
2. Executional cost drives.

  Structural Cost Drivers. The first category is what are called "structural" cost drivers, drawing upon the industrial organization literature [Porter, 1985; Scherer, 1980]. From this perspective, there are at least five strategic choices by the firm regarding its underlying economic <u>structure</u> that drive cost position for any given product group:

- *Scale* - Size of operation. How big an investment to make in manufacturing, in R&D and in marketing resources.
- *Scope* - Degree of vertical integration; Degree of sharing of activities (such as manufacturing, R&D, marketing, sales, and distribution) across business units within the firm.
- *Experience* - How many times in the past the firm has already done what it is doing again.
- *Technology* - What process technologies are used in each step of the firm's value chain.
- *Complexity* - Number of product lines. How wide a line of products or services to offer to customers.

Each structural driver involves choices by the firm that drive product cost. Given certain assumptions, the cost calculus of each structural driver can be specified (Ghemawat, 1986). Recently, there has been a great deal of interest in activity-based costing (ABC) (Cooper, 1989; Cooper & Kaplan, 1988; Kaplan & Johnson, 1987; Shank & Govindarajan, 1988). The ABC analysis is a framework to operationalize "complexity", one fundamental structural cost driver.

Executional Cost Drivers. The second category of cost drivers, "executional" drivers [Riley, 1987], are those determinants of a firm's cost position which hinge on its ability to *execute* successfully. Whereas "structural" cost drivers are <u>not</u> monotonically scaled with performance, "executional drivers" are. That is, for each of the structural drivers, <u>more</u> is not always <u>better</u>. There are diseconomies of scale, or scope. A more complex product line is not necessarily better or necessarily worse than a less complex line. Too much experience can be as bad as too little in a dynamic environment. Texas Instruments emphasized the learning curve and became the world's lowest cost producer of obsolete microchips. Technological leadership versus followership is a legitimate choice for most firms.

In contrast, for each one of the "executional" drivers, more is always better. In other words, better execution always contributes to performance. The list of basic executional drivers includes at least the following:

- *Work force involvement* ("participation") - the concept of work force commitment to continuous improvement (*Kaizen* in Japanese).
- *Total quality management* (beliefs and achievement regarding product quality). The manner in which quality is implemented in the factory will affect the cost structure.
- *Capacity utilization* (given the scale choices on plant construction).
- *Exploiting linkages* with suppliers and/or customers, per the firm's value chain.

Operationalizing each of these drivers also involves specific cost analysis issues. Many strategy consultants maintain that the SCM field is moving very quickly toward "executional" drivers because the insights from analysis based on "structural" drivers are too often "old hat."

As of this writing, there is no clear agreement on the list of "fundamental" cost drivers. For example, two different lists are proposed in one single publication [Booz, Allen, Hamilton, 1987]. However, those who see cost behavior in strategic terms are clear that output volume alone does not typically catch enough of the richness. How unit cost changes as output volume changes in the short run is seen to be a less interesting question than how cost position is influenced by the firm's comparative position on the various drivers that are relevant in its competitive situation.

Whatever items are on the list of cost drivers, the key ideas are as follows:

1. Value chain is the broader framework; the cost driver concept is a way to understand cost behavior in each activity in the value chain. Thus, ideas such as ABC are only a subset of the value chain framework.
2. For strategic analysis, volume is usually not the most useful way to explain cost behavior.
3. What is more useful in a strategic sense is to explain cost position in terms of the structural choices and executional skills which shape the firm's competitive position. For example Porter [1986] analyzes the classic confrontation between General Electric and Westinghouse in steam turbines in 1962 in terms of the structural and executional cost drivers for each firm.
4. Not all the strategic drivers are equally important all the time, but some (more than one) of them are very probably very important in every case. For example, Porter [1986] develops a strategic assessment of Dupont's position in Titanium dioxide based primarily on scale and capacity utilization issues.
5. For each cost driver, there is a particular cost analysis framework which is critical to understanding the positioning of a firm.

6. Different value activities in the value chain are usually influenced by different cost drivers. For instance, the relevant cost driver for advertising is market share whereas promotional costs are usually variable. Coca Cola, for example, can realize economies of scale in advertising because of its large market share. A price-off, by contrast (an example of a sales promotion activity), is strictly a variable cost per unit.

Cost drivers are discussed in more depth in Chapter 9.

Develop Sustainable Competitive Advantage

Once the firm has identified the value chain and diagnosed the cost drivers of each value activity, the firm can gain sustainable competitive advantage in one of two ways:

(i) By controlling those cost drivers better than competitors; or
(ii) By reconfiguring the value chain.

Control Cost Drivers Better Than Competitors. For each value activity, the key questions to ask are:

1. Can we reduce costs in this activity, holding value (revenues) constant?
2. Can we increase value (revenues) in this activity, holding costs constant?
3. Can we reduce assets in this activity, holding costs and revenues constant?

By systematically analyzing costs, revenues, and assets in each activity, the firm can achieve differentiation-cum-cost advantage--something which Japanese manufacturers have been able to achieve. An effective way to accomplish differentiation-cum-cost advantage is to compare the value chain of the firm with the value chains of one or two of its major competitors and identifying the actions needed to manage the firm's value chain better than those of its competitors. In short, competitive advantage is purely relative. What matters is not how fast the firm runs but whether or not the firm is running faster than its competitors. The dynamics of competition automatically lead to continuously shifting benchmarks. The firm can be rest assured that its average competitors will be smarter tomorrow than they are today. As such, on-going *competitor cost analysis* is crucial to developing and sustaining competitive advantage.

Reconfigure the Value Chain. While continuing the focus on managing the firm's existing value chain better than competitors, greater efforts need to be spent on redefining the value chain where payoffs could be even more significant. For instance, in the mature and tough meatpacking industry, Iowa Beef Processors has performed exceptionally well by controlling their processing, distribution, and labor costs. They accomplished these cost reductions by *redefining* the traditional value chain in this industry. To quote Stuart (1981, pp. 67-73):

> Earnings per share (of Iowa Beef Processors) have soared at a compound annual rate of over 23 percent since 1973. The company has achieved this remarkable record by never wavering from its strategy and obsession - to be the low-cost producer of beef.
>
> To that end, it rewrote the rules for killing, chilling, and shipping beef. It built plants on a grand scale, automated them to a fare-thee-well, and now spends up to $20 million a year on renovation to keep them operating efficiently. The old-line packers shipped live animals to the abattoirs at such rail centers at Chicago, but Iowa Beef brought the plant to the cattle in the sprawling feedlots of the High Plains and Southwest. This saved on transportation and avoided the weight loss that commonly occurs when live animals are shipped. Iowa Beef also led the industry in cleaving and trimming carcasses into loins, ribs, and other cuts, and boxing the pieces at the plant, which further reduced transport charges by removing excess weight.
>
> The company has fought tenaciously to hold down labor costs. Though some of its plants are unionized, it refused to pay the wages called for in the United Food & Commercial Workers' expensive master agreement, which the elders of the industry have been tied to for 40 years. Iowa Beef's wages and benefits average half those of less hard-nosed competitors.

Calculational Difficulties

We do not wish to imply that constructing a value chain for a firm is easy. There are several thorny problems to confront: calculating value (revenues) for intermediate products, isolating key cost drivers, identifying linkages across activities, and computing supplier and customer margins, and constructing competitor's cost structures.

The analysis starts by segmenting the chain into those components for which some firm somewhere does make a market, even if other firms do not. This will catch the segments outlined in Exhibit 1 for the paper industry, for example. One could start the process by identifying every point in the chain at which an external market exists. This gives a good first cut at identifying the value chain segments. One can always find some narrow enough stage such that an external market does not exist. An example would be the progress of a roll of paper from the last press section of a paper machine to the first dryer section on the same machine. There is obviously no external market for paper halfway through a continuous flow paper machine! Thus, seeing the press section and the dryer section of the paper machine as separate stages in the value chain is probably not operational.

Part of the "art" of strategic analysis is deciding which stages in the value chain can meaningfully be decoupled conceptually and which cannot. Unless some firm somewhere has decoupled a stage by making a market at that stage, one cannot independently assess the economic profit earned at that stage. But the opportunities for meaningful analysis across a set of firms that have defined differently what they make versus what they buy and what they sell are often very significant.

Despite the calculational problems, we contend that every firm should attempt to estimate its value chain. Even the process of performing the value chain analysis, in and by itself, can be quite instructive. Such an exercise forces managers to ask 'how does my activity add value to the chain of customers who use my product (service)?' and 'how does my cost structure compare with those of my competitors?'.

STRATEGIC POWER OF VALUE CHAIN ANALYSIS: CASE STUDIES

In the next two sections, we present two examples to illustrate further the value chain perspective and how it differs from conventional management accounting analysis.

- The first example is drawn from the telecommunications industry; this example describes value chains of three competitors in this industry in qualitative terms.
- The second example is drawn from the airline industry; here, we contrast the cost/differentiation positioning of United Airlines and People Express by comparing the cost per seat mile of these two airlines in the

different components of their value chains.

THE TELECOMMUNICATIONS INDUSTRY

Exhibit 2 contains the value chains of AT&T, NYNEX, and IBM in the telecommunications industry. To quote Hax and Majluf (1991, pp. 80-81):

AT&T is a dominant firm in U.S. telecommunications, NYNEX is one of the leading Bell operating companies serving the New York and New England area, and IBM is a growing force in this industry.

The telecommunications industry is in a state of flux, due to the rapid progress in technology and changes in the regulatory and competitive environment. The increasing technological sophistication in many telecommunication networks has expanded the range of products being offered. It has also increased the pressures on major players to maintain their technological edge as a competitive tool. There are three classes of products: public networks (for example, telephone lines, satellites), customer-premise equipment (CPE, ranging from answering machines to sophisticated PBXs), and value-added network services (VANs, like electronic mail, videotext, voice messaging).

The comparative value chains of AT&T, NYNEX, and IBM (Exhibit 2) highlights their different competitive strategies in this industry. AT&T has a nation-wide presence, a strong technological and procurement leadership through Bell Labs and Western Electric, the strongest telecommunications network, and a great reputation for high-quality service. NYNEX enjoys a regional monopoly, freedom to use any suppliers, proximity to the customer, as well as a service image. IBM is attempting to position itself in this important industry using its enormous world-wide reputation for excellence in computers, that gives it easy access to most major corporations. Its alliance with ROLM and MCI, and its strong capabilities in software and hardware technologies, provide IBM a solid foundation to launch a competitive assault in telecommunications.

It is hard to predict the final competitive position of these three corporations in the telecommunications industry. It will depend eventually on a variety of outside factors, such as government regulation, technological development, evolution of customers' expectations, and most importantly the exact scope of the market in which the three firms compete. There are two trends which seem to define this scope: the blurring of the computer and communications industry into a still nebulous information society, and the trend toward globalization of major markets.

In the case of the telecommunications industry, the value chain differences among AT&T, NYNEX, and IBM were explained in qualitative terms. In the next section, we describe the value chains of competitors in the airline industry, both qualitatively and in dollar terms.

Strategically, Ajax seems to be hoping that a small increase in aggregate (but not per unit) customer service expenditures and a better ticketing and reservation system will justify higher prices in an aging fleet. But increased aircraft operations costs wiped out most of the profit impact of the increase in revenue per seat mile flown from $0.126 in 1987 to $0.135 in 1988 (see "Revenue per seat mile flown" in Exhibit 5). This hardly seems to fit the "success story" told by the conventional financial analysis. Value chain analysis can yield very

different insights. We believe that the linking of financial analysis to strategic positioning in this way is a critical element in effective financial analysis.

Value Chains of United Airlines versus People Express

It should also be noted that the ability to present value chain analyses that are comparative across competing firms further enhances the value of the technique. As one simple example of the comparative value chain perspective, consider the chart prepared from publicly available information for two very different major airlines, United Airlines and People Express (in its heyday) (See Exhibit 7).

Structured in this way, the difference in strategies between the two airlines becomes apparent. The "no frills" concept of People Express shows through clearly. Specifically, strategic decisions in five areas listed in the "Value Chain Elements" column of Exhibit 8 account for the $13,100 difference in the cost per 10,000 seat miles between these two airlines.

We will turn in the next chapter to a field study to illustrate how value chains are prepared and used.

EXHIBIT 6
Ajax Airlines: A Value Chain Analysis

	1988	1987
Sales	$8800	$7200
Expenses		
Tickets and Reservations	320	300
Aircraft Operations	4980	3900
Customer Service	2600	2400
Total Expenses	$7900	$6600
Identifiable Property, Plant, and Equipment Assets		
Tickets and Reservations	$2000	$1000
Aircraft Operations	5000	5300
Customer Service	0	0
Total	$7000	$6300

		Per Seat Mile Flown		Per Available Mile	
		1988	1987	1988	1987
Costs:	Tickets & Reservations	$.005	$.005	$.003	$.003
	Aircraft Operations	.077	.069	.049	.044
	Customer Service	.040	.042	.025	.027
	Total	$.122	$.116	$.077	$.074
Assets:	Ticket & Reservations	$.031	$.018	$.020	$.011
	Aircraft	.077	.093	.049	.060
	Customer Service	0	0	0	0
	Total	$.108	$.111	$.069	$.071

EXHIBIT 7
Value Chain Configurations: A Comparison Between
People Express and United Airlines

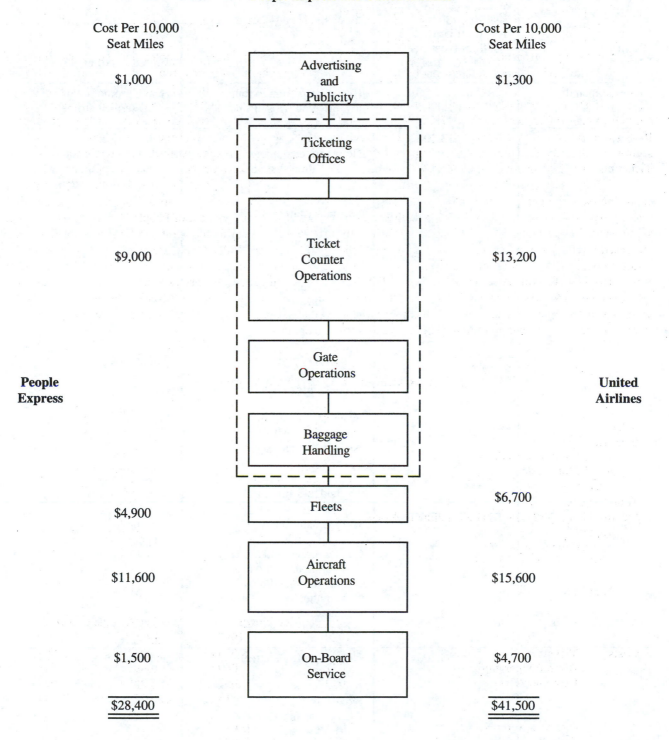

Cost Per 10,000 Seat Miles		Cost Per 10,000 Seat Miles
$1,000	Advertising and Publicity	$1,300
	Ticketing Offices	
$9,000	Ticket Counter Operations	$13,200
	Gate Operations	
	Baggage Handling	
$4,900	Fleets	$6,700
$11,600	Aircraft Operations	$15,600
$1,500	On-Board Service	$4,700
$28,400		$41,500

People Express

United Airlines

EXHIBIT 8
Strategic Inferences From the Value Chains of People Express and United Airlines

Value Chain Elements	People Express less than United Airlines (cost per 10,000 seat miles)	Strategic Differences	
		People Airlines	**United Airlines**
Advertising and Publicity	$300	Heavy promotion to tout low price/no frills airline	Heavy promotion of full service airline
Reservations and Ticketing	$3,200	No ticket offices No separate computer reservation system	Ticket offices in downtown locations Extensive computer reservation system
		Secondary airports and terminals No ticket counters (check-in only) Purchase tickets on board the aircraft or from machines No interline tickets Few fare options	Full service
		First come, first serve seating No ticketing at gates	Full service
		Provide carry-on space Charge for checked baggage No interline baggage	Free baggage checking
Fleet Costs	$1,800	Used aircraft ("budget" airplanes)	New aircraft
Flight Operations	$4,000	High-density seating Non-union pilots Smaller crews and more flying hours per day Flight crews paid on dramatically lower scale Flight crews double on ground duties	Union pilots Bigger crews Crews paid on higher scale
Cabin Operations	$3,200	Non-union flight attendants Lower pay scale No first class No meals Charge for snacks and drinks served	Full service

A/S DANSK MINOX*

This case is set in Denmark in 1967 when the "boom" in consumer food products was just beginning—more working mothers, more disposable income, more choices in convenience food products. Should the company, a food products manufacturer, introduce "complete meal" products to enhance the product line?

A/S Dansk Minox in Copenhagen, specialized in branded vacuum-packed meat and other food products. For many years it had sold vacuum-packed sliced pork in gravy, a very popular dish in Denmark. In 1965 the product represented about 15% of the firm's total sales in the country in a product line which comprised 30 products. The Danish house-wife very often serves this dish together with a red cabbage salad. Because this salad is rather time-consuming to prepare at home, certain competitors of A/S Dansk Minox had recently introduced red cabbage salad in either vacuum-packed, canned, or frozen form. However, A/S Dansk Minox estimated that the major part of the red cabbage sold was still prepared at home. Although sales of ready-made red cabbage salad were expanding rapidly, it was confirmed by consumer research that there was still a great untapped potential for such a product.

At the end of 1965 A/S Dansk Minox had not marketed vacuum-packed red cabbage salad. But in view of existing market potential, and since it was so often eaten together with sliced pork, the company management considered introducing vacuum-packed red cabbage salad in 1966. A/S Dansk Minox was also considering introducing a specialty line of complete meals, which were to be sold in an attractive carton containing vacuum-sealed bags with the different ingredients for the meal. The management decided that the first product in this specialty line was to be "sliced pork in gravy with red cabbage". The product was to be packed in a carton containing the standard vacuum-sealed bag of sliced pork plus another bag with the red cabbage. Cost allocation problems arose in this connection, leading to long discussions between the marketing and finance departments of the Danish company.

The standard product, "sliced pork in gravy", was sold in a 450-gram bag at a consumer price of D.Cr. 4.85. This was the "ideal" quantity for an average family, giving between 3 and 4 servings. Therefore, when considering the "complete meal" product, the marketing department did not wish to change the quantity of sliced pork in gravy. Extensive testing showed that the average family consumed between 500 and 600 grams of red cabbage salad with 450 grams of sliced pork in gravy. It was therefore decided to sell the "complete meal" product in a 1-kilogram pack, containing the standard 450-gram bag of sliced pork in gravy plus another vacuum sealed bag with 550 grams of red cabbage salad.

The marketing department received a preliminary selling price recommendation from the finance department, based on the assumption that the new product should produce approximately the same profit per kilogram as the standard pork in gravy [i.e., D.Cr. 0.30 per kilogram per Exhibit 1].

---

* This case was written by Professor Gordon Shillinglaw of Columbia University. It is reproduced here, with minor editing, with permission from the author.

The difference in consumer price between the two packs as proposed by the finance department meant that the consumer would have to pay D.Cr. 3.35 (8.20 - 4.85) for the red cabbage salad, since the sliced pork in gravy content of the two packs was the same. The marketing department protested that this price difference was prohibitive, since the ingredients for making the red cabbage salad at home could be bought for approximately D.Cr. 1.10 and the labor costs at home (if counted at all) would not amount to more than approximately 0.70. The marketing department argued that A/S Dansk Minox could not expect the consumer to pay more than D.Cr. 2.00, at the most, for the red cabbage salad and added convenience, thus showing a consumer price for the new pack of 4.85 + 2.00 or 6.85. The marketing department contended, furthermore, that the finance department's selling price calculation showed that the raw material and labor costs amounted to only 0.75 for the red cabbage salad and that it was unreasonable that the addition of the other cost elements should result in a total consumer price difference of 3.35. The marketing department then proposed its own price calculation, based on the assumption that the consumer price for the "complete meal" would be D.Cr. 6.85 as indicated above (see Exhibit 2).

There was no disagreement between the marketing and finance departments with regard to the raw material, labor, packaging material, transport and storage, and sundry variable costs. The item "Other product-related fixed expenses" covered mainly advertising. Consequently, the marketing department could not argue with the finance department about this item, either, since it was under the control of the marketing department. The two items "Margins and discounts" and "General overheads" are, as a standard rule in the company, calculated as fixed percentages of the price to the retailer (8% and 4%, respectively). Although this procedure might be open to question, the marketing department was satisfied that the costs allocated to this product would decrease automatically if a lower selling price could be agree upon.

The main discussion, therefore, centered upon the item "Production fixed expenses." After internal agreement on the sales budget every year, the total production fixed expenses were divided by the total sales quantity, expressed in kilograms. This computation had resulted in a rate of D.Cr. 1.20 per kilogram for the year 1966. This rate was then applied to all products from the company's factory. There was no need to buy any new equipment for making the red cabbage salad and there was spare capacity available for the estimated production of the new "complete meal" product. The estimated sales of the new product were included in the budgeted sales quantity for 1966.

The finance department claimed that any departure downwards from the rate of D.Cr. 1.20 per kilogram for production fixed expenses would result in an under coverage of fixed expenses. The marketing department replied that a strict application of this rule would lead to unreasonable consequences in this case, where a relatively cheap component (red cabbage) is added to an expensive component (sliced pork in gravy), and where the cheap component more than doubles the weight of the new pack and thus also doubles the fixed overhead charged to the product. The finance department stated that it would be impractical to use different overhead rates per kilogram for different products. It was supported in this view by the managing director who said that the product should not be introduced if a normal selling price calculation did not show a reasonable operating profit.

The marketing department responded that selling the new product at D.Cr. 8.20 per pack was out of the question; therefore, only two alternatives remained:

(a)   Abandon the whole project

(b)   Establish a consumer price of D.Cr. 6.85 and a price to the retailer of D.Cr. 4.78. The 8% margins and discounts to wholesalers and the 4% general overhead would then amount to 0.38 + 0.19 instead of 0.46 + 0.23, a reduction of 0.12. The production fixed expense would need to be reduced from 1.20 to 0.54, the same amount as for one standard pack of sliced pork in gravy.

The managing director decided, in spite of the marketing department's arguments, that the new product should not be introduced without full coverage of fixed expenses. It was introduced at a consumer price of D.Cr. 8.20, and the sales budget was set at 85 tons. This was about forty-five percent of the budgeted sales of the standard pack of sliced pork in gravy, which reflected the assumption that the upward sales trend of recent years would continue. In other words, the company did not expect that the new "complete meal" product would steal sales from the standard pack. Some customers would certainly switch over from the old product to the new, but these losses would be offset by the added sales resulting from greater consumer awareness of A/S Dansk Minox products due to the planned advertising campaign for the "complete meal" item.

In the months that followed, a number of complaints about the high price of the new product were received from retailers and consumers, and sales for 1966 amounted to only 30 tons in contrast to the budgeted 85 tons. Sales of the standard pack, on the other hand, exceeded the budgeted volume by a small percentage.

ADDITIONAL INFORMATION

Assume that 1 ton = 1000 Kg. (a "metric ton")

The budgeted sales volume for standard pack pork with gravy for 1966 was 189 tons.

Budgeted production fixed expenses for the company for 1966 was Cr. 1.51 million.

Budgeted direct labor expense for the company for 1966 was Cr. 700,000.

Assume the cost item "other product related fixed expenses" is advertising and that the annual budget for the item must be committed at the beginning of the year for any product that will be sold that year.

The cost item "transportation, storage" represents an allocated share of the expense for operating a fleet of company owned delivery trucks and a company owned finished goods warehouse. The company believes these expenses should be considered volume dependent because the alternative to company ownership would be use of public freight companies and a public warehouse, both of which charge a price per kilo of product handled.

QUESTIONS:

1) Once the decision was made to introduce the "complete meal" product and to advertise it according to the plan, what was the impact on profit in 1966 (before taxes) of selling 30 tons at a retail price of Cr. 8.20?

2) Once the decision had been made to introduce the "complete meal" product and to advertise it according to plan, what would have been the impact on profit in 1966 (before taxes) if 85 tons had been sold at a retail price of Cr. 6.85?

3) Combining questions 1 and 2, which retail price would produce more incremental profit for the firm in 1966, and how much more?

4) What sales volume is required at a retail price of Cr. 6.85 to give the same profit impact in 1966

(before taxes) as selling 30 tons at a retail price of Cr. 8.20?

5) What is the total unit cost and per unit profit for 1 Kg of "complete meal" at a retail selling price of Cr. 6.85 and with an allocation of Cr. 1.20 for production fixed expenses?

6) How much production fixed expense should be allocated to 1Kg of "complete meal"? Give a specific number and your logic to support the number.

7) What is your recommendation to management regarding the new "complete meal" product for 1967?

A/S DANSK MINOX
Exhibit 1
Finance Department Proposal

	New Pack	Std. Pack	Difference
Consumer Price	8.20	4.85	3.35
Turnover Tax (12.5% of consumer price before tax)	.91	.54	.37
Consumer Price Before Tax	7.29	4.31	2.98
Retailer's Margin (27.5% of price to retailer)	1.57	.93	.64
Price to Retailer 5.72	3.38	2.34	
Material: Pork	1.67	1.67	
Labour: Pork	.25	.25	
Material: Cabbage	.50		.50
Labour: Cabbage	.25		.25
Packaging	.26	.11	.15
Transportation, Storage	.20	.09	.11
Margins and Discounts to Wholesalers (8%)	.46	.27	.19
Sundry Variable Costs	.10	.04	.06
Total Variable Costs	3.69	2.43	1.26
Production Fixed Expenses (D.Cr. 1.20 per kilogram)	1.20	.54	.66
Other Product Related Fixed Expenses	.30	.14	.16
General, Selling and Administrative Expenses and Overhead (4% of Price to Retailer)	.23	.14	.09
TOTAL COST 5.42	3.25	2.17	
PROFIT	.30	.13	.17

A/S DANSK MINOX

Exhibit Two
Marketing Department Proposal

	New Pack	Std. Pack	Difference
Consumer Price	6.85	4.85	2.00
Turnover Tax (12.5% of consumer price before tax)	.76	.54	.22
Consumer Price Before Tax	6.09	4.31	1.78
Retailer's Margin (27.5% of price to retailer)	1.31	.93	.38
Price to Retailer 4.78	3.38	1.40	
Material: Pork	1.67	1.67	
Labour: Pork	.25	.25	
Material: Cabbage	.50		.50
Labour: Cabbage	.25		.25
Packaging	.26	.11	.15
Transportation, Storage	.20	.09	.11
Margins and Discounts to Wholesalers (8%)	.38	.27	.11
Sundry Variable Costs	.10	.04	.06
Total Variable Costs	3.61	2.43	1.18
Production Fixed Expenses	.54	.54	
Other Product Related Fixed Expenses	.30	.14	.16
General, Selling and Administrative Expenses and Overhead (4% of Price to Retailer)	.19	.14	.05
TOTAL COST 4.64	3.25	1.39	
PROFIT	.14	.13	.01

Dartmouth "Wireless Cable"

This case is set in 1990. It deals with "technology costing"—strategically astute financial analysis for new technology introduction.

John Green, an entrepreneurially oriented MBA, had twenty years experience in various telecommunications projects throughout the state of Vermont including an engineering management job in a cable television system. Through his contacts in the telecommunications industry he had learned about "wireless cable." He thought this new technology had promise for rural New England. With the help of an engineering firm that was eager to sell wireless transmission equipment, John conducted a feasibility study for a small system in the "Upper Valley" region of Vermont and New Hampshire bordering the Connecticut River. He chose the name "Dartmouth Wireless Cable" for his proposal in order to draw upon the prestige of the local college. The name was not copyrighted, being used locally by everything from a travel agency and bookstore to a "Christian" school.

The Coax Competition. A traditional (coaxial) cable television system collects "over the air" and satellite signals from a set of "headends", which are combinations of "over-the-air" antennas and satellite dishes. From each headend, these signals are distributed through a coaxial cable to system subscribers. A basic fact of cable system economics is the fewer headends, the better. Rather than build an additional head end for $44,000 it is favorable to extend cable at a cost of $10,000 to $12,000 per mile. However there are limits to how far a strand of cable can extend. Every 500 feet of cable requires an amplifier which introduces "noise" into the signal and reduces picture quality. The noise is then reamplified over the entire cascade. In general, one can only place 40 to 45 amplifiers on one strand of cable before signal degration overcomes the economics of avoiding a new head-end. A second problem with coax is its shortcoming in reaching rural areas. Each mile of cable represents up to $20,000 of total capital investment (headend and cable). Unless there is enough population density to support a given mile of plant it will not be built. Traditionally, systems were not built in areas with fewer than 25 feasible residences per mile. New techniques, incorporating fiber optic trunks (which do not require amplifiers) allow cables to reach further. Through headend consolidation, fiber optic trunks make systems with as few as 12 to 15 homes per mile feasible. Even with this technology in place, tens of millions of American residences are unable to receive cable television.

This case was written by Professor John Shank of the Amos Tuck School with the assistance of Mr. Fred Buddemeyer (T'90).

Appendix A is a brief overview of the cable industry. As one indication of the profitability of cable systems in a rural area, John Green looked at the financial projections for a recent start-up in central Vermont, Valley Cable. Although Valley was independently owned and operated by private investors, John Green was able to obtain the original financial projections filed with the Vermont Public Service Board (Exhibit 1) in order to obtain its 11 year franchise. This data was a matter of public record. Making extensive use of fiber optic trunks, the system passed more than 18,000 rural homes, using about 1020 miles of cable, for an average density of 18 homes per mile. Only 24 headends were required, due to the longer extensions made possible by the use of fiber optics. The system had capacity of thirty six channels although only thirty were used for entertainment programming. The other six were allocated to government mandated public access and future use including pay-per-view. The system charged a basic monthly rate of $19.95 and enjoyed basic service penetration rates of 65% on average.

The Wireless Alternative. "Wireless Cable," an oxymoron, is the popular description of a new alternative technology. Instead of using coax cable, a wireless cable system places a microwave transmitter at each headend. This transmitter rebroadcasts the television signals to subscribers equipped with special antennas. This technology addresses both of the problems mentioned above. Signals are not reamplified by power-consuming and signal-deteriorating devices but with simple mirrors. Rural areas are particularly well suited to this technology because the potential subscriber market is based on "line of sight" from the headend rather than homes per linear mile. There is no cost to the operator from building additional miles of plant; the system's ultimate capacity is established the first day of operation. The technology has much lower capital costs per subscriber. Headends are much more expensive, but the system does not require hundreds or thousands of miles of cable. Yet it is still not clear whether the technology represents a competitive advantage. Programming costs, which make up the most significant aspect of operating costs, are a problem for wireless cable due to discriminatory pricing. Programmers charge lower prices to coax systems. This is partially explainable by extensive vertical integration in the industry between programmers and cable systems.

Valley projected operating margins (revenues - operating costs/revenues) of 44% in the second year of operation (after construction is completed), in line with industry averages. A large proportion of costs were for programming (see Exhibit 2 for Valley's programming costs and related prices charged to wireless operators). For premium services such as HBO Valley paid only for those subscribers that pay additional fees to receive it.

Without a "short cut" metric, John Green didn't have a quick way to analyze the feasibility of his proposed system. The wireless engineering firm had told him that 11 headends would be required to cover his 27,000 potential subscribers. On flat land, one wireless headend can reach an area of 3,000 square miles. But, in hilly terrain like the Upper Valley, one headend could only cover about 30 square miles. Of the 27,000 homes, 18,000 were reachable by coax cable and 9,000 were not. This area covered territory served by 2 different non-overlapping cable companies.

Green's system would only have broadcasting capacity of thirty two channels. In order to lock up even this many channels, Green would have to acquire frequencies that the FCC had allocated to educational institutions. In return for entertainment use of these frequencies, Green would broadcast educational programming at various times in the day. Green believed that a deal with local educators would result in 27 stations left for full time entertainment programming. With fewer channels than his cable competitors (30 each), Green believed he should charge only $15 for basic cable and $32 for a premium package including basic, Showtime, NESN and Disney. For individual premium services he would match Valley's prices: $10.95 for HBO, $9.95 for Showtime, and $6.95 each for Cinemax, Disney, NESN and SportsChannel. At these prices he hoped to gain a 25% share of cable feasible homes and a 65% penetration of cable infeasible homes. Green's programming costs are outlined in Exhibit 2. Green's only advantage in operating costs was in maintenance. The wireless system would only require one technician for every 1,700 subscribers compared to 1 per 1,000 in traditional cable systems. This was due to the lack of amplifiers that require frequent adjustment.

As Green began his analysis he was curious why the wireless industry was off to such a slow start. Wireless systems seemed to be an excellent idea for rural areas. He knew that the traditional cable business wanted to make things difficult for wireless, but he also felt that superior technology must be the way of the future. Wireless definitely looked like a superior technology, at least until the new DBS technology arrived.

DIRECT BROADCASTING SATELLITES (DBS)

In 1990, major cable companies such as TCI, Time-Warner, and CableVision began two different direct broadcast satellite (DBS) consortia in an attempt to maintain control over a new distribution technology. One of the consortia, SkyCable, is a billion dolar joint venture among NewsCorp (Rupert Murdoch), NBC, CableVision and Hughes Communication. Experts predict a start up no earlier than 1996.

Simply stated, DBS satellites send a much stronger signal than existing satellites. This allows reception with a home antenna as small as a dinner napkin. Technologically, this makes coax obsolete. Even consumers in apartment buildings could place an antenna in a window sill with no need for headends or coaxial cable.

However, both of the consortia consist of companies with a major stake in existing coaxial systems. Rather than becoming a competitor to coax, it appears that the technology will represent a supplemental service. Entirely new cable networks could be placed on the DBS satellites and the antennae necessary to receive them would only be available through existing cable companies. While many of the details of DBS distribution remain vague, it is clear that this technology is superior to wireless in almost every respect (greater channel capacity, smaller size of subscriber equipment, no need for re-broadcast sites). Yet a DBS entry by major cable companies would not be a threat to wireless as long as cable operators are legally precluded from owning wireless licenses.

QUESTIONS

1. Prepare a DCF analysis of the Dartmouth Wireless Cable System proposal, starting in 1990 (FCC licenses cover an 11 year period). Use the format in Exhibit 1. Round the numbers as much as you like. Think about how to estimate the cash flows before you jump into a big spreadsheet here. Keep the calculations as simple as possible. Use information from Exhibits 2 & 3, where applicable, with additional information from Appendix B.

2. Can you construct a "metric" for evaluating the attractiveness of a given market area for a wireless system? What does this metric suggest about the Upper Valley area?

3. Is there a good business venture here?

4. What SCM issues are raised in the case?

5. What is your advice for John Green?

EXHIBIT 1
Valley Cable—Financial Plan*

	1986	1987	...	1996
Subscribers	0	908		14,127
Revenues	0	$469,000		$6,431,000
Operating Costs	0	$258,000		$2,392,000
Operating Income	0	$211,000		$4,039,000
Depreciation	0	$266,000		$851,000
Capital Expenditure	$1,332,000	$2,565,000		$96,000
Net Cash Flow	$(1,322,000)	$(2,346,000)		$2,859,000

11 Year IRR = 17+%, real
Estimated Cost of Capital = 10%, nominal

*Details for all of the above calculations are shown in the spreadsheet in Appendix B.

EXHIBIT 2

	Programming Costs Per Sub.	
	Cable	Wireless
ESPN	0.38	0.57
WTBS	0.10	0.15
FNN	0.06	0.08
Discovery	0.13	0.20
MTV	0.18	0.27
Nickelodeon	0.18	0.27
VH-1	0.02	0.03
CNN	0.23	0.35
TNT	0.20	0.30
USA	0.18	0.27
A&E	0.11	0.17
Comedy Channel	0.18	0.27
Lifetime	0.14	0.21
Learning Channel	0.12	0.18
C-Span	0.00	0.00
Weather Channel	0.07	0.11
Subtotal	2.28	3.43
Premium Channels		
HBO	6.25	
Cinemax	4.50	
Disney	3.46	*
NESN	3.55	
Showtime	4.69	
Sports Channel	4.10	

* Estimated at a 40% premium over the price charged to small cable operators.

Because many programming suppliers are closely linked with the cable system operating business they also see wireless operators as competitors rather than new customers. Currently wireless operators pay programming prices comparable to individual satellite dish owners, about 50% higher than prices to the smallest coax operators. Cable programmers seem to be able to legally price discriminate between different distribution technologies. Several networks, including HBO, which is linked to Time-Warner's cable systems, have only recently agreed to sell to wireless operators at any price. There is a strong possibility of federal regulation in this area (known as "must sell") by 1992.

Exhibit 3

Assumptions for a Wireless System

Revenues

Assume a .8% population growth for the wireless territory.

There is no "construction period" for a wireless system. As soon as the head end is completed, the system can serve its entire territory. Assume penetration rates increase 2% a year, starting from a 36% penetration in year 1.

Installation price is $29.95 per home, which has nothing to do with cost.

All subscribers require converters/antennas which are rented for $3 per month, total.

Expenses

Assume 6 office workers in year 1; 7.5 each year thereafter.

Monthly basic programming costs are outlined in Exhibit 2.

Assume $4,900 annual vehicle expenses.

Green believes he can operate his office and insure his operation for $20,000 annually. His insurance cost is lower because of his lack of plant.

Green plans to spend $10,000 annually on advertising. Assume $28,000 per year for utilities.

No franchise fee or public access expense is necessary.

Assume maintenance expense of $61,000 in year 1 and $122,000 in year 2. Later years grow with the subscriber base.

Capital Expenditures

The headends, at $668,000 each, are much more expensive than in a conventional system because they also include the broadcasting equipment.

Green needs 5 trucks at $15,000 each. His needs are less than coax because he does not need to periodically maintain miles of cable.

Subscriber equipment is also more substantial than with coax. Each subscriber must be equipped with both an antenna and a descrambling unit, at a combined cost of $150 per home.

Assume no spare parts are needed.

APPENDIX A

The Cable TV Industry—An Overview—1990

Until the 1970's, cable television was merely a means for improving the quality of television reception. The industry abbreviation that is still used, CATV, stands for Community Antenna TV, an accurate description of the industry's origins. Early systems were built by local appliance dealers in an effort to boost the sale of TV sets. The builder would simply construct a small "headend" consisting of VHF and UHF antennas. The headend was then connected to nearby homes via coaxial cable. These systems had the blessing of broadcasters because they increased the size of a television station's market. The penetration rate for these early systems was a direct inverse of television reception quality. From the start, cable was a "natural monopoly" as a distributor of television programming in those areas of the country where it is impossible to get decent television reception. Cable system operators were strengthened in the 1980s as stations available only on cable (CNN, ESPN, or MTV, for example) became as important to Americans as the traditional broadcast networks. Also, while there are a handful of communities with two competing parallel cable systems, it is typically infeasible to run a second coax cable down a street because of limited utility pole space or low densities. Because of its quasi-monopoly status, cable was a regulated industry prior to 1984. In that year, the powerful cable lobby was able to convince Congress that the industry no longer needed regulation, citing home satellite dishes as a source of potential competition. Between 1985 and 1990, the average price of basic cable has risen over 70%, with doubling and even tripling of rates in some areas, including the Upper Valley.

In the 1980s, satellite programming became the most important offering for cable operators. Even in the earliest cable systems, there was significant capacity on the coax for channels beyond local UHF and VHF signals. At first, these extra channels were filled with programming from existing libraries. Cable operators often operated their own movie channels or would resell the satellite feed of HBO, the nation's first cable programmer, at a premium. Using satellite technology, early entrepreneurs such as Ted Turner turned existing local independent stations into "Superstations". Turner's TBS represented the beginning of the economics that would come to characterize cable programming. WTBS was a typical independent broadcaster in Atlanta. It would serve standard re-run fare like Andy Griffith along with Braves and Hawks games. In the late 70's Turner bought a satellite uplink and sold access to TBS to cable operators across the country. Hungry for programming, thousands of cable systems bought it, and TBS was instantly transformed into an outlet for national advertisers. Thus unlike a broadcast television network, TBS enjoyed what is now termed "dual revenues". It earned the advertising revenues of a traditional network and carriage fees from cable operators.

During the 1980's the programming industry integrated substantially with the nation's cable operators. A new cable network needs massive distribution to build both of its sources of revenues. Rather than compete on price to gain carriage with cable operators, a cable network can achieve instant distribution through alliances with a few of the largest operators. Once the network is carried on a critical mass of systems, enough recognition is built so that consumers eventually demand that the network be added to their local system. Then, the network can extract a premium from the remaining systems and simultaneously build its viewer base for advertising revenues.

Again, the launch of a new Turner Broadcasting network characterizes the dynamics of the industry. Turner Network Television, or TNT, started in 1988, was by 1990 carried on over 75% of the nation's cable systems.. It is the network's integration with cable operators that brought it such rapid success. Several of the nation's largest operators (often called multi-system operators) have a significant financial interest in Turner Broadcasting. The Wall Street Journal reported in 1990 that CableVision owns 25% of TBS. Today, multi-system operators account for half of the TBS board of directors. These operators quickly agreed to carry TNT, instantly giving it a large national audience. With this audience guaranteed, Turner was able to move his NBA coverage from TBS to TNT. This created tremendous demand for the service among those cable systems that were not already linked with TNT. As this demand continues to grow, Turner is able to raise both carriage fees and advertising rates.

Capital expenditures for a system are driven largely by overall coverage rather than subscribers. The drops and converters required for each subscriber represent only 5% of construction cost. If the 1,000 miles of plant in the Valley system passed 180,000 subscribers instead of 18,000 there would be little additional cost. The only difference would be in expected revenues! Looking at Appendix B, we can derive the logic behind the "homes per mile" metric that is used in the industry. Dividing Valley's third year operating income of $2.9 million by its 10,800 average subscribers brings an operating profit of $269 per subscriber. In this system, a mile of cable (including cable "drops" for each subscriber) costs $11,598 (providing no fiber optics are involved). Thus after a headend is built, an extra mile of cable must generate at least $9,600 in present value; net of the tax shelter, to justify construction. With a $269 operating margin each year, each subscriber can be expected to generate about $1,150 in after tax present value (11 years at 10% with a 34% tax rate). Thus 8+ subscribers or 14 homes (at a 60% penetration rate) are needed to justify an extra mile of plant.

The Government's Role in Cable TV

Because of the price increases possible through the monopoly power, re-regulation by Congress and the FCC appeared likely in 1990. However, the FCC's most significant act to this date has been to encourage development of wireless systems. Wireless began as a technology for educational television. In the late 70's the FCC reserved part of the microwave broadcast spectrum for the exclusive use of U.S. schools. After several years, it has become clear that school's have extremely limited interest in the technology's potential. Some schools applied for channels and then used them. Many schools did not even apply for channels. But many schools did apply for and received channel allocations which they never actually used. In the last 3 years, some of this third group of school's have made deals with entrepreneurs that result in "leasing" their allocated channels for entertainment programming (Norwich University in Vermont, for example). This came with the blessings of the FCC, as the agency quickly realized that the technology represents needed competition for coax cable operators.

Today the FCC is trying to improve the viability of the wireless industry. It will not grant wireless operating licenses to coax operators and it is considering allocating additional channels directly to wireless entertainment programming. Thus wireless technology can not be used by coax operators as a supplement to existing systems As far as the government is concerned, wireless is a competing distribution system.

In September, 1990 the House, in a strong show of bipartisan support, passed on a voice vote a bill that would reregulate cable television rates for basic service and assist emerging competitors. Under the House-passed bill, the Federal Communications Commission would establish a maximum fee that cable operators could charge for retransmission of broadcast signals.

To discipline so-called "bad actors," the FCC would develop guidelines to identify exorbitant rates, and local or state authorities would be allowed to step in on a case-by-case basis when they suspect price "gouging." Local cable authorities would also monitor customer service standards developed by the FCC. The bill requires operators to provide their signals to competitors, such as satellite and microwave services, in a "reasonable" and "nondiscriminatory" fashion.

The National Cable Television Association, the industry's main trade association, expressed dismay with the legislation but didn't say it would oppose the bill. NCTA President James Mooney said his group "continues to be deeply troubled by the legislation" and it remains "an open question whether a reasonable cable bill can be enacted this year. What began as a consumer issue is now turning into an effort by other industries to pile on, and hobble cable as a competitor," he said.

House passage puts pressure on the Senate to take up its version of cable revision soon, but whether Congress can pass cable legislation this year remains uncertain. The Senate measure, which has cleared the Commerce Committee, includes tougher language on providing programming to competitors but gives cable operators more leeway to raise rates. Even if the Senate acts soon, the measures will have to go through a conference committee to iron out details.

APPENDIX B
Detailed Spreadsheet Projections for the Valley Cable Start-Up

Revenues

#	Subscribers	1987	1988	1989	1990	1991	1992	1993	1994	1995	1996
1	Total Homes Passed	4,462	18,018	18,366	18,721	19,084	19,454	19,833	20,220	20,615	21,020
2	Residences Passed	4,190	16,923	17,250	17,584	17,925	18,273	18,629	18,993	19,365	19,745
3	Penetration Rate	40.8%	60.5%	62.5%	65.0%	66.3%	67.6%	69.0%	70.3%	71.7%	72.8%
4	Less Disconnects	0	-68	-203	-296	-356	-461	-476	-495	-515	-535
5	**Ending Subscribers**	**1,711**	**10,171**	**10,583**	**11,130**	**11,525**	**11,893**	**12,371**	**12,865**	**13,379**	**13,839**
6	**Average Subscribers**	856	5,941	10,377	10,857	11,327	11,709	12,132	12,618	13,122	13,609
7											
8	Summer Homes Passed	271	1,095	1,116	1,137	1,159	1,181	1,204	1,227	1,250	1,274
9	Penetration Rate	46.0%	47.1%	47.9%	48.4%	48.9%	49.4%	49.9%	50.4%	50.9%	51.4%
10	Less Disconnects	0	-4	-17	-17	-18	-18	-19	-19	-20	-20
11	**Ending Subscribers**	**104**	**426**	**429**	**441**	**454**	**468**	**481**	**496**	**510**	**525**
12	**Average Subscribers**	52	265	427	435	448	461	475	488	503	518
13											
14											
15											
16	**Revenues**	**1987**	**1988**	**1989**	**1990**	**1991**	**1992**	**1993**	**1994**	**1995**	**1996**
17	Basic Cable	104,717	727,175	1,270,168	1,328,873	1,386,484	1,433,187	1,484,979	1,544,446	1,606,140	1,665,776
18	Premium Package 1	186,130	1,292,518	2,257,661	2,362,006	2,464,407	2,547,419	2,639,477	2,745,177	2,854,836	2,960,835
19	Summer Members	9,617	48,996	79,020	80,477	82,865	85,290	87,789	90,364	93,017	95,751
20	Additional Units	10,263	70,800	123,495	129,145	134,715	139,243	144,260	150,012	155,979	161,752
21	HBO	17,368	119,816	208,992	218,554	227,979	235,642	244,132	253,867	263,965	273,734
22	Cinemax	7,368	50,831	88,663	92,720	96,719	99,970	103,571	107,701	111,985	116,129
23	Disney	7,368	50,831	88,663	92,720	96,719	99,970	103,571	107,701	111,985	116,129
24	NESN	7,368	50,831	88,663	92,720	96,719	99,970	103,571	107,701	111,985	116,129
25	Showtime	10,526	72,616	126,662	132,457	138,169	142,814	147,959	153,859	159,979	165,899
26	SportsChannel	7,368	50,831	88,663	92,720	96,719	99,970	103,571	107,701	111,985	116,129
27	CVN	770	5,347	9,339	9,771	10,195	10,538	10,919	11,356	11,810	12,248
28	Installations	63,345	323,177	32,863	41,602	38,649	41,933	46,902	48,626	50,556	49,804
29	Converter Rentals	36,660	254,156	443,317	463,598	483,593	499,848	517,856	538,505	559,925	580,647
30	**Total Revenues**	**468,872**	**3,117,925**	**4,906,171**	**5,137,363**	**5,353,931**	**5,535,792**	**5,738,557**	**5,967,015**	**6,204,147**	**6,430,963**

	1987	1988	1989	1990	1991	1992	1993	1994	1995	1996
31 **Income**										
32										
33 **Operating Costs**										
34 Office Compensation	20,800	83,200	135,200	135,200	135,200	135,200	135,200	135,200	135,200	135,200
35 Compensation 2	31,875	42,500	42,500	42,500	42,500	42,500	42,500	42,500	42,500	42,500
36 Basic Programming	23,947	165,201	288,156	301,339	314,335	324,901	336,606	350,028	363,952	377,421
37 HBO	9,868	68,077	118,746	124,178	129,534	133,888	138,711	144,242	149,980	155,531
38 Max	4,737	32,677	56,998	59,606	62,176	64,266	66,581	69,236	70,859	74,655
39 Disney	21,488	148,238	258,568	270,397	282,059	291,540	302,043	314,087	326,581	338,667
40 NESN	22,047	152,094	265,293	277,431	289,396	299,123	309,900	322,257	335,075	347,476
41 Showtime	29,127	200,935	350,486	366,521	382,329	395,180	409,417	425,742	442,677	459,060
42 Sportschannel	4,316	29,773	51,931	54,307	56,649	58,554	60,663	63,082	65,591	68,019
43 Maintenance	32,100	149,800	235,400	235,400	235,400	235,400	235,400	235,400	235,400	235,400
44 Pole Rental	5,069	30,128	31,351	32,970	34,139	35,230	36,646	38,109	39,632	40,995
45 Franchise Fee	3,000	3,000	3,000	3,000	3,000	3,000	3,000	3,000	3,000	3,000
46 Utilities	9,902	20,000	20,000	20,000	20,000	20,000	20,000	20,000	20,000	20,000
47 Vehicles Expense	10,000	10,000	10,000	10,000	10,000	10,000	10,000	10,000	10,000	10,000
48 Office & Insurance	10,000	62,000	62,000	62,000	62,000	62,000	62,000	62,000	62,000	62,000
49 Public Access Expenses	15,000	15,000	15,000	15,000	15,000	15,000	15,000	15,000	15,000	15,000
50 Advertising, Promotion	5,000	7,000	7,000	7,000	7,000	7,000	7,000	7,000	7,000	7,000
51 **Operating Expenses**	258,277	1,219,624	1,951,629	2,016,848	2,080,717	2,132,781	2,190,668	2,256,883	2,324,447	2,391,922
52 Total Revenues	468,872	3,117,925	4,906,171	5,137,363	5,353,931	5,535,792	5,738,557	5,967,015	6,204,147	6,430,963
53 **Operating Income**	210,594	1,898,301	2,954,542	3,120,514	3,273,214	3,403,011	3,547,889	3,710,132	3,879,700	4,039,042
54										
55 **Depreciation Schedule**										
56 Head End	70,499	70,499	70,499	70,499	70,499	70,499	70,499	70,499	70,499	70,499
57 Optical Transmitter	12,000	12,000	12,000	12,000	12,000	12,000	12,000	12,000	12,000	12,000
58 Optical Receivers	6,000	6,000	6,000	6,000	6,000	6,000	6,000	6,000	6,000	6,000
59 Optical Splitter	267	267	267	267	267	267	267	267	267	267
60 Optical Cable	5,638	22,552	22,774	22,976	23,178	23,380	23,581	23,783	23,985	24,187
61 Coaxial Cable	59,041	236,163	238,419	240,674	242,930	245,186	247,441	249,697	251,952	254,208
62 Vehicles	9,000	39,000	39,000	39,000	39,000	37,500	39,000	39,000	39,000	39,000
63 Construction Labor	103,379	413,515	417,434	421,353	425,272	429,191	433,110	437,029	440,948	444,867
66 **Total Depreciation**	265,824	799,997	806,393	812,770	819,146	824,022	831,899	838,275	844,651	851,028

	1987	1988	1989	1990	1991	1992	1993	1994	1995	1996
67										
68 **Income Statement**										
69 Operating Income	210,594	1,898,301	2,954,542	3,120,514	3,273,214	3,403,011	3,547,889	3,710,132	3,879,700	4,039,042
70 Interest Expense	0	0	0	0	0	0	0	0	0	0
71 Depreciation	265,824	799,997	806,393	812,770	819,146	824,022	831,899	838,275	844,651	851,028
72 Miscellaneous										
73 Income Taxes	-18,778	373,424	730,371	784,633	834,383	876,856	923,437	976,431	1,031,917	1,083,925
74 **Net Income**	**-36,451**	**724,881**	**1,417,778**	**1,523,111**	**1,619,685**	**1,702,133**	**1,792,554**	**1,895,426**	**2,003,132**	**2,104,089**
75 **Capital Expenditures**										
76 Head End	1,057,488									
77 Optical Transmitter	180,000									
78 Optical Receivers	90,000									
79 Optical Splitter	4,000									
80 Optical Cable	84,570	253,710	3,331	3,028	3,028	3,028	3,028	3,028	3,028	3,028
81 Coax Cable & Amps	885,612	2,656,837	33,834	33,834	33,834	33,834	33,834	33,834	33,834	33,834
82 Vehicles	45,000	150,000				37,500	157,500			
83 Construction Contracting-Buried	1,222,722	3,668,166	46,352	46,352	46,352	46,352	46,352	46,352	46,352	46,352
84										
85										
86 Construction Contracting Aerial	327,960	983,881	12,433	12,433	12,433	12,433	12,433	12,433	12,433	12,433
87 **Total**	**3,897,353**	**7,712,595**	**95,949**	**95,646**	**95,646**	**133,146**	**253,146**	**95,646**	**95,646**	**95,646**
88 **Cash Flow From Operations**	**229,372**	**1,524,878**	**2,224,172**	**2,335,881**	**2,438,831**	**2,526,155**	**2,624,452**	**2,733,701**	**2,847,784**	**2,955,117**
89 **Net Cash Flow**	**-3,667,981**	**-6,187,718**	**2,128,223**	**2,240,235**	**2,343,185**	**2,393,009**	**2,371,306**	**2,638,055**	**2,752,138**	**2,859,471**
90										
91 **IRR**	17.63% (Estimated Cost of Capital 9.5%)									
96 **Additional Miles Coax**	208.478	625.433	7.965	7.965	7.965	7.965	7.965	7.965	7.965	7.965
97 **Additional Miles Fiber**	29.175	87.525	1.045	1.045	1.045	1.045	1.045	1.045	1.045	1.045

Explanations for Appendix B.

All amounts are in 1990 dollars. For purposes of simplification, assume all equity financing. Cash flows are 11 years to match term of franchise.

After two year construction period , half of subscriber growth comes from plant growth, half from population growth on existing plant.

Penetration rates increase at 2% a year.

Total homes passed = residences passed + summer homes passed
Disconnects = .04 * previous years ending subscribers
Summer homes passed = 6% of total homes passed. The Valley system provides a 5 month service for these uninsulated vacation homes.

Revenues

(Slight discrepancies exist from calculation of displayed numbers versus stored numbers in spreadsheet.)

The number refers to the Line Item in the spreadsheet.

17.   Basic cable revenues = (51% of premium package subscribers)*basic rate of $20 *average residence subscribers*12 months.

1989 example- (.51)*20*10,377*12=$1,270,145

18.   Premium Package 1(includes both basic and premium) subscribers = 49% * average res. subs. * $37 rate*12.

1989- (.49)*10,377*37*12=$2,257,620

19.   Summer Members = $37* avg. summer subs*5.

1989- 37*427*5=$78,995

20.   Additional units (65% of subscribers rent unlimited additional units at a cost of $1.50 per month)= $1.50((65%*avg res Subs*12) +(65%*avg summer subs*5)

1989- 1.5*((.65*10,377*12)+(.65*427*5))=$123,493

21.   HBO= same calculation as above with 15% penetration and $11 premium

1989- 11*((.15*10,377*12))+(.15*427*5))=$208,987

22.   Cinemax= same calculation as above with 10% penetration and $7 premium.

1989- 7*((.1*10,377*12))+(.1*427*5))=$88,662

23.   Disney= same calculation as above with 10% penetration and $7 premium

24.   NESN= same calculation as above with 10% penetration and $7 premium

25.   Showtime= same calculation as above with 10% penetration and $10 premium

26.   Sportschannel= same calculation as above with 10% penetration and $7 premium

27.   CVN (Cable Value Network, shopping channel) revenues =5% "commission" rate*average residential subscribers*$18 average annual purchases.

1989- .05*10,377*18=$9,339

28.   Installations = $29.95, including any additional units

1989- ((10,583-10,171+203)*29.95)+((429-426+17)*29.95)=$19,018

29.   35% of subscribers need converters to receive cable on their sets. Converter rentals = 35% * $10 a month for both residence and summer subscribers.

1989- (.35*10,377*$10*12)+(.35*427*$10*5)=443,306

Expenses

34.   Each office compensation worker receives $20,800 in cash and benefits. In 1987, there is 1, 1988: 2, 1989-1997: 6.5.

35.   Compensation 2 is for the system manager who receives $42,500 per year.

36.   Basic Programing is calculated using the costs in Exhibit 2, which total $2.28 per subscriber.

1989- (2.28*12*10,377)+(2.28*5*427)=288,782

37.   HBO costs $6.25 per month, per subscriber with a 15% penetration.

1989- (6.25*12*.15*10,377)+(6.25*5*.15*427)=118,743

38.   Cinemax costs $4.50 pre month with a 10% penetration.

1989- (4.5*12*.1*10,377)+(4.5*5*.1*427)=56,997

39.   Disney costs $3.46 with a 59% penetration (49% from Premium Package, 10% from additional)

1989-   (3.46*12*.59*10,377)+(3.46*5*.59*427)=258,561

40.   NESN costs $3.55 with a 59% penetration (49% from Premium Package, 10% from additional)

1989-   (3.55*12*.59*10,377)+(3.55*5*.59*427)=265,288

41.   Showtime costs $4.69 with a 59% penetration (49% from Premium Package, 10% from additional)

1989-   (4.69*12*.59*10,377)+(4.69*5*.59*427)=350,478

42.   Sportschannel costs $4.10 with a 10% penetration rate.

1989- (4.1*12*.1*10,377)+(4.10*5*.1*427)=51,930

43.   Each maintenance worker receives $21,400 in cash and benefits. In 1987, there is 1.5, 1988: 7, 1989-1997: 11.

44.   Pole rental = $6 per pole, 25 poles per mile of plant.

45.   Franchise fee of $3,000 per year is paid to the Public Service Board.

46.   Utilities are $20,000 per year, 9,902 during first year.

47.   Vehicles Expense is $10,000 per year.

48.   Office expenses and insurance are $62,000 per year, $10,000 first year.

49.   Public access expenses (government mandated access to a channel) are $15,000 per year.

50.   Advertising expenses are $7,000 per year.

55.   Straight-Line Depreciation (15 year life except for vehicles at 5 years)

75.   Capital Expenditures:

76.   24 Headends at $44,062 each.

77.   10 optical transmitters (one for each of the 10 headends that uses fiber) at $18,000 each.

78.   Eight of the systems require two optical receivers ($5,000 each) and one splitter, two require only one receiver and no splitter.

79.   Each splitter costs $500.

80.   Optical cable costs $2,898.72 per mile. An extra 10% of third year requirements is purchased as spare parts in the third year only. <u>Mileage is outlined each year.</u>

1989-   2899*1.045*1.1=3,332

81.   Coax cable and amplifiers cost $3,540 (plus 20% for subscriber drops) per mile. Assume this number covers all necessary subscriber converters.

1989- 3540*1.2*7.965=33,835.

82.   Vehicles cost $15,000 each. 3 are purchased in the first year and an additional 10 are purchased in the second year.

83.   70% of construction is buried plant which costs $7,350 per mile.

1989-   9.01 total miles (coax+fiber)*.7*7350=46,356

86.   Aerial construction (30% of plant) costs $4,600 per mile.

1989-   9.01 total miles (coax+fiber)*.3*4600=12,434

The Forbes and White Insurance Group—The DMO Project*

The case, set in 1987, considers project economics, financial accounting results, and strategic issues for a new product venture by a property and casualty insurance company.

The Company. Forbes and White Insurance Group operates as a wholly-owned subsidiary of a major industrial products company. It offers a full line of property and casualty insurance policies for sale through independent agents and is recognized as a leader in the personal-lines (auto, homeowners, and "umbrella" liability insurance) segment. In recent years, however, many agency-based insurance companies such as Forbes and White have been slowly but steadily losing market share in the personal-lines marketplace to companies that are characterized as "direct writers." Direct writers use direct response mass marketing techniques and/or a captive agency sales force to circumvent the traditional independent agency distribution system. Direct writers enjoy an "expense ratio" advantage over agency companies of approximately 10 percentage points, basically because they do not pay commissions to independent agents. Exhibit 1 is a summary of insurance terminology. This expense advantage allows direct writers to charge lower premiums. They captured 58.3 percent of industry-wide personal lines written premium in 1985, as compared to 57.3 percent in 1981. This one percent change represents a $400 million swing in premium dollars from agency companies to direct writers.

Despite this encroachment by direct writers, Forbes and White is committed to the personal-lines marketplace with products among the best in the industry. It's strategic plan is to increase its market share in personal-lines. Their challenge in the current environment is how to implement a growth strategy in a mature industry where they are a high cost player. Stimulating growth via the independent agency system was studied and dismissed as not viable because of the expense disadvantage and the fact that most agents simply do not make enough profit on personal-lines products to warrant marketing them more aggressively.

Another alternative would be to enter the direct-response market and aggressively target specific groups, vs. individuals. The rationale for targeting groups is that, historically, direct writers have less favorable underwriting results than agency companies because they operate in a less controlled underwriting environment. They cannot evaluate each potential policy holder as carefully as does the independent agent. This potential underwriting disadvantage can be alleviated if one targets a segment that traditionally has produced favorable loss experience (for example, mature Americans 50 years and older). The combination of expense reductions from direct-response marketing with the favorable underwriting environment created by niching could represent a viable entry strategy.

Forbes and White was not concerned that competing against its own agents with a direct marketing product would hurt its agency-based business.

---

* This case was adapted by Professor John Shank of the Amos Tuck School from an earlier one collected by Professor Shane Moriarty of the University of Oklahoma under a grant from the Institute of Management Accountants.

The DMO Project. In early 1986, Forbes and White was presented with an opportunity to bid on a contract that would enable the winner to market an auto insurance policy on an exclusive direct response basis to the members of a 20 million member professional association, The Golden Age Confederation [GAC]. In response to this opportunity, a task force was formed to prepare a proposal and an implementation plan for the project. The financial viability of the project was of particular concern to senior management as the project represented a major new strategic thrust for the company.

The task force completed its report for the project, termed the DMO (Direct Marketing Opportunity) Project in mid 1986. A presentation of the financial viability of the project was made to senior management who found the projections reasonable and acceptable. After a review of the proposal and the implementation plan, senior management gave their approval to submit the proposal to the professional association. The association selected Forbes and White from several competitors as its endorsed carrier shortly thereafter and gave the go-ahead to start soliciting its members in 1987.

Forbes and White had a three year exclusive with GAC. Obviously, GAC expected them to accept most members who applied and to only drop the very bad drivers.

Management's Problem. The scene is a meeting in the home office in late November of 1987; those present were:

Frank Donahue—President
Ward Delaney—Senior Vice President, Marketing
Mary Thomas—Senior Vice President, Underwriting
Mike Thurz—Vice President and Comptroller

Frank Donahue opened the meeting, "Good morning. As you all know, I called this meeting to discuss the latest five-year financial projections for our DMO project. I think we have to reconcile some issues before we finalize these projections and submit them to corporate management in our 1988 strategic plan. Quite frankly, the results are not acceptable. When we initially approved this project, we projected declining losses in 1987, 1988 and 1989, due to start-up costs, then a growing earnings stream with a reasonable 6% after tax ROE in the sixth year, and better thereafter. All I see on the latest projections (Exhibit 3) are bottom line numbers with brackets around them and a fifth year return on equity of negative 6 percent! Obviously, our original projections were wrong. Can we still expect this venture to produce a reasonable profit in line with our original profitability objectives? Ward, why don't you brief us on the situation."

Ward responded, "Frank, Mary and I believe we can resolve your concerns regarding DMO's profitability. First of all, our first year loss and loss expense ratio of 95 percent is much worse than our projected ratio of 90 percent. Second, our first year expense ratio of 25 percent is higher than our initial assumption of 20 percent. Third, our actual new business compound growth rate of 25 percent is blowing our initial assumption of 10 percent out of the water. These three changes taken together are the reason we aren't showing profit on this venture on a GAAP basis. The second point I want to make is that we are trying to look at a new method of conducting business using traditional short-run financial measures. The profitability of this project is based on the long-term economics; therefore, we should measure the overall benefit accruing to us on that basis."

At this point in the conversation, Mike Thurz broke in, "Ward, conceptually, I agree with you. However, Frank and I have to make the presentation to top management in the format they are familiar with, which is return on shareholder's equity. In that format, we are now looking at a financial picture that doesn't even remotely resemble the financial projections supporting our initial go-ahead decision. I can already see J. Gregory Lankford (corporate controller) raising his eyebrows when I tell him that, even though on paper we're not making money, intuitively we believe that this is a money making proposition. In addition, at the rate DMO and our other businesses are growing, we're going to need additional statutory surplus to support the growth. We had better make sure we have a good idea what our profit margin on this business is before we float an issue of preferred stock that cold cost us up to 8 percent in after-tax dividends."

"How do you think I feel," responded Ward. "Here we are entering a direct marketing world that is totally new to us and we are making operational decisions about our new marketing approach based on very soft information.

Mary Thomas, who had been silent until this point, spoke. "Clearly, GAAP financials, however useful they may be for public financial reporting and for internal management reporting, can be misleading as a guide to operating decisions; at least on a short-term basis. In evaluating the DMO contract, we can, and should, compare the contract to the financial results of our traditional lines of business with which we have long experience. However, our analysis should also take into account the risk and uncertainty characteristics that make this contract distinct from our traditional lines of business."

"As I see it, the real value of the DMO project

lies in the value of the renewal policies for which we are incurring the high first-year marketing costs and suffering the high first-year loss ratio. We have to keep in mind that our expenses on renewals will drop drastically in the years following the initial policy year. After the first year, we will be performing only a maintenance function on these policies.

In addition, our latest actuarial studies show that the loss experience on renewal policies can be improved each year the policy is renewed. We now believe that we can reduce the Loss and Loss Adjustment Expense Ratio by 5 percentage points each year and still maintain a 90% renewal rate. We will constantly work to eliminate those policies with high claims and high administrative costs.

The key to the economic profitability of the policies in force for a number of years is the renewal rate. And, we're doing that with 25% growth in new policies! This is a very popular policy with GAC members and a great piece of business for us, over time. Our best thinking, now that we have about a year's experience, is shown in the revised report (Exhibit 2). Actually, based on our current estimates, the project, overall, still earns a return well above our 8% hurdle rate!"

"The problem is how do we quantify, portray and monitor what I have just said. From an actuarial point of view, I believe we should look at each year's new policies separately and value the cash flows generated on this business over a time horizon that reasonably reflects the life expectancy of the renewals, say ten years."

Mike Thurz, slowly shaking his head, responded, "I'm not so sure I'd want to present top management with projections regarding the DMO project's profitability that are based on ten year cash flow projections. They are used to GAAP-based presentations. We've spent a lot of time in recent years convincing them to stop looking at regulatory statements (SAP) and focus instead on GAAP. Now you want me to tell them to stop looking at GAAP and focus instead on ten year cash flow projections. Aren't we going to look a little foolish for changing the measurement scheme when we don't like the story it tells?"

At this point, Frank Donahue broke in. "Why don't we try to develop something using the methodology that Mary has mentioned? Once we have the model, we can compare GAAP results versus the model's results and determine which way to proceed. Should we continue full speed with DMO, revise our program somehow, or begin "damage control" while we back out as gracefully as possible? I think that you three should get together and each assign one of your best people to a task force to develop this model. We will meet in two weeks to monitor their progress. I expect we should be able to resolve this issue by the end of the month."

REQUIRED

1. Based on the information in the first column of Exhibit 2, prepare the five year strategic plan for the DMO project as it was originally presented to senior management at Forbes and White.

2. What format would you recommend for summarizing the profitability of the DMO project?

3. Using the format you recommend in question 2, what is your estimate of the overall profitability of the project under:

   a. The original projections?
   b. The revised projections?

4. How would you resolve the problem of presenting the DMO project to parent company management and public shareholders when a "project return" format does not match a "GAAP-based return" format and the two formats show conflicting views of the project?

5. What business issues are raised for Forbes and White by this new venture? Is it a good strategic fit?

6. What is your recommendation to Frank Donahue regarding the future of the DMO project? Why?

EXHIBIT 1
A Primer on Insurance Terminology and Accounting Principles

The insurance industry uses two sets of accounting principles, Statutory Accounting Principles (SAP) and Generally Accepted Accounting Principles (GAAP). SAP regulations are promulgated by the National Association of Insurance Com-missioners in co-operation with the State Insurance Commissioners in the various states. They are the accounting principles used to prepare annual financial reports required for state regulatory purposes. SAP's intent is to measure the liquidity or solvency of the insurer. No deferral of expenses is allowed and emphasis is centered on the liquidity of the balance sheet. For example, all fixed assets and any receivables over 90 days old are not considered assets for statutory purposes.

GAAP, on the other hand, allows a more liberal recognition of expenses. For instance, expenses such as policy acquisition costs and agent commissions are deferred and amortized over the life of the policy. All assets are recorded net of appropriate allowances, and deferred taxes are recorded on the balance sheet. GAAP's primary emphasis is on the matching of expenses with related revenues. GAAP is used by all publicly-traded insurance companies for external financial reporting purposes and by most insurance companies for internal management reporting purposes.

Since the case employs terminology unique to the insurance industry, a listing of common terms and definitions follows:

- Written Premium—The total premium charged by an insurance company to provide a policyholder with coverage over a specified period of time (typically, one year). In other words, this is the insurance industry's equivalent to "orders" in manufacturing.

- Earned Premium—The portion of the written premiums earned during the insurance company's fiscal year. This is the equivalent to "sales" in manufacturing.

- Unearned Premiums—The portion of the written premiums that are not earned during an insurance company's fiscal year. This is the equivalent to "order backlog" in manufacturing.

- Loss Ratio—The claims expense for policies, expressed as a percentage of earned premium.

- Loss Adjustment Expense (LAE) Ratio—All costs associated with the settlement of claims (except the claim payment itself) expressed as a percentage of earned premiums.

- Expense Ratio—Marketing and Administrative expenses (other than loss adjustment expenses) incurred during a specific period of time divided by premiums earned during the same period.

- Combined Ratio—The sum of the loss, loss adjustment expense, and the expense ratios. The combined ratio is generally considered the "rule of thumb" for evaluating the current "underwriting" performance of an insurer. A combined ratio under 100 percent indicates that an insurer is operating at an underwriting profit. A ratio above 100 percent indicates an underwriting loss. Because of investment earnings from the premiums collected long before claims are paid, it is possible to earn steady overall profits on policies which show negative underwriting margins.

- Capacity Ratio—The ratio of written premium to owners' equity. As a general "rule of thumb," insurance regulators do not like to see a capacity ratio above 3 to 1. "Statutory Surplus" is the industry term for owners' equity that is committed to support a given level of annual written premium revenue.

- Personal Lines—Insurance coverages that are primarily related to individuals, such as auto, homeowner, and umbrella policies.

- Commercial Lines—Insurance coverages that are primarily related to businesses, such as workers compensation, commercial multi-peril, general liability, and medical malpractice.

- GAAP Profit on Underwriting—Earned Premium minus Losses (claims) minus Loss Adjustment Expense (claims processing) minus Other Expense (all other accrued expenses).

EXHIBIT 2
Assumptions for the DMO Project

	Original	Revised
Average Premium—Year 1	$500.00	$500.00
Premium Growth Rate	5%	5%
New Policies Written—Year 1	100,000	100,000
New Policies Growth Rate	10%	25%
Renewal Retention Rate—All Years	90%	90%
Loss and Loss Expense—Year 1	90%	95%
Annual Improvement in Loss and Loss Expense	90% again in year 2 Then 80% in years 3, 4 and 5 and 75% thereafter	-5% each year, capped at 50%
Operating Expense		
- Year 1	20%	25%
- Subsequent Years	10%	10%
Capacity Ratio (Written Premium divided by shareholders' equity) [A bookkeeping requirement for insurance regulation]	2.8	2.8
Project "Hurdle" Rate (after taxes)	8%	8%
Federal Income Tax Rate	34%	34%

Assume that Cash Flows for a given policy year all occur on January 1 of the applicable year (A simplifying, but unrealistic, assumption, See Exhibit 4) To further simplify the analysis, also assume that investment income on "surplus" is not considered

EXHIBIT 3
GAAP Basis Income Statement
Revised Strategic Plan—DMO Project

	1987	1988	1989	1990	1991
Net Written Premium	$50,000,000	$112,875,000	$192,799,688	$295,244,035	$427,382,564
Loss & Loss Adj. Expense	47,500,000	104,868,750	175,593,796	264,222,336	376,697,915
Operating Expense	12,500,000	21,131,250	32,199,891	46,481,772	64,994,760
Underwriting Income/(Loss)	(10,000,000)	(13,125,000)	(14,993,999)	(15,460,073)	(14,310,111)
Federal Income Tax/(Benefit)	(3,400,000)	(4,462,500)	(5,097,960)	(5,256,425)	(4,865,438)
Net Income/(Loss)	$(6,600,000)	$(8,662,500)	$(9,896,039)	$(10,203,648)	$(9,444,673)
Aggregate Loss & Loss Adj. Expense Ratio	95.0%	92.9%	91.1%	89.5%	88.1%
Aggregate Expense Ratio	25.0%	18.7%	16.7%	15.7%	15.2%
Aggregate Combined Ratio	120.0%	111.6%	107.8%	105.2%	103.3%
Statutory Surplus (Premium÷2.8)	17.9	40.3	68.9	105.5	152.6
ROE%	(36.9)	(21.6)	(14.3)	(9.7)	(6.2)

EXHIBIT 4

The Cash Flow Economics of a Typical Agency-based Policy

The <u>basic</u> cash flow profile of an insurance project like DMO is very different from that of an industrial business project which has the cash outflow up front, followed by a series of cash inflows over time. For an insurance project, the cash <u>inflows</u> are up front, followed by a series of cash <u>outflows</u> over time.

If there is a <u>cash bind</u> in a "normal" business it occurs <u>up front</u>.

If there is a <u>cash bind</u> in an insurance venture it occurs at <u>the end</u>.

As shown below, the <u>cash flow</u> profile for the DMO project is very likely to be <u>positive</u> from just about day 1. Any cash problems from the project, should they arise, will be in subsequent years if growth stops and the combined ratio remains above 100%.

CASH PROFILE OVER 6 QUARTERS FOR AN AGENCY-BASED POLICY
($500 annual premium, paid semi-annually, in advance)

		First Policy Year				Second Policy Year	
Quarters	0	1	2	3	4	5	•••
Premium Collected	250		250		250		
Loss & LAE (85%)			(100)	(100)	(100)	(125)	
Other Expense							
Commission							
(15%; 5% on renewal)		(75)				(25) 5%	
Policy Acquisition (10%)	(50)				(50)		
Policy Admin. (5%)	—	(5)	(5)	(5)	(5)	(5)	
Net Cash Flow	200	(80)	145	(105)	95	(155)	•••
Cumulative Cash Flow	200	120	265	160	255	100	

THE POLICY SHOWS CUMULATIVE <u>POSITIVE</u> CASH AFTER EACH QUARTER

NOTE: Even though the combined ratio is 115% for Year 1 and 100% for Year 2, the Cumulative Underwriting Cash Flow from the policy, with renewals, will stay positive until the policy is cancelled, unless the combined ratio jumps a lot above 100% in the future.

Graham, Inc.*

This case is a "timeless" exercise in the logic of product costing systems for profit determination. The problem is easy to see, difficult to explain and analyze, and impossible to resolve!

The new president of Graham, Inc., Tom Graham, Jr. was very pleased with the turnaround in sales in August. August sales were $200,000 greater than in July, so he had every reason to expect the income statement to show a healthy increase over July's profit of $14,036. When the August report came in showing a loss of $22,928, he was shocked (Exhibit 1). After the initial shock, thinking there must be some mistake, Graham called the controller, Andy Derrow, for an explanation. Derrow assured him, however, that the figures were correct. The reason for the loss was that the company had reduced production levels well below normal. This resulted in an unabsorbed production volume variance which more than offset the impact of the increase in sales. He said that the rate of sales must equal factory production or the same thing would happen every month. As it was, factory operations were out of phase with sales. As long as the company followed GAAP accounting and charged the under- or overabsorbed manufacturing overhead to the current income statement, the type of distortion which occurred in August would happen.

The president had recovered totally from his initial shock: "You always seem to be able to talk your way our of a jam, but I don't care about your fancy accounting principles. Common sense indicates to me that when sales go up, and other things are reasonably the same, profit should also rise. If your reports can't reflect this simple idea, why do I pay you so much money?"

Derrow had been troubled by the same question himself, but from a different angle. He took the opportunity to suggest a different approach to the problem. He wanted to charge all fixed manufacturing overhead for the current month to the income statement in a lump sum, the same as selling and administrative expenses. Then there would be no problem with variations in under- or overabsorbed overhead when the production volume changed. Cost of goods sold would reflect only variable costs, which Derrow called "direct costs."

---

* This case was suggested by a similar exercise written by Professor Robert Anthony of Harvard Business School in 1956. The case was written by Thomas Graham under the supervision of Professor John K. Shank.

To illustrate, he reworked the August statement and found that the loss turned into a profit (Exhibit 2). He showed this to the president and quipped, "You want profit for August—I'll give you profit!" Graham's response was, "That's more like it!" But, after some consideration about the corresponding increase in taxes and demands for wage and dividend increases resulting from big profit, he said, "Maybe this idea isn't so good after all."

Derrow was in favor of the idea chiefly because it simplified accounting procedures. He was always one for simple methods. Omission of fixed overhead costs from the product cost would eliminate the tiresome and expensive task of determining an acceptable allocation of overhead to each product. The change was doubly desirable to Derrow, since the current standard cost allocations were out of date and were due to be recalculated anyway. He could neatly avoid the extra work by doing away with the system!

The president wondered whether the proposed system might have any impact on cost control or marketing efforts. Certainly, product costs would be lower now by the amount of fixed manufacturing cost previously assigned to each unit.

QUESTIONS

1. Approximately how busy (realtive to a normal month) was the factory in August?

2. Can you construct an income statement for a "normal" month under both absorption costing and direct costing? Analyze the profit variance for August versus a normal month.

3. Be prepared to explain the profit differences shown in Exhibits 1 and 2 ($-22,928 vs. $+34,272) and in Ehxibit 3 ($+14,036 vs. $-59,432).

4. Could the problem in the case ever arise with respect to annual income statements?

5. From a managerial perspective, how does Graham, Inc. earn a profit? Which costing system best reflects the basic economics of the business?

6. What do you recommend?

EXHIBIT 1
Graham, Inc.
Condensed Income Statement
for August, 1993

Sales	$1,347,000	
Standard Cost of Goods Sold	712,000	
Standard Gross Margin		$635,000
Less Manufacturing Variances		
Labor	(17,200)	
Material	15,800	
Overhead		
Volume	107,480	
Spending	5,380	111,460
Overall Gross Margin		523,540
Selling Costs		
Sales Expenses	338,056	
Sales Taxes	13,900	
Freight Allowed	28,780	380,736
Administrative Costs		
General and Administrative	108,060	
Interest Expense	57,672	165,732
Profit (Loss)—Before Taxes		$(22,928)

EXHIBIT 2
Graham, Inc.
Condensed Income Statement (Proposed)
for August, 1993

Sales	$1,347,000	
Cost of Goods Sold (Standard "Variable" Cost)	492,000	
Standard Contribution Margin		$855,000
Selling Expenses		
Sales Expenses	338,056	
Sales Taxes	13,900	
Freight Allowed	28,780	380,736
Merchandising Margin		474,264
Administrative Expenses		
General and Administrative Expense	108,060	
Interest Expense	57,672	165,732
Factory Overhead		270,280
Manufacturing Variances		
Labor	(17,200)	
Material	15,800	
Overhead Spending	5,380	3,980
Profit (Loss)—Before Taxes		$34,272

EXHIBIT 3
Graham, Inc.
Condensed Income Statement
for July, 1993

	As Actually Prepared	Under Proposed Method
Sales	$1,132,112	$1,132,112
Cost of Sales at Standard	610,416	418,648
Gross Margin	521,696	713,464
Less Manufacturing Variances		
Labor	(21,704)	(21,704)
Material	20,324	20,324
Overhead		
Volume	(1,788)	--
Spending	8,692	8,692
Fixed Factory Overhead	--	263,448
Profit before Administrative and Selling Expenses	516,172	442,704
Selling Expenses (Total)	341,928	341,928
Administrative Expenses (Total)	160,208	160,208
Profit (Loss)—Before Taxes	$14,036	$(59,432)

A Note On GAAP Accounting ("Absorption Costing")versus Throughput Accounting ("Direct Costing")*

(For use with Graham, Inc. case)

ABSORPTION COSTING

Under Generally Accepted Accounting Principles (GAAP) and IRS rules, raw material, direct labor, and manufacturing overhead are all treated as product costs. All three cost components are assigned to inventory for units produced. All three cost components flow through the income statement as cost of good sold for units sold to customers. All nonmanufacturing expenses are treated as period expenses. They flow through the income statement in the accounting period in which they are incurred. Common examples of period expenses are selling, general, and administrative expenses. This traditional approach to product costing, "absorption costing," classifies costs by function (i.e., manufacturing, selling or administration).

An Example. Assume that a firm called the All-Fixed Company has discovered a process that transforms air into a new product called Super-air. The manufacturing process consists of a machine that is fully automated and requires no direct labor or purchased materials. The only production ingredient required in the process is air for which we assume there is no cost. The annual production costs are $12,000 (all fixed) for factory rental, machine depreciation, and maintenance. Selling and administrative costs are constant each month at $200, regardless of sales or production volume. These costs are all assumed to be constant within a range of 1 to 25,000 units of production. The normal level of production is 16,000 units per year. The normal overhead absorption rate is $.75 per unit ($12,000 of production overhead costs divided by the normal volume of 16,000 units). The following data pertain to the first 3 months of operations:

	January	February	March	3-Month Total
Units Sold (at $1 per unit)	1,000	1,000	2,000	4,000
Units Produced	2,000	1,000	1,000	4,000
Production Costs (All Fixed)	$1,000	$1,000	$1,000	$3,000
Selling and Administrative Expenses (All Fixed)	$200	$200	$200	$600

---

* This note was prepared as a basis for class discussion by Professor John K. Shank.

155

Profit over the three months can be calculated as follows:

Conventional GAAP Accounting (Absorption Costing)

	January	February	March	Total
Sales	$1,000	$1,000	$2,000	$4,000
Cost of Goods Sold:				
Beginning Inventory (At Standard)	0	750	750	0
Production Cost	1,000	1,000	1,000	3,000
Available to Sell	1,000	1,750	1,750	3,000
Less Ending Inventory (at Standard)	(750)	(750)	0	0
Total CGS*	250	1,000	1,750	3,000
Gross Margin	750	0	250	1,000
Selling and Administration	200	200	200	600
PROFIT (Before Taxes)	$550	$(200)	$50	$400

*An alternative way of thinking about the CGS calculation:

	January	February	March	Total
1. Standard CGS ($.75 per unit sold)	$750	$750	$1,500	$3,000
2. Production Volume Variance:				
Production Cost Incurred	1,000	1,000	1,000	3,000
Production Cost Absorbed	(1,500)	(750)	(750)	(3,000)
Volume Variance	500F	250U	250U	0
1. + 2. = Total CGS	$250	$1,000	$1,750	$3,000

The "Profit Model." Under absorption costing, reported profit varies partly with sales and partly with production. For every unit sold, reported profit goes up by the difference between sales price and standard manufacturing cost—call this the "sales effect." In addition to this "sales effect," for every unit produced the production volume variance is reduced by the amount of fixed production overhead absorbed for that unit—call this the "production effect." This means, in effect, that every unit produced increases reported profit by reducing the production volume variance. This amount for each unit produced is just the fixed manufacturing overhead absorption rate.

An alternative way of looking at absorption costing, therefore, is to say that reported profit equals the "sales profit" (standard profit margin per unit X units sold) plus the "production profit" (fixed manufacturing overhead absorption rate X units produced), less the total fixed cost incurred. We can illustrate this for the All-Fixed Company as follows:

	January	February	March	Total
Sales Profit ($.25 per Unit Sold)	$250	$250	$500	$1,000
Production Profit ($.75 per Unit Produced)	1,500	750	750	3,000
Less All fixed Costs Incurred	(1,200)	(1,200)	(1,200)	(3,600)
Reported Profit	$550	$(200)	$50	$400

Many trained accountants will dispute the idea that production level influences profit under absorption costing. They don't think about the "profit model" as being affected by the production profit. Nevertheless, it is true.

DIRECT COSTING

Many people believe that reported profit should be affected only by the sales level and <u>not</u> by the production level as well. They argue that allowing managers to "earn" a profit by producing products that are not sold creates a dysfunctional incentive to build inventory levels. There is an alternative accounting system, called "direct costing," in which profit is only influenced by sales.

This result is achieved by reclassifying production costs according to their <u>behavior</u> (fixed versus variable) rather than their <u>function</u>. Manufacturing overhead costs that don't vary with production are included with the traditional period costs—selling and administration. Product costs then include only items that vary directly with volume, such as direct material, direct labor (if any), and variable manufacturing overhead. The distinction between the conventional product costing system (known as absorption or full costing) and this alternative product costing system (known as direct, variable, or marginal costing) lies in the treatment of fixed manufacturing overhead costs.

Absorption costing treats all factory overhead as product cost, ignoring the fixed/variable distinction. Direct costing includes as product costs only those manufacturing costs that vary directly with production. The following table illustrates direct costing for the All-Fixed Company:

Direct Costing

	January	February	March	Total
Sales	$1,000	$1,000	$2,000	$4,000
Cost of Goods Sold*	0	0	0	0
Contribution Margin	1,000	1,000	2,000	4,000
Fixed Expenses:				
Production	1,000	1,000	1,000	3,000
Selling and Administration	200	200	200	600
Total	1,200	1,200	1,200	3,600
Profit Before Taxes	$(200)	$(200)	$800	$400

*Since there are no volume dependent production costs in this example, there is no CGS. Profit contribution here equals 100% of sales

The "Profit Model." Under direct costing, profit varies directly with sales volume and only with sales volume. Since cost of goods sold includes only variable manufacturing costs, gross margin is really the same as profit contribution. Reported profit thus equals total profit contribution (contribution per unit times units sold) less total fixed costs.

COMPARING THE TWO SYSTEMS FOR THE ALL-FIXED COMPANY

Under absorption costing, cost of goods sold and ending inventories consist only of fixed factory overhead. The ending inventory is valued at standard cost of $.75 per unit. Under direct costing, there is no product cost to assign to cost of goods sold or inventories because there is no variable cost of production.

Over the 3-month period, both product costing alternatives result in the same total earnings of $400 because production equals sales. However, in January, absorption costing shows a profit of $550, whereas direct costing results in a loss of $200. In February, absorption costing shows the same loss ($200) as direct costing. In March absorption costing profit is only $50, while direct costing shows $800 profit. Can we explain these differences?

The key to understanding the effect on earnings and inventories lies in the accounting for fixed factory overhead. Under direct costing, the income statement each period includes the fixed manufacturing overhead actually incurred that period. Under absorption costing, the situation is more complicated. The income statement will include the fixed manufacturing cost which is part of the standard cost of goods sold (normal fixed manufacturing overhead costs per unit times units sold). However, the income statement will also include the production volume variance for the period. This represents under or over absorbed fixed manufacturing overhead during the period depending on whether production is below or above normal, respectively. <u>The difference between profit reported under the two systems is always equal to the difference in the amount of fixed manufacturing overhead charged in the income statement</u>. For our example, this can be illustrated as follows:

	January	February	March	Total
Profit under Direct Costing	$(200)	$(200)	$800	$400
Profit under Absorption Costing	550	(200)	50	400
Profit Difference	$750	0	$(750)	0
Fixed Manufacturing Cost Included in the Income Statement:				
Direct Costing	$1,000	$1,000	$1,000	$3,000
Absorption Costing				
Standard Cost of Goods Sold	$750	$750	$1,500	$3,000
Production Volume Variance	500F	250U	250U	0
	$250	$1,000	$1,750	$3,000
Difference	$750	0	$(750)	0

THROUGHPUT ACCOUNTING

In the current environment, many firms consider only raw material cost to be volume dependent in the short run. In this case the only "direct cost" is raw material and profit contribution equals sales less material cost. All cost other than raw material is considered to be operating expense or overhead and flows through the income statement each month as period expense. This version of direct costing is called "throughput accounting." Throughput is just defined as sales minus materials cost.

SUMMARY

Accounting theory favors absorption costing under the argument that the unit of product should carry a share of all the costs (fixed and variable) incurred to make it. Proponents of direct costing argue that reported profit should vary only with sales, not with the level of production. They reject the accounting theory argument about "full" cost because of the resulting impact on profit measurement—the level of production affects the level of profit.

The direct costing method also has broad appeal for product costing and cost control purposes because of its close relationship to contribution analysis, break-even analysis, and to flexible budgets. Grouping all fixed costs together leads at once to break-even analysis for decision making (cost-volume-profit analysis) and to flexible budgets for cost control.

The managerial significance of direct versus absorption costing is beyond the scope of this note. This note is intended only to clarify calculational issues—not to propose an answer as to which approach is "better." In fact, in practice, both systems are widely used for internal reporting purposes.

Jones Ironworks, Inc.*

This case is set in Detroit, Michigan in 1973 when the minimum wage was $1.75 per hour. It is about people who do hard, dirty, dangerous work for low wages.

Jones Ironworks is a job shop specializing in heavy duty gray iron castings which is not a "growth industry" in Detroit in 1973. One particularly troublesome department is the raw castings foundry. The average hourly wage rate in the foundry is approximately $3.85 and the fringe-benefit package is about 20%, based on paid wages. The base rate is $3.75 and there is a $.50 per hour raise after four months, for those who stick around that long. The job requires a very strong back, a high tolerance for dismal working conditions, and very little else. The foundry is hot, dirty, dark (except for the blinding flames from the furnaces) and rat infested. The normal production crew is 125 men on each of two shifts, or 250 men in total. Usually, about 122 of the 125 scheduled workers actually come to work. Profit margins have been steadily declining in recent years and are now at a dangerously low point. Gray iron foundries in Detroit are closing in droves in the early 1970s due to the declining auto industry, the move to lighter materials (aluminum vs. iron) induced by the oil "crisis," the depressed "rust belt" economy in general, and a trend to new materials technologies. Those foundries that remain have good backlogs because they are picking up the extra volume from those that close. But, trying to raise prices just increases the rate of defecting customers even more. For companies that want to stay in the business, the trick is to accept iron casting prices (or maybe even cut them!) and learn how to make a profit ("price based costing").

Freddie Jones, son of the founder, has just returned from two years in a well-known rural eastern business school and is convinced "new management ideas" can turn around the company's declining fortunes. He would like the company to switch from an hourly pay system to a unit of production pay system for the foundry workers. He is suggesting a rate of $10.00 for every unit that passes inspection. He tells his father that this change wouldn't cost the company a penny. He substantiates his claim with the following information:

1. There is presently no financial incentive for an employee to produce efficiently. The piece rate will encourage higher efficiency and increased production.

2. The present pay rate of $3.75 or $4.25 per hour is much too low. The work is hard, dirty, and hot. Many employees don't even stay on the job 3 weeks. There is a steady stream of new applicants every week sent from the State Unemployment Bureau. However, these applicants typically represent the least skilled and least desirable candidates from the unemployment rolls. During the first 6 months of the current year, the payroll department shows that 750 different production employees were paid. Freddie says this 400% labor turnover rate is a disgrace which must be corrected.

---

*This case is adapted by Professor John K. Shank of the Amos Tuck School, with permission, from an earlier case written by Professor Felix Kollaritsch of the Ohio State University.

3. The $10.00 per unit represents only a 13% increase over the present actual cost per hour, demonstrated as follows:

Current Year

6 Months Total Labor Hours	253,750
(244 men x 26 weeks x 40 hours/week)	
6 Months Total Units Produced	110,000
	2.30 hours/unit

Suggested Pay per Unit	$10.00
Labor Hours Per Unit	2.30
New Pay Rate per Hour	$4.35
Pay Increase ($4.35/$3.85)	13%

4. The incentive system and the increase in pay will dramatically reduce the turnover problem and thus save the company money in training and in outfitting new employees. Eliminating the wasted time from hundreds of new workers learning the job will save the company more than 10% in labor productivity. If the incentive system reduces the current 2.3 labor hours per unit to 2.00 hours on average, the productivity savings is 12.5%. The reduction in "outfitting," which is legally required, would save an additional 6% of the total payroll, as follows:

Outfitting per Person (asbestos gloves, protective goggles, asbestos fiber coveralls, steel toed work boots)	$150
Annualized Turnover(500 each 1/2 year)	x 1,000 workers
Total Cost Per Year	$150,000
Yearly Pay (507,500 labor hours x $3.85)	$1,954,000
Savings (150,000x80%/1,954,000)	6%

Freddie's father sees the piece-rate idea from an entirely different perspective. He thinks it is a bad idea. He rebuts Freddie's argument as follows:

1. The proposal represents a 25% increase in labor cost per unit, as follows:

Standard Cost now (Standard hours (2.1) per unit x standard rate $3.85)	$8.085 per unit
Proposed piece rate	$10.00

Pay increase ($10.00/$8.085)	~25%

2. The increased productivity and decreased turnover are speculation without evidence. As a matter of fact, the evidence is to the contrary. Mr. Jones tells Freddie that he tried a profit sharing plan for workers in the early 1960s and it did not work.

3. He says the claimed turnover-rate decrease is wishful thinking. Admittedly, this company has a high labor turnover rate; however, the industry as a whole has a turnover rate of 50%. Foundry jobs are not attractive and higher pay isn't going to change that. It isn't fun to mix and pour vats of molten iron, pack sand around heavy molds, and drag around castings averaging 220 pounds. This is, at best, a low pay job for low value-added work. It is not a "career." People will still come and go every day. The savings due to outfitting and training are "wishful thinking."

4. The company is already experiencing a profit squeeze. Labor cost and material cost are each about 24% of sales. Any increases could well put the company, as well as the employees, out of business. If anything, a pay cut is more in order!

5. Mr. Jones also feels that the company cannot afford the pay increase from a balance sheet perspective. Although there is excess demand, he does not want to expand capacity because of the declining profitability of the business. Higher wages would mean reduced cash flow and thus more pressure on working capital.

Freddie and his dad do agree on some things. The yearly production demand is currently running about 250,000 to 300,000 units, spread fairly evenly over the months of the year. Raw castings can be stocked (stored) if necessary. Production has varied between 215,000 and 220,000 units in the past three years. The present backlog of orders is 150,000 units. Deliveries are running behind schedule by several weeks, but that is a normal occurrence.

The company needs 125 men on the foundry floor each shift to attend the available work stations. On average about 3 men fail to show up for a scheduled shift, so 122 are working. A third shift is not possible because the furnaces need substantial daily cleanup and maintenance. The production process is subject to an "80% learning curve"—(1) each time production doubles, the time per unit should come down to a factor of .8 of the prior time; (2) a fully experienced worker should be able to produce a casting in 20% of the time it takes a new worker. A new worker spends the entire first day (8 hours) producing one good unit and 6.4 hours (80%) to produce the second good unit. Thereafter, every time production doubles, the normal labor time per unit should be reduced to 80% of the previous level until maximum efficiency of 1.6 hrs. per unit is achieved after 64 units have been produced in total. This "learning curve" can be summarized as follows:

Units Produced		Average Labor Time per Unit (Hours)	Cumulative Labor Time (Hours)
first	1	8.0	8
next	1	6.4	14.4
next	2	5.1	24.6
next	4	4.0	40.6
next	8	3.2	66.2
next	16	2.5	106.2
next	32	2.0	170.2
	64 total		

During this learning period, weekly output should be as follows:

Week 1	8 good units
Week 2	14 good units
Week 3	17 good units
Week 4	20 good units
Week 5	24 good units

After week 5, each unit should only take 1.6 hours. An experienced worker should thus produce 25 units a week. All units are inspected before leaving the department and many are rejected as inadequate. These reject units are melted down for scrap.

Of course, hard working and experienced workers can sometimes do even better than 1.6 hrs/unit, but this isn't normal. On a typical shift, 10 workers of the 122 might average 26 or 27 good castings per week, but many others would average fewer than 20. Using the "standard" productivity measure of 2.1 hours, approximately 121,000 units should have been produced (253,750/2.1 hours) in the first six months. Management uses 2.1 hrs/unit as the norm for production scheduling and product costing purposes, but this was not presented to the workers as an acceptable level of productivity. Yet, many of the workers seem to have figured out that if they average only 18 or 19 good units per week, they are not challenged by the foremen for poor performance.

On the shop floor, of the 122 men working, about 40 are still in the five week "learning curve" phase. Of the 82 who are beyond week five, 72 level off at about 17 to 20 units per week versus the "standard" of 19 [40÷2.1]. They get no incentives for higher output, get

progressively more alienated by the job and the working conditions, and leave between six weeks and six months. About ten workers are "high output/low pay" anomalies who stay around for reasons only they know (remember Boxer in Animal Farm?).

REQUIRED

Freddie and his father are genuinely perplexed about this labor productivity problem. Can the company expect a better result if it manages compensation better? Or, is low productivity a fact of life for which low pay is the consequence in a business where "committed and motivated" workers are just not necessary?

Your assignment is to evaluate the various claims and counterclaims and to recommend a course of action. Exhibits 1 and 2 are reference sources on the "philosophy" of work and workers.

1. Comment on the arguments presented by Freddie Jones in support of a $10 piece rate.

2. Comment on the counter-arguments by Freddie's father in support of the current pay system.

3. What are your recommendations and why do you make them?

EXHIBIT 1
JAMES F. LINCOLN'S OBSERVATIONS ON MANAGEMENT (CIRCA 1905)*

- Some think paying a man more money will produce cooperation. Not true. Many incentives are far more effective than money. Status is a much greater incentive.

- The public will not yet believe that our standard of living could be doubled immediately if labor and management would cooperate.

- If those crying loudest about the inefficiencies of labor were put in the position of the wage earner, they would react as he does. The worker has the same needs, aspirations, and reactions as the industrialist. A worker will no cooperate on any program that will penalize him. Does any manager?

- The industrial manager is very conscious of his company's need of uninterrupted income. He is completely oblivious, though, to the worker's same need. Management fails—i.e. profits fall off—and gets no punishment. The wage earner does not fail but is fired. Such injustice!

- Higher efficiency means fewer man-hours to do a job. If the worker loses his job more quickly, he will oppose higher efficiency.

- There never will be enthusiasm for greater efficiency if the resulting profits are not properly distributed. If we continue to give it to the average stockholder the worker will not cooperate.

- A wage earner is no more interested than a manager in making money for other people. The worker's job doesn't depend on pleasing stockholders, so he has no interest in dividends. Neither is he interested in increasing efficiency if he may lose his job because management has failed to get more orders.

- If a manager received the same treatment in matters of income, security, advancement, and dignity as the hourly worker, he would soon understand the real problem of management.

- There is all the difference imaginable between the grudging, distrustful, half-forced cooperation and the eager, whole-hearted, vigorous, happy cooperation of men working together for a common purpose.

- Continuous employment of workers is essential to industrial efficiency. This is a management responsibility. Laying off workers during slack times is death to efficiency. The worker thrown out is a trained man. To replace him when business picks up will cost much more than the savings of wages during the layoff. Solution? The worker must have a guarantee that if he works properly his income will be continuous.

- The calling of the minister, the doctor, the lawyer, as well as the manager, contains incentive to excel. Excellence brings rewards, self-esteem, respect. Only the hourly worker has no reason to excel.

- Do unto others as you would have them do unto you. This is not just a Sunday school ideal, but a proper labor-management policy.

- An incentive pay should reward a man not only for the number of pieces turned out, but also for the accuracy of his work, his cooperation in improving methods of production, his attendance.

- There should be an overall bonus based on the contribution each person makes to efficiency. If each person is properly rated and paid, there will not only be a fair reward to each worker but friendly and exciting competition.

- The present policy of operating industry for the stockholder is unreasonable. The rewards now given to him are far too much. He gets income that should really go to the worker and the management. The usual absentee stockholder contributes nothing to efficiency. He buys a stock today and sells it tomorrow. He often doesn't even know what the company makes. Why should he be rewarded by large dividends?

---

*James Lincoln was the founder of Lincoln Electric, the very successful and widely heralded company in Cleveland, Ohio known for highly motivated, highly productive workers who are paid "incentive" pay. In 1905, the sexist tone of his views was not seen as an issue. Try to ignore the sexism and focus on the philosophy.

EXHIBIT 2

LABOR INTENSIVE

That people love their work, who work a drill
Or run a lathe, sounds alien to some
Who see in them "the robots they've become"
Automatons bent to assembly's will.

And some are that, who welcome programmed steel,
Greet automation heralded as Change—
But others feel an intimate exchange,
The tiniest components but a field

As varied as a single breed of snail,
With textures, contours hidden from all eyes
Save those communing daily half their lives
With parts they know like totems. They have nailed

That one philosophy, have made the grade
Who see in work their lives, and love their trade

Elissa Malcohn

Kinkead Equipment, Ltd.*

This case is set in a specialty manufacturer of industrial measuring instruments in Scotland in 1979. The topic is profit variance analysis.

THE FIRM

Kinkead has been a leading UK firm since World War II in specialty instruments for measuring electric current characteristics (voltmeters, ohmmeters, ammeters...). Kinkead's products are grouped into two main lines of business for internal reporting purposes (electric meters and electronic instruments). Each line includes many separate products, which are averaged together for purposes of this case. The EM and EI products are substitute products for the customer (both are industrial measuring instruments). They represent two stages of the technology. EM is the older, but still dominant technology. The EI technology is new and still experimental. An analogy is the mechanical wrist watch versus the digital watch.

1978 RESULTS

Andrew MacGregor, Managing Director of Kinkead Equipment, Ltd., glanced at the summary profit and loss statement for 1978 which he was holding (Exhibit A), then tossed it to Douglas McCosh and looked out the window of his office overlooking the industrial center of Glasgow.

As you can see Douglas, we beat our turnover goal for the year, improved our trading margin a bit, and earned more profit than we had planned. Although our selling costs did seem to grow faster than our turnover, all things considered, I would say 1978 was a good year for the firm.

Douglas McCosh, a recent graduate of a well-known European business school, was serving a training period as Executive Assistant to Mr. MacGregor. He looked over the figures and nodded his agreement.

"Douglas, I'd like you to prepare a short report for the managing committee meeting next week summarizing the key factors which account for the favorable overall profit variance of 24,000 pounds. That might not be much for a firm like ours, but it would still pay your salary for quite a while, wouldn't it," he laughed. "I think you're about ready to make a presentation to the committee if you can pull together a good report.

"Check with the financial director's staff for any additional data you may need or want. Just remember to keep it on a commonsense level—no high-powered financial double-talk. How about giving me a draft to look at in a day or so?"

Douglas McCosh smiled somewhat meekly as he rose to return to his office. "I'll give it a try, sir," he said. His first step was to gather the additonal information shown in Exhibit B.

REQUIRED

Prepare the report which you feel Douglas McCosh should present to Andrew MacGregor.

---

*This case was prepared by Professor John Shank of the Amos Tuck School based on materials originally collected by Professor Frank Aguilar of the Harvard Business School.

EXHIBIT A
KINKEAD EQUIPMENT, LTD.
Preliminary Operating Results
15 January, 1979
(Thousands of Pounds)

	Budget 1978		Percent of Turnover	Actual 1978		Percent of Turnover
Turnover		£6,215	100		£6,319	100
Trading Margin		2,590	41.7		2,660	42.1
Less Other Expenses						
Selling	£706		(11.4)	£740		(11.7)
Administrative	320		(5.1)	325		(5.1)
Research	318	1,344	(5.1)	325	1,390	(5.1)
Profit before Taxes		£1,246	20.05		£1,270	20.10

Summary for 1978

	Budget	Actual	Variance
Turnover	£6,215	£6,319	104F
Expenses	4,969	5,049	80U
Profit before Taxation	£1,246	£1,270	24F

Remarks

Good Sales Performance (1+% above plan)
Good Manufacturing Cost Control (margins percent above plan)
Selling Overspent a bit (up .3% of Sales)
Administration and R&D Overspent a bit

Overall—Performance essentially on target with profit above plan.

EXHIBIT B
Additional Information

	Electric Meters (EM)	Electronic Instruments (EI)
Selling Prices per Unit		
Average Standard Price (Kinkead ≅ Competition)	£30.00	£150.00
Average Actual Prices, 1978	29.00	153.00
Product Costs per Unit		
Average Standard Variable Manufacturing Cost	15.00	40.00
Average Actual Variable Manufacturing Cost	16.00	42.00
Average Standard Selling Commission	1.00	15.00
Average Actual Selling Commission	.98	14.90
Volume Information		
Units produced and sold -- Actual	65,369	28,910
Units produced and sold -- planned	82,867	24,860
Total Industry Turnover, 1978 -- Actual	£26 million	£36 million
Kinkead's Share of the Market (% of Physical Units)		
Planned	10%	10%
Actual	10%	8%

Fixed Expenses at Kinkead—1978
(Thousands of Pounds)

	Planned	Actual
Fixed Manufacturing Expenses	£1,388	£1,399
Fixed Selling Expenses	250	245
Fixed Administrative Expenses	320	325
Fixed Research Expenses	318	325

M-L Fasteners GmbH*

This case is set in West Germany in 1986 in the apparel fasteners industry. The issue is cost analysis for a "bundled" business.

INTRODUCTION

My biggest concern is keeping prices up in the face of Japanese competition. We do not want to lose market share to them, but their prices are so much lower than ours that matching them would be too expensive. They do not present an immediate threat because our quality is so much higher. However, even though our customers who carefully analyze the situation decide to stay with us, they are left wondering if they might be better off buying Japanese.

The worst scenario I can think of is the Japanese importing thousands of their attaching machines and pricing their fasteners below cost in an attempt to dominate the European market. If they did that, Europe would become a battlefield.

Mr. Brune
European Sales Manager

THE BUSINESS

Snap fasteners are a substitute for buttons in the garment industry. ML produced about 700 different fasteners in four major product lines: "SS," "rings," "prongs," and "tacks." In 1985, ML introduced a new fashion line of prong and tack fasteners that were manufactured from a wider range of materials in a broader variety of shapes and finishes. Mr. Esslinger, the company's marketing manager, wanted to convince the market that snap fasteners could be a fashionable replacement for conventional buttons in a wide array of clothing. Fasteners were customized by color or finish or by embossing the customer's logo on the cap.

As part of their strategy to expand the market for high-end snap fasteners, ML also manufactured the machines that attach fasteners to the fabric. In 1986, ML manufactured six different attaching machines, three manual and three automatic (Exhibit 2). Each of the machines could be modified to attach any of the company's fasteners. An operator using a manual machine placed the two parts of the fastener into the machine by hand, positioned the material, and activated the machine. In an automatic machine, one or more of the parts was positioned automatically, but the operator still had to position the material manually. The type of garment application determined whether a customer would pay the extra cost for an automatic machine.

---

* This case is adapted by Professor John Shank of the Amos Tuck School, with permission, from an earlier version prepared at Harvard Business School under the supervision of Professor Robin Cooper who is now at the Claremont Graduate School.

Over the years, the firm had developed a policy of selling manual machines and leasing automatic ones. Manual machines, unlike automatic machines, were inexpensive to produce, did not require service, and were easily and inexpensively modified to attach different fasteners. Automatic machines were rented on an annual basis, though ML was willing to take them back at any time. On average, 10% of the 7,000 rented machines were returned each year. The company inventoried these machines until new orders arrived. They then modified the old machines to attach a different fastener. Modification was expensive, as it required replacing all components specific to the fastener. The company estimated that an average modification cost $2,000.

It was industry practice to provide preventive maintenance and emergency service at no charge. Even though most large customers had downtime insurance, ML viewed reliability and fast service response as important sales tools. It was not unusual for service personnel to fly to a customer site within hours of an emergency call. In 1986, service was expected to cost about $4.5 million. To partially make up for this cost, ML required that only ML fasteners be used on the machine. The average rented machine attached about $7,000 of fasteners per year.

The European market was mature (1% growth) and could be characterized as a "stable oligopoly" in which four firms together accounted for 65% of sales (Exhibit 3). An additional 13 firms (including the Japanese) accounted for the remaining sales. Most firms sold fasteners and attaching machines, but there were several companies who only produced attaching machines. Their machines were usually cheaper and of inferior quality to ML's. About 10% of ML's fastener sales were to customers using third-party machines. The exact percentage was unknown because ML could not be certain on which machines their fasteners were actually used.

The four major players all provided comparable services, never initiated price wars, and rarely tried to steal each other's customers. Customers sourced from multiple suppliers, but the companies developed long standing personal relationships with their customers. Also, the policy of renting machines and of designing fasteners that could only be used in the supplier's machines made switching an expensive undertaking. In addition, there were virtually no standard prices, with each customer paying whatever could be negotiated. This made it difficult to compete on price. The firms competed primarily on three dimensions:

1. The quality of the fasteners and, in particular, the tolerance to which they were manufactured. The higher the quality, the less likely fasteners were to cause machine downtime and the longer their life expectancy once fastened.
2. The performance of the attaching machine; in particular speed, reliability, safety, noise level, and ability to attach fasteners without scratching the surfaces.
3. The quality of service provided.

ML sold fasteners through agents in some countries, distributors in others, and regional sales offices in yet others. Attaching machines were always purchased or rented directly. In countries where ML maintained a regional sales office, large customers could purchase directly from the firm at reduced prices.

THE PRODUCTION PROCESS

ML's production facility was a four story building located next to the head office in Duesseldorf. The top floor of the building contained the machining and tooling departments and was primarily dedicated to the production of attaching machines.

Machining. The machining department labor force produced new attaching machines, refitted returned attaching machines and repaired machinery for fastener production. Except for refitting costs, 80% of the work was on attaching machines.

Tooling. The tooling department designed, manufactured, and repaired all the tooling that was used in the production of both fasteners and machines. Tools used in the production of fasteners were very costly and were frequently reworked. Tools used in the production of attaching machines were relatively inexpensive and were usually replaced when they showed signs of wear. Perhaps 20% of the cost of this department related to attaching machines production.

The other three floors of the factory were each dedicated to one of the three major steps in fastener production: stamping, assembly, and finishing.

Stamping. In stamping, the material components were stamped out of large coils of various metals. If the fastener was being produced in very large quantities, automated machines were used that could produce up to 12 components with a single stamp. At low production volumes, less sophisticated machines were used. The stamping department contained 47 different types of machines, and it was not unusual for a single operator to run several machines simultaneously.

Assembly. In assembly, the stamped components were combined by machine to make the top piece and bottom piece of a fastener. The type of machine used to assemble the components again depended on the production volume. There were 112 different types of machines in assembly. Once assembled, the parts were chemically washed and, if required, heat treated before being sent to finishing.

Finishing. Several different processes were used to produce different surface treatments, including plating, painting or enameling, tumbling, and polishing. There were 15 different types of machines in the finishing department.

General. Only minimum work in process and finished goods inventories were maintained, because most fasteners were produced to order. While fasteners appeared to be simple products, in fact, they had to be machined to within a hundredth of a millimeter. This required precision stamping and high quality control. Similarly, the attaching machines were on the forefront of automated material handling technology. To maintain their technological superiority, ML maintained a strong research and development department. The recent introduction of the fashion line required significant R&D resources. Management estimated that about 75% of current R&D projects were related to the new high fashion prong and tack fasteners.

THE COST ACCOUNTING SYSTEM

The cost accounting system for ML had recently been overhauled with the help of a leading consulting firm because the old system, which consisted of about 70 cost centers, failed to differentiate appropriately between automatic and manually operated machines. The new system contained 174 separate cost centers: one per machine group.

Materials Cost. Material, after adjustment for normal scrap, was charged directly to the product. The new cost system also identified a material overhead charge, which included the costs associated with purchasing, material handling, and inventory storage. Products were allocated material overhead on the basis of the material dollars they consumed.

Labor Cost. Labor costs, after dividing by the number of machines the operator was running, were charged directly to each product. Setup labor costs, after dividing by the lot size to yield a per part setup charge, were also charged directly.

Overhead was divided into two sections: machines overhead and general overhead. Each product was charged machine overhead and general overhead based on the labor hours it spent in each machine group cost center.

Machines Overhead. Machine costs were those costs that could meaningfully be assigned directly to the machine, such as floor space, energy, maintenance, or depreciation. The total costs of these items for each machine group was divided by the projected direct labor hours (including setup hours) expected to be worked in that cost center for the coming year to yield a machine overhead rate per labor hour. Thus, there were 174 separate machines overhead rates, one for each cost center.

General Overhead. General overhead, where possible, was traced directly to the fastener production departments; otherwise it was allocated to departments on the basis of direct labor hours (including setup hours). The general overhead pool for each fastener production department was then divided by projected direct labor hours, yielding a general overhead rate per labor hour. There were also 174 different general overhead rates, one for each cost center.

Total product cost was the sum of material, labor, machines overhead and general overhead. A schematic of the cost system is shown in Exhibit 6. While the different products looked similar to the inexperienced eye, they could actually have significantly different cost structures. Exhibit 4 shows cost structures for representative products from the four major categories.

THE JAPANESE COMPETITION.

Hiroto Industries (HI), the major Japanese competitor in Europe, was a trading company that sold a broad range of fashion accessory products to the shoe, leather goods, and garment industries. Typical products included belts, buckles, and zippers. HI was about ten times as big as ML, but the two firms competed in only 20% of HI's markets. Unlike ML, HI purchased approximately 85% of the products it sold. The 15% it produced were all high volume, low complexity product lines.

Japan, with 120 million people, and Germany, with 60 million, were not large enough to support multiple domestic producers without significant export sales. The larger Japanese market with its tradition of high tariff barriers and strong cultural aversion to imported products provided Japanese producers with a significant economic advantage. The high price that Japanese garment manufacturers paid for their fasteners (120% of German prices) reflected the isolation of the Japanese market.

When HI entered the European market in 1973, the substantial entry barriers it faced included the long standing relationships of European companies with customers, HI's lack of high quality attaching machines, and the absence of a network of distributors and service personnel. To help mitigate these barriers, HI focused on high volume niches, such as workwear and babywear, where the market consisted of a few customers ordering in very large volumes. HI identified distributors who were willing to purchase attaching machines elsewhere and then rent them to their customers. HI then supplied these dealers with fasteners at about a 20% discount from current European prices. This strategy had several advantages for HI. Not owning the machines meant it did not have to provide service and could keep invested capital to a minimum. Also, HI did not bear the risk of returned machines. The dealers benefited because they could now compete against companies like ML by using their significant price advantage to solicit those customers who were not contractually obligated to use a specific firm's fasteners.

While most fasteners were customized, some of the really high volume fasteners, such as "SS" fasteners, were sufficiently standardized to run on anyone's equipment. Certain ML customers, even though contractually obligated to ML, were known to experiment with the Japanese product. ML had threatened to cancel the equipment leases if they caught any firm violating the contract. Recently, one firm had been caught, but immediately agreed to stop "experimenting" with Japanese fasteners.

In its 13 years in Europe (1973 to 1986) HI had achieved only about a 6% overall market penetration (Exhibit 3). ML did not consider HI to be a major threat, but they were a constant factor in the market for new customers and high volume users.

ASSIGNMENT QUESTIONS

1. Break the 1986 profit of $9.5 million down between fasteners and attaching machines (rough approximation to the nearest million is sufficient). What inferences do you draw about the relative profitability of these two segments of the business?

2. One can view the production and leasing of an (automatic) attaching machine as a multi-period "annuity". Money is spent in year zero in order to generate a stream of cash flows (positive net cash flows, hopefully) over an average of ten years. After ten years, a machine is renovated and then generates positive cash flows again for another ten years, on average. Try to structure the time-phased cash flows for this annuity for an "average" automatic attaching machine using 1986 costs and prices. Estimate the Internal Rate of Return (Economic Rate of Return)

for the annuity. How does this calculation change your thinking, if at all, about the profitability of the attaching machines segment of the business?

3. How would you characterize ML's business strategy in 1986? Is it reasonable?

4. A. Calculate profitability for the four products in Exhibit 4 excluding the impact of attaching machines cost which is part of general manufacturing overhead. The calculations here require more thinking than crunching.

    B. Following on from 4(A), what is your assessment of the overall relative profitability of the four product categories?

5. What is the annual attaching capacity for all the ML machines in the field? Compare this to ML's unit sales volumes for all four categories together. What inferences do you draw?

6. Consider the pricing issues and product line issues for fasteners and machines by focusing on Exhibit 5 and Question 5.

7. What specific recommendations do you have for management regarding "bundling," pricing for fasteners, and pricing for attaching machines?

Note: Suggested answers to Questions 1 and 2 are attached to help you get started on the case.

EXHIBIT 1

Operating Budget for 1986
($000)

Turnover			$103,000
Cost of Goods Sold			
Material (including material overhead of $2,500)		$31,000	
Direct labor		1,610	
Machines overhead		4,400	
General overhead[1]			
Factory support and supplies	$3,490		
Technical administration	6,500		
Support departments	6,500		
Machining department	13,450		
Tooling department	3,050	32,990	70,000
Trading Margin			$33,000
Research and development			5,800
Sales, General and Administration[2]			
Administration	2,760		
Marketing & Selling	7,930		
Shipping & Distribution	3,170		
Commissions Expense	3,840		17,700
INCOME BEFORE TAXATION			$9,500

[1]GENERAL OVERHEAD DEPARTMENTS

Factory Support and Supplies included the unallocated supervision, floor space, supplies, and janitorial services that were consumed by fastener production. Production management was also included in this account.

Technical Administration included $4,500 for attaching machine service costs. The balance was engineering costs related to attaching machines manufacturing and production machinery repair . About 20% of engineering cost was for fastener production.

Support Departments included costs for production scheduling, quality control, fastener inventory control, the apprentice workshop, and the worker council.

Machining Department included material, labor, supervision, depreciation, and space costs for the manufacture and refitting of attaching machines and some repair of production machinery ($2.4M). The entire cost of this department in a given year was charged to expense immediately as part of the overhead of the fastener business.

Tooling Department included material, labor, and overhead costs for the manufacture of tools and dies for fastener and machines manufacturing.

[2]SALES, GENERAL AND ADMINISTRATION

Management estimated that the high fashion prongs and tacks segment of the business, which they saw as the high growth segment, absorbed 75% of marketing and selling expense, 75% of shipping and distribution, 80% of Administrative effort, and 90% of commissions.

EXHIBIT 2

Attaching Machines

Model #	M1	M2	M3	A1	A2	A3
Operation Mode	Manual	Manual	Manual	Semi-Automatic	Automatic	Automatic
Motive Force	Hand	Foot	Pneumatic	Pneumatic	Pneumatic	Electronic
Sale Price	$200	$250	$500	---	---	---
Annual Lease Rental	---	---	---	$300	$500	$1,500
Attaching Speed (fasteners attached per minute)	5/min.	6/min.	15/min.	15/min.	25/min.	50/min.
1986 Production	35	70	105	350	280	420
Total Machines in Use	700	1,400	1,575	1,350	2,250	3,500

Fastener Sales Breakdown

Through Automatic Machines	$49,000	
Through 3rd Party Machines	9,600	
Through Manual Machines	37,400	96,000

EXHIBIT 3

Sales Statistics

COMPETITIVE SITUATION - SALES BY FASTENER PRODUCT LINE ($ MILLION)

Company	Country of Origin	SS	Ring	Prong	Tack	Total
ML	Germany	$ 12	$ 9	$ 60	$ 15	$ 96
Piloni	Italy	44	30	16	2	92
Berghausen	Germany	63	11	11	2	87
Yost & Co.	Germany	12	21	46	4	83
Hiroto	Japan	15	9	5	4	33
Other	Various	46	37	58	19	160
		$192	$117	$196	$ 46	$551

COUNTRY DEMOGRAPHICS

Country	Population (000,000)	Estimated Fastener Market ($000,000)	ML Sales ($000,000)	ML Share	Estimated Market Growth %*	ML Sales through Distributors
France	54	$84	$24	29%	+1%	100%
Germany	62	82	30	37%	-1%	20%
UK	56	56	19	34%	+1%	0%
Finland	5	12	4	33%	+2%	60%
Netherlands	14	82	4	5%	+1%	50%
Belgium	10	9	4	44%	0%	0%
Spain	38	14	3	21%	+1%	100%
Italy	57	138	2	1%	+1%	65%
Yugoslavia	22	23	2	6%	+2%	60%
Other	362	51	4	8%	+1%	---
	680	$551	$96			

* This assumes no major breakthrough in replacement of buttons as the major fastening device.

EXHIBIT 4
Product Cost Information for Representative Products
($ per 1000 units)

	SS (S-Spring)	Ring	Prong	Tack
AVERAGE SELLING PRICE	$46.75	$39.83	$17.80	$38.40
Price versus the major European Competitors	A little higher		A little lower	
PRODUCT COST				
Material Cost (including materials overhead)	$11.20	$10.09	$6.02	$14.18
Direct Labor (including set-up charge)	$1.32	$1.43	$.21	$.66
Overhead				
Machines	2.06	2.29	.82	1.80
General	27.75	25.31	4.42	14.10
Total Overhead	$29.81	$27.60	$5.24	$15.90
TOTAL	$42.33	$39.12	$11.47	$30.74

For cost analysis and decision-making purposes, it was assumed within ML that only material cost was volume dependent in the short run.

EXHIBIT 5

CHOICE OF AN ATTACHING MACHINE DEPENDS ON THE ATTACHING APPLICATION AND IS ESSENTIALLY INDEPENDENT OF SNAP VOLUME PURCHASED.

Example 1—A high volume application using manual machines.
- Labor rate = $5.00 per hour
- Labor time to cut and sew = 1 hour
- Each garment has 2 snaps
- Excluding fastener attaching, labor cost per garment = $5.00
- Attaching costs:

The range = .6% of Labor Cost
- If use M1 (5/minute) = 2/5 minutes = $.033/garment
- If use A3 (50/minute) = 2/50 minute = $.003/garment
- M1 costs $200 once & no maintenance (say $20/year)
- A3 costs $1,500 and no maintenance
- Cost difference ~$1,480/year
- It takes ~49,000 garments to pay back the A3 cost increment
  49,000 garments = 49,000 labor hours!
- In this example, each worker should very probably have an M1 machine, even if the company made 500,000 garments and bought 1,000,000 snaps/year!

Example 2—A low volume application using automatic machines.
- Labor rate = $5/hour
- Labor time to cut & sew = 3 minutes (20/hour)
- Each garment has 6 snaps
- Excluding attaching, labor/garment = $.25
- Attaching costs:

The range = 36% of Labor Cost
- If use M1 (5/minute) = 6/5 minutes = $.10/garment
- If use A3 (50/minute) = 6/50 = .010/garment
- It takes only ~16,000 garments to pay back the $1480 A3 cost increment for this example
- 16,000 garments = 96,000 snaps and only 800 labor hours
- In this example, each worker will probably have an A3 machine, even if snap volume was only 96,000 per year!

EXHIBIT 6
The Cost Accounting System

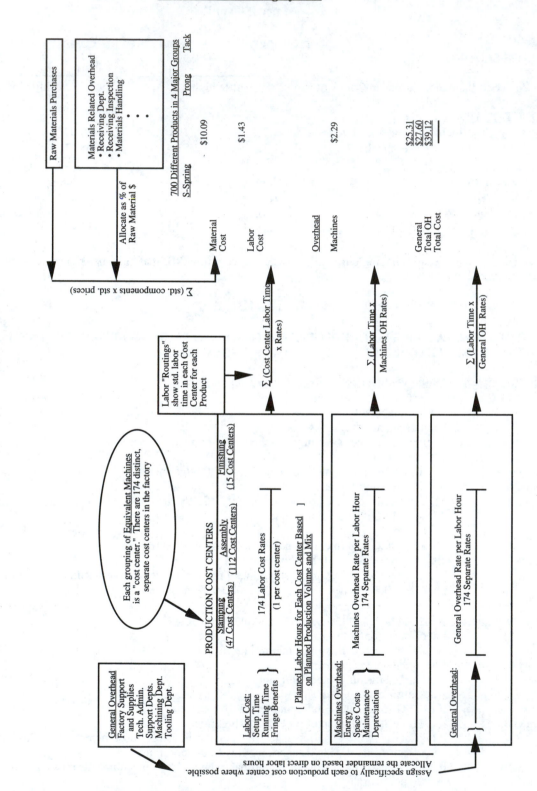

A "TYPICAL" COST SYSTEM FOR A COMPLEX (700 DIFFERENT PRODUCTS, 174 SEPARATE COST CENTERS) MANUFACTURING COMPANY

Suggested Answer to Question 1

"Product Line" Profitability

	Attaching Machines		Fasteners	
Turnover	$7.0		$96.0	
Costs				
Materials (& Materials OH)	---		31.0	
Labor	---		1.6	
Machines OH	---		4.4	
General OH				
Factory Support and Supplies	---		3.5	$52.2
Tech. Administration	{ 4.5 /Service			
	1.6		.4*	
Support Departments	---		6.5	
Machining Department	{ 1.4 /refitting			
	9.7		2.4*	
Tooling Department	.6		2.4	
R&D	---		5.8	
Selling, General & Administration			17.7	
Administration	---	2.8		
Marketing	---	7.9		
Shipping	---	3.2		
Commissions	---	3.8		
Total Costs	17.8		75.7	
Profit (Before Taxation)	($10.8)		$20.3	

Combined $9.5

* These are costs related to production machinery for fasteners.

_____

1. The <u>primary</u> business is fasteners.

2. Machines are just the "delivery system."

3. Charge to machines only the costs clearly and directly related to machines.

4. When in doubt, charge the cost to the primary business—fasteners.

SUGGESTED ANSWER TO QUESTION 2

> This is one way of viewing the machines business, from a multi-year perspective

The "Annuity" for One Automatic Attaching Machine

			Mfg. Cost
			$17.8M
Year 0	Build the machine	($11,333) ← $\dfrac{\$11.9M}{1,050}$ ←	-4.5M
			-1.4M
			$11.9M

Years 1 through 10

a) Rental income $833 ← (weighted average)

b) Average service cost   ($643) ← $\dfrac{\$4.5M}{7,000}$

c) Margin on fastener sales $2,660 ← $7,000 Sales x 38%*

$$* \quad \text{Mfg. Cost} = \frac{52.2}{96} = 54{+}\%$$

$$\text{Shipping \& Commission} = \frac{7.0}{96} = \underline{7{+}\%}$$

$$\sim 62\%$$

$$\underline{\text{Margin}} = 38\%$$

d) Marketing & Administration   ($800) ← $\begin{cases} \$10.7 \text{ x } 52\%* = \$5.6M \\ \$5.6/7,000 \end{cases}$

* [51% of fastener sales are for automatic fasteners]

NET $2,050   Each Year

Year 10   Rebuild the machine for a new application ($2,000)

Years 11 through 20   NET $2,050   Each Year

	Recap	
Year 0	($11,333)	
Years 1-10	$2,050	Economic Rate
Year 10	($2,000)	of Return?
Years 11-20	$2,050	

<u>This ignores all inflation in costs & prices.</u>

Majestic Lodge*

This case study is set in 1962 in rural Vermont. The Majestic Lodge is an old, but well-maintained property that has changed ownership several times over the years. It has no restaurant or bar. It is positioned as a mid-price, good quality "destination" resort lodge.

The Majestic Lodge is open only during the skiing season. It opens on December 2 and closes the last day of March. The ski mountain it serves operates on a permit from the state which allows only 120 days of operation per year. Each of the 50 rooms in the east wing rents for $15 for single occupancy or $20 for double occupancy. The west wing of the lodge has 30 rooms, all of which have spectacular views of the skiing slopes, the mountains, and the village. Rooms in this wing rent for $20 and $25 for single or double occupancy, respectively. The average occupancy rate during the season is about 80% (typically, the Lodge is full on weekends and averages 50 to 60 rooms occupied on week nights). The ratio of single versus double occupancy is 2:8, on average.

Operating results for the last fiscal year are shown in Exhibit 1. Mr. Kacheck, the manager of the lodge, is concerned about the off-season months, which show losses each month and reduce the high profits reported during the season. He has suggested to the owners, who acquired this lodge only at the end of the 1961 season, that to reduce the off-season losses, they should agree to keep the west wing of the lodge operating year-round. He estimates the average occupancy rate for the off-season to be between 20% and 40% for the next few years. Kacheck estimates that with careful attention to the off-season clientele a 40% occupancy rate for the 30 rooms during the off-season would be much more likely if the owners would commit $4,000 for advertising each year ($500 for each of 8 months). There is no evidence to indicate that the 2:8 ratio of singles vs. doubles would be different during the remainder of the year or in the future. Rates, however, would have to be drastically reduced. Present plans are to reduce them to $10 and $15 for singles and doubles.

The manager's salary is paid over 12 months. He acts as a caretaker of the facilities during the off-season and also contracts most of the repair and maintenance work during that time. Using the west wing would not interfere with this work, but would cause an estimated additional $2,000 per year for repair and maintenance.

Mrs. Kacheck is paid $20 a day for supervising the maids and helping with check-in. During the season, she works 7 days a week. The regular desk clerk and each maid are paid on a daily basis at the rate of $24 and $15 respectively. The payroll taxes and other fringe benefits are about 20% of the payroll. Although depreciation and property taxes would not be affected by the decision to keep the west wing open, insurance would increase by $500 for the year. During the off-season, it is estimated that Mr. and Mrs. Kacheck could handle the front desk without an additional person. Mrs. Kacheck would, however, be paid for 5 days a week.

---

* This case is adapted by Professor John Shank of the Amos Tuck School, with permission, from an earlier version written by Professor Felix Kollaritsch of the Ohio State University.

The cleaning supplies and half of the miscellaneous expenses (room supplies) are considered a direct function of the number of rooms occupied. The other half of the miscellaneous expenses are fixed and would not change with 12 month operation. Linen is rented from a supply house and the cost also depends on the number of rooms occupied, but is twice as much, on average, for double occupancy as for single occupancy. The utilities include two items: telephone and electricity. There is no electricity expense with the motel closed. With the motel operating, electricity expense is a function of the number of rooms available to the public. Rooms must either be heated or air-conditioned. The telephone bills for each of the four seasonal months were as follows:

80 Telephones @ $3.00/month	$240
Basic Service Charge	50
	$290

During the off-season, only the basic service charge is paid. The monthly charge of $3 is applicable only to active telephones.

An additional aspect of Mr. Kacheck's proposal is that a covered and heated swimming pool be added to the lodge. Mr. Kacheck believes that this would increase the probability that the off-season occupancy rate would be above 30%. Precise estimates are impossible. It is felt that although the winter occupancy rate will not be greatly affected by adding an indoor pool, eventually such a pool will have to be built to stay even with the competition. The cost of such a pool is estimated to be $40,000. This amount could be depreciated over 5 years with no salvage value ($15,000 of the $40,000 is for a plastic bubble and the heating units, which would be used nine months of the year). The only other costs associated with the swimming pool are $400 per month for a lifeguard, required by law during the busy hours; additional insurance and taxes, estimated to be $1,200; heating cost of $1,000; and a yearly maintenance cost of $1,800. If the pool is covered, a guard would be needed for 12 months. If it is not covered, a guard would be needed only for 3 summer months (from 15 June to 15 September, the warmest period of the year), and there would be no heating expense.

EXHIBIT 1
Majestic Lodge
Operating Statement, For the Fiscal Year ended 3/31/62

Revenues		$160,800
Expenses		
Salaries		
Manager	$15,000	
Manager's Wife	2,400	
Desk Clerk	2,880	
Maids (four)	7,200	
	$27,480	
Payroll Taxes and Fringe Benefits	5,496	
Depreciation (15 year life)	30,000	
Property Taxes	4,000	
Insurance	3,000	
Repairs and Maintenance	17,204	
Cleaning Supplies	1,920	
Utilities	6,360	
Linen Service	13,920	
Interest on Mortgage(5% interest rate)	21,716	
Miscellaneous Expenses	7,314	
Total Expenses		138,410
Profit before Federal Income Taxes		$22,390
Federal Income Taxes (48%)		10,747
Net Profit		$11,643

ASSIGNMENT QUESTIONS

1. List all the relevant decision alternatives in Mr. Kacheck's proposal.
2. For each alternative from question 2, list the annual expenses that are incremental to that decision alternative but are not related to the room/days occupied.
3. What is the incremental contribution margin per occupied room/day during the off-season?
4. For each decision alternative calculate the occupancy rate necessary to break even on the incremental annual expenses.
5. What alternative do you recommend? Why?
6. Evaluate the profitability of the Lodge as an investment for its owners. Does this affect your answer to question 5?
7. Do you have any other recommendations for the owners?

Mavis Machine Shop*

The case is set in a metalworking job shop in West Virginia, one of whose products is drill bits for oil exploration. The time is 1980, in the midst of an oil drilling boom resulting from the oil crises of 1973 and 1979.

Early in 1980, Tom Mavis, President of Mavis Machine Shop was considering a project to modernize his plant facilities. The company operated out of a large converted warehouse in Salem, West Virginia. It produced assorted machined metal parts for the oil and gas drilling and production industry in the surrounding area. One of Mavis' major customers was Buckeye Drilling, Inc., which purchased specialized drill bits and replacement parts for its operations. Mavis had negotiated an annual contract with Buckeye to supply its drill bit requirements and related spare parts in each of the past 8 years. In 1978 and 1979 the requirements had been about 8,400 bits per year. All Buckeye's rigs were busy. Mavis knew there were 30 rigs operating in the state in 1979, up from 17 in 1972. Wells drilled was up even more, from 679 in 1972 to 1,474 last year.

The arrangement of the machine shop included four large manual lathes currently devoted to the Buckeye business. Each lathe was operated by a skilled worker, and each bit required machining at all four lathes. Mavis was considering replacing these manual lathes with an automatic machine, capable of performing all four machining operations necessary for a drill bit. This machine would produce drill bits at the same rate as the four existing lathes, and would only require one operator. Instead of skill in metalworking, the job would now involve more skill in computerized automation.

The four existing manual lathes were 3 years old and had cost a total of $590,000. Together they could produce 8,400 drill bits on a two-shift, 5-day/week basis. The useful life of these lathes, calculated on a two-shift/day, 5-day/week basis, was estimated to be 15 years. The salvage value at the end of their useful life was estimated to be $5,000 each. Depreciation of $114,000 had been accumulated on the four lathes. Cash for the purchase of these lathes had been partially supplied by a 10-year, unsecured, 10% bank loan, of which $180,000 was still outstanding. The best estimate of the current selling price of the four lathes in their present condition was $240,000, after dismantling and removal costs. The loss from the sale would be deductible for tax purposes, resulting in a tax savings of 46% of the loss.

The automatic machine being considered needed only one skilled operator to feed in raw castings, observe its functioning, and make necessary adjustments. It would have an output of 8,400 drill bits annually on a two-shift, 5-day basis. Because it would be specially built by a machine tool manufacturer, there was no catalog price. The cost was estimated to be $680,000, delivered and installed. The useful life would be 15 years. Using a 12 year life (the remaining life of the current lathes), the estimated salvage value would be 10% of cost.

---

*This case was written by Tom Graham under the supervision of Professor John Shank.

The automatic lathe was first introduced in 1975 at a cost of $750,000. It was expected that as the manufacturing techniques became more generally familiar, the price would continue to drop somewhat over the next few years. This price decline was in stark contrast to the inflation in oil services products and supplies which was 18% in both 1978 and 1979.

A study prepared by the cost accountant to help decide what action to take, showed the following information. The direct labor rate for lathe operations was $10 per hour including fringe benefits. Pay rates for operators would not change as a result of machining changes. The new machine would use less floor space, which would save $15,000 annually on the allocated charges for square footage of space used, although the layout of the plant was such that the freed space would be difficult to utilize and no other use was planned. Miscellaneous cash expenses for supplies, maintenance, and power would be $20,000 less per year if the automatic machine were used. The purchase price was subject to the 10% investment tax credit which did not reduce the depreciable cost.

If purchased, the new lathe would be financed with a secured bank loan at 14%. Some additional financial data for the company are given in Exhibit 1. This information is considered to be typical of the company's financial condition, with no major changes expected in the foreseeable future.

REQUIRED

1. Summarize the net cash flows for the proposed project.
2. For the project, calculate the internal rate of return, the accounting rate of return, the payback period, the net present value and the profitability index.
3. What qualitative factors should be considered in evaluating this project?
4. What decision would you recommend?

EXHIBIT 1
Mavis Machine Shop
Selected Financial Information

Condensed Income Statement, 1979

Net Sales	$5,364,213
Cost of Goods Sold	3,494,941
Selling, General & Administrative	643,706
Profit before Taxes	$1,225,566
Income Taxes	602,851
Net Income	$622,715

Condensed Balance Sheet, 12/31/79

Cash	$532,122	Current Liabilities	$930,327
Accounts Receivable	662,107	Long-Term Notes Outstanding (at 10%)	500,000
Inventory	1,858,120	Common Stock	1,000,000
Property Assets	4,390,701	Retained Earnings	5,011,723
	$7,442,050		$7,442,050

Montclair Paper Mill—The "Deep-Color" Grades*

This disguised case set in 1992 illustrates target cost, standard cost, ideal cost and value chain analysis, some of the tools of "strategic cost management."

As Tim Winton looked out the window of his office overlooking the sprawling complex of the Montclair Paper Mill, an "eighteen wheeler" pulled away from the loading dock. It carried 20 tons of Montclair products which represented a little more than 100th of one percent of the mill's yearly output. Where was it headed, he wondered. In the end, it is the final consumer of the paper product that "pulls" the paper through the value chain. Paper is sold by Montclair to merchants, who sell to printers, who sell to end-users. By understanding each "link" in this chain, each value chain stage as both supplier and customer, Winton was trying to understand his overall business opportunities. Previous mill managers at Montclair hadn't thought much about this external perspective, focusing instead on the "value added" of the mill-- sales less pulp purchases. But Winton was determined to take a broader viewpoint. He really had no choice since the mill was falling far short of its profit goals. He had to try something more imaginative than "sell harder and control spending".

Only three months into the job as mill manager, Winton was trying to gather enough information to evaluate the current state of the business and formulate appropriate actions. He was specifically focusing on one product, "Forest Green Uncoated Cover Paper", as representative of the problems the entire mill faced.

The Mill. Montclair is the oldest and smallest of the 10 mill's owned by the General Paper Company. There has been a paper mill on this site since the 1890s. The mill's huge paper machines are some of the oldest in the industry, but they are well-maintained and still run very well. The Montclair Mill buys dry pulp which it converts to an assortment of coated and uncoated fine papers for premium or "high-end" applications in brochures, catalogues, magazines, annual reports and labels. The trick is to create viable strategies for Montclair's grade-lines (1500 different products in total) which play to the mill's strengths and to available market niches.

Paper Machines. Montclair operates six paper machines with "trim" ranging from 124 to 154 inches and run speeds from 1500 to 2000 feet per minute. The width(trim) and the speed of a machine determine its capacity. The machines can produce different colors, weights and grades depending upon pulp mix, additives, machine design, and machine settings.

The machines run continuously, three shifts a day, 365 days a year. It is widely believed in the industry that you can't make money unless the mill is running. What a machine runs is secondary to that it runs. Changing products "on the run" (grade, weight, color, texture) produces waste while the machine is trying to get "on grade". The cost of that waste in lost materials, sewage disposal, operating costs, and opportunities missed is perhaps 30% of overall mill cost. The common wisdom is, "the fewer changes, the better."

---

* This case was written by Professor John Shank with the assistance of Tom Wisniewski (T'93) and with the cooperation of Champion International. All financial information in the case is disguised to protect proprietary information.

Montclair's "premium papers" competitors have smaller capacity machines. Although Montclair's machines are narrow, old, and slow by General's standards, they are new, wide, and fast for a premium papers niche mill. Montclair's machines average 90 tons per day each, whereas a typical premium papers machine might run 30 tons per day, ranging down to 10 tons per day. It isn't clear whether Montclair's "large" small machines constitute a plus or a minus in the premium niches. That is, are there scale economies or diseconomies for machines of this size in this niche?

Converting. Converting is the process of changing the large rolls of paper that come off the paper machines into finished goods. This includes coating, supercalendering, rewinding, slitting, sheeting, embossing, and packaging. The processes vary widely from product to product. Some paper is sold as machine rolls; some products use nearly all these processes. The converting area operates like a job shop. In the premium segment, converting is essential for a mill to provide each customer exactly what they need.

The converting area is characterized by a great deal of "WIP" inventory. Large quantities of WIP between departments serve as buffers to make day to day mill operations run more smoothly. Minimizing WIP has never been a management priority. But the excess WIP is costly in terms of high opportunity for damage and waste, delayed feedback on upstream quality problems, and low urgency for first pass quality.

Very little of the converting equipment would be considered state-of-the-art. Even the modern Sheet Packers and Precision Sheeters do not perform up to their rated capacity because of the large number of changeovers. Some operations are 100% non-value added, such as the machine which flips huge stacks of sheets back to "face up" after a manual inspection operation flips them, one at a time, "face down." It was widely known at the mill that outside contractors charged prices for converting operations which were less than half of Montclair's costs.

Distribution Center. Montclair maintains one of the country's largest premium paper warehouses. The Distribution Center (DC) comprises 300,000 sq. ft. of old warehouse space containing over 20,000 tons of finished goods spread among 1000 products. Montclair sells about 100,000 tons per year through the DC and about 100,000 tons in manufacturing orders.

Each product has a stocking zone from which orders are filled. Any inventory over the amount that can fit in this zone is held in an excess area. Between daily and weekly peaks in order filling activity, the DC staff restocks zones from the excess area and shuffles pallets within the zones to make the oldest stock most accessible. Order fillers "pick" stock daily from the zones using order

lists, then apply bar code stickers that identify the stock and move it to the truck pit where shippers assemble the stock into complete orders, arrange the orders into truck loads, and load the trucks.

Uncoated "Text and Cover" grades. The mill produces over 1000 different products in the Uncoated grade line, involving combinations of color, size, finish texture, weight, and package type. Uncoated paper is usually sold through "merchant" distributors to job shop printers who contract with end-use customers for brochures, catalogues, corporate letterhead, or reports.

In this segment, products and companies are highly differentiated; many product attributes are judged; small quantities are sold to a large number of customers; brand names and "image" are important; and the industry is highly fragmented with dozens of niches players.

Deep Colors. Dark or "deep" colors is one niche believed to be vital in the premium segment to be considered a serious player. Deep colors increase the visual appeal of the mill's swatch books which are a critical selling tool with printers and graphic designers. Deep colors are produced on #2 paper machine with frequent grade changes to produce the large variety of weights, colors and textures demanded by end-users. The darkest colors are run less frequently because there is limited demand. Annual demand is only about 4 to 6 tons for any one deep color product (color/size/texture) and a typical mill order from a "merchant" is one ton or less. Deep color production runs are also scheduled infrequently because they are difficult and extremely costly to run. Long runs allow averaging of the high set-up waste.

Sixty-Five Pound "Carnival" Grade Uncoated Sheets - "Forest Green" Color. Tom Winton knows very well that an uncoated grade such as "Carnival" in a heavy basis weight (cover stock) in a "deep" color is difficult to run, difficult to sell in "reasonable" quantities, and difficult to position in the market place. Exhibit 1 shows the value chain for one specific use of this one specific product. The stages in this value chain are the end-use (an odd shaped, folded sales brochure for Reebok shoes), the commercial printer, the merchant, and the paper mill. Analysis of those value chain stages upstream from the paper mill (pulp mill and wood suppliers) is beyond the scope of this case which focuses on cost issues at the paper manufacturing stage of the chain.

Exhibit 2 shows the standard cost report for this product in the conventional format. The report shows what the mill is "supposed" to spend making one ton of the product, if it meets the "allowed standards". At the "standard cost" of $2900, there is a loss of over $700 on every ton. After considering the warehousing costs in the DC, the loss is $900 on every ton.

The cost analysis supervisor at the mill was convinced that any problem with this grade [product] was in the marketplace and not in Montclair's manufacturing process. The standard cost of $2,900/T for Forest Green was solidly constructed:

- union wage rates for all labor costs ("pattern bargaining" virtually assured comparable labor costs across all mills of the major firms, all of whom were unionized),
- standard yield rates for all conversion steps, based on latest performance against long-standing norms in the mill,
- current market prices for all purchased components,
- generally accepted industry procedures for building the "normal" cost of scrap into the standard, after deducting the offset for the market value of the scrap generated.

The standards were updated once a year for changes in purchase prices, process flows and yield targets. With over 1500 products in the mill, more frequent updating was not deemed feasible.

The standard cost represented "best practices" for the mill. It was accepted by manufacturing management and the mill manager as an appropriate basis for monitoring manufacturing performance. There was month to month stability in allowed cost because standards were only updated once a year. This stability was seen by management as a positive feature in monitoring monthly performance against the annual plan.

In short, this was a typically derived standard cost for a product which is infrequently produced and very hard to make. Also typical was the high level of skepticism among financial management, manufacturing management and general management that a substantially lower cost was feasible in this mill.

The belief at the mill was that the loss per ton was a price problem rather than a cost problem. Mill management believed that Montclair's $2200/T selling price shown in Exhibit 2 was kept artificially low by the sales department's need to compete against firms which operated out of very old, small, fully-depreciated and obsolete mills, using non-union labor and following a marginal cost pricing strategy, just to keep their mills running.

Sales management saw pricing as given, based on market competition. They were already achieving prices for the Carnival grades that were several hundred dollars per ton higher than competitors such as Ajax Paper Company charged. Further price increases were just not feasible. To them, the loss was not a sales problem. Manufacturing saw costs as given, based on well established production processes and materials requirements. To them, the loss was not a manufacturing problem. Financial management saw the standard cost as the appropriate measure for monitoring mill production performance. To them, the loss was certainly not an accounting problem.

In this situation, the standard costs were useful in the mill principally to simplify calculating cost of goods sold and cost of inventories month-by-month for financial statements. The standard cost was not helpful at all in resolving the management problem of deep color uncoated cover grades.

Exhibit 3 shows some additional information for the merchant segment of the value chain. One issue here is that Montclair also stocks inventory, as well as the merchant, whereas most niche manufacturers do not operate large warehouses themselves.

THE ASSIGNMENT

1. What can the mill do about this "problem"?

The following questions deal with some calculations that may help you think about question 1.

2. Can you calculate a "target cost" at the Montclair mill for the product described in Exhibits 1 and 2? So what? Assume here that the "referent" product is the one made by our competitor—Ajax Paper. For this particular end-use our "higher value" is not "worth it" to the customer (Reebok).

3. Can you calculate the "ideal cost" for this product? So what?

4. Suppose Montclair could use 75% scrap in the raw material mix, and could use green* scrap paper (reduce dye cost from $500 to $250), and could achieve 75% yield at the paper machine. How would the $2,276 standard cost (at the machine) change? So what?

5. Suppose Montclair changed its distribution strategy to "steam-line" DC operations and eliminate inventory at the merchant. Then, the merchant would treat Montclair products as "mill direct" items rather than "stocking" items. How would this change in the "value chain" affect the mill target cost for the product described in the case? So what?

*The standard cost presumes using white scrap paper in the raw material mix.

EXHIBIT 1
Value Chain for One Use of One Ton of One Uncoated, "Deep" Color Grade

<u>**Customer**</u>   (Reebok - for a sales promotion brochure, 20,000 copies; 2 pieces per 23"x35" sheet; the paper came from Ajax Paper Company's mill in Middletown, Ohio)

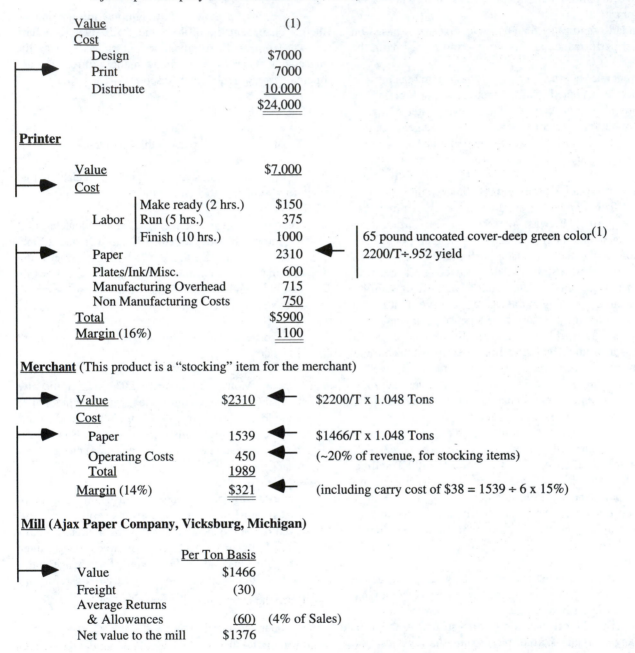

<u>Value</u>   (1)
<u>Cost</u>
   Design $7000
   Print   7000
   Distribute   <u>10,000</u>
                   <u>$24,000</u>

<u>**Printer**</u>

<u>Value</u>   <u>$7,000</u>
<u>Cost</u>
           Make ready (2 hrs.) $150
   Labor   Run (5 hrs.)   375
           Finish (10 hrs.)   1000   65 pound uncoated cover-deep green color[1]
   Paper   2310   2200/T÷.952 yield
   Plates/Ink/Misc.   600
   Manufacturing Overhead   715
   Non Manufacturing Costs   <u>750</u>
<u>Total</u> $5900
<u>Margin</u> (16%)   1100

<u>**Merchant**</u> (This product is a "stocking" item for the merchant)

<u>Value</u> $2310 $2200/T x 1.048 Tons
<u>Cost</u>
   Paper   1539 $1466/T x 1.048 Tons
   Operating Costs   450   (~20% of revenue, for stocking items)
   <u>Total</u>   <u>1989</u>
<u>Margin</u> (14%)   <u>$321</u>   (including carry cost of $38 = 1539 ÷ 6 x 15%)

<u>**Mill**</u> (Ajax Paper Company, Vicksburg, Michigan)

              <u>Per Ton Basis</u>
Value $1466
Freight   (30)
Average Returns
   & Allowances   <u>(60)</u>   (4% of Sales)
Net value to the mill $1376

---

(1) For this job the customer chose $2200/T paper made by Ajax Paper Co. for which the merchant pays $1466/T. For the comparable paper made by Montclair (Carnival Grade - Forest Green), the printer pays $3300/T ($2200/T to the merchant). The customer might also have chosen grades costing up to $3600/T. An unanswered question is how the customer (Reebok) decides to spend $2200, $3300, or $3600 per ton for the paper.

EXHIBIT 2
Standard Cost
65 Pound Carnival Cover (Uncoated) - Forest Green Color - Sheets Pack

Fiber

	% Mix	Market Price
Virgin Hardwood (for opacity and smoothness)	.63	$425/T
Virgin Softwood (for strength)	.15	$475/T
Scrap	.22	$60/T
	$352/T	

Paper Machine (Yield = 46%)

Fiber ($352 ÷ .46 - $61 credit for scrap generated)	704
Other Materials & Dyes (550 ÷ .46)	1196
Machine Conversion ($520 per running hour ÷ 3 tons per hour ÷ .46)	376
	$2276/T

Converting (Yield = 88%)

Paper ($2276 ÷ .88)	2586
Sheeting & Packing ($600 per hour ÷ 2.25 tons/hour ÷ .88)	303
Pack & Ship to the DC	11.
	$2900/T

Manufacturing Cost Summary (Yielded)

Materials	$2159	← [(704 + 1196) ÷ .88]
Paper Machine	427	← (376 ÷ .88)
Conversion	303	← (a competitor cost survey showed
Ship to DC	11	"best practices" of $150/T)
	$2900	

Overall Cost Summary

	Per Ton	
Manufacturing	$2900.	
DC Operating Costs	25.	
DC Carry Cost	145.	($2900; 3 turns; 15% carry cost)
Freight to Merchant	30.	
	$3100.	
Selling Price	2200.	(to the merchant)
Loss	$(900.)	

Also note that the mill has $160 million invested (including working capital). This is $800 per ton of annual throughput. To earn a 15% return on investment the mill would have to raise the price by $1,020/T (the $900 loss plus $120 profit—$800/T x 15%).

EXHIBIT 3
Capital Paper Merchants
(Millions of $)

Income Statement - Condensed

Sales -	From Stock (12,000 Tons)	$23	
	Mill Direct (15,500 Tons)	23	$46
Gross Margin (14.5%)	"Stocking" Business (22%)	5.1	
	"Mill Direct" Business (7%)	1.6	$6.7
Administration Costs			$5.5*
Personnel Cost (7.25%)	(Sales/Customer Service/		
	Distribution/Purchasing/		
	Administration/ Management)	$3.4	
Other Cost (4.75%)		$2.1	
Margin (2.5%)			$1.2

* No more than $1 million (4.5% of sales) of this $5.5 million relates to the "mill direct" segment of the business. The balance of $4.5 million (20% of sales) relates to the "stocking" segment.

Asset Base

> A/R (45 Days) | Stocking Items - 60 Days
> | Direct Mill Ship- 30 Days

> Inventory (6 turns)
> Warehouse 100,000 ft.^{2} x $40/ft.^{2} $4.0
> Other Space 10,000 x $70   .7
> Equipment (warehouse handling & shipping)   1.1

The Capital Paper Company operate a regional chain of 5 fine paper warehouses in the Northeast. The chain provides classic break-bulk, full line and quick response value as a reseller. With $46 million in sales and 50,000 sq. ft. of warehouse, the Boston operation (CP Boston) is about average in size for Capital and the industry. They stock 2400 different sku's from 10 major suppliers and a dozen other minor ones. The majority of sku's are fine paper products.

Peter Johnson, Manager of the Boston operation, described the merchant business: "It's quite simple really, we buy low and sell higher. We earn our cut by being middlemen that provide service to our customers. CP offers one stop shopping for fine paper. We give technical advice on the products. And we will sell any amount -- from one ream right up to 100 tons. Our customers don't want to deal with 10 or 20 different mills for their paper needs. From the manufacturer's perspective, I just don't think most of them are ready to give the extended credit and all the advice and hand holding for such small orders."

"To sell paper we can either stock it and fill a order from our floor, or we can have it shipped directly from the supplier. The general rule is we stock at a level to meet demand for smaller orders and use mill-direct for the larger ones. It all depends on the individual product and customer's needs. Printers will call up for a few cartons of paper and want delivery today. If we don't have it in stock, we don't get the order. They don't hold inventory; they expect us to. On the other extreme, we have manufacturers who call up for 50 tons of a single product and don't need shipment for weeks. They don't expect or need us to stock at that level."

Sole supplier relationships are not uncommon. The manufacturer will supply only one merchant in the area with a product line. In return the merchant will stock the product at a higher level and limit the number of competitive products it carries.

Customers often get competitive bids from several merchants. The salesmen are given a lot of leeway in price setting because they are paid on straight commission. A standard price book exists, but is a guideline only. One salesman noted: "The reality is that CP is bidding on orders. I offer a price based on our product costs, the size of the order, the customer and the competitive situation.

Question: Does the merchant do better on the "stocking" business or the "mill direct" business? So what?

National Paper's Timberlands: Wither and Whence?*

In 1987 National Paper, a major forest products company, was also one of the largest private landowners in the US. National Paper owned or controlled 4.6 million acres of timberland, an area larger than Massachusetts and Rhode Island combined. This case considers the financial and strategic aspects of that investment.

TIMBERLANDS AS AN INVESTMENT

Paper mills and solid wood products mills generally complement each other in terms of the kind of raw material demanded. "Roundwood" sourcing to paper mills typically consists of poor quality, low valued, small size bolts (or logs) that cannot be profitably milled by saw mills or plywood mills. Mill waste (e.g., edgings, trim, slabs, and "peeler cores") can be so readily chipped and processed into paper that sawmill waste is often the preferred source of raw material for paper mills. It is widely viewed that processing roundwood into paper is the least profitable use of the tree.

Beginning in 1983, following a dramatic drop in land and stumpage values (Exhibit 2) and an increased emphasis on white paper manufacturing, National began to seriously question the need for its extensive land holdings. In fact, about 1 million of the acres no longer serviced any National operations at all. Exhibit 1 is a recap of the largest American corporate landowners in 1984 and their paper-making capacity. James River Corporation is included as one firm following a zero timber ownership strategy. In spite of the massive holdings reflected in Exhibit 1, forest products firms control only 14% of the timberland in the U.S. (68.5 million acres). The federal government controls 21% (102.4 million acres), other governmental units 6%, and other private owners 58% (285.6 million acres). Even with 4.6 million acres, National typically supplies less than 50% of its fiber requirements from its own land.

---

* This case was written by Professor John Shank of the Amos Tuck School and Dr. William Berry while he was a visiting professor at Tuck, with the cooperation of a major forest products firm that wishes to remain anonymous. All information in the case is disguised.

NATIONAL PAPER TIMBERLANDS

EXHIBIT 1

THE LARGEST CORPORATE OWNERS OF U.S. TIMBERLAND
AND THEIR PAPER MAKING CAPACITIES -- 1984

| Company | Millions of Acres | | 1984 Capacity (000 tons) |
	Owned	Controlled	Paper & Board
Champion International	5.2	1.6	5,557
International Paper	6.4	0.4	3,760
Weyerhaeuser	6.0	0	2,890
National Paper	4.4	0.2	3,760
Georgia-Pacific	4.2	0.5	2,477
Boise Cascade	3.2	0.5	2,890
Great Northern Nekoosa	2.8	0.1	2,129
Crown Zellerbach[1]	1.7	0.3	1,834
Scott	1.8	0.1	1,690
Mead	1.7	0.1	2,564
Union Camp	1.6	0.1	2,148
Burlington Northern	1.5	0.0	0
Potlatch	1.4	0.0	0
Westvaco	1.3	0.0	1,872
James River Corporation	0.0	0.0	1,324

1   Acquired by Sir James Goldsmith in 1985. He retained the timber holdings and sold the paper mills to James River Corporation

At the broadest level, there are four reasons for a paper and wood products company to own timber acreage:

1. Owned timber is an insurance policy to guarantee a source of supply for at least part of the basic raw material source. Fiber accounts for 15 to 25% of the manufacturing cost for a paper mill and a much larger percent for a lumber or plywood mill. The issue here is clearly a cost-benefit tradeoff and a hedge against future uncertainty in raw material supply over the 30 to 50 year growing cycle.

2. Owned timber is a cash flow "smoothing" device. When demand is weak and cash flow is tight, a company with large timber holdings can use a higher than normal proportion of its own timber. This reduces corporate cash outflows since there is very little marginal outflow associated with harvesting trees that are mature.

3. Owned timber is a device to "smooth" reported earnings. When demand is weak, reported earnings are also lower than normal. Earnings can be increased by using a higher than normal proportion of owned timber which always shows a much lower cost than purchased timber. The book value of standing timber includes only the original planting costs. All annual upkeep costs are expensed as incurred. Thus, the book value of a mature stand of timber is almost always much lower than the market price of the wood.

4. Timberland ownership can be viewed as a business of its own. The cash flows associated with ownership over the growing cycle would have to show an adequate rate of return on the invested capital, after allowing for the risks of the business, under this rationale for ownership.

It is interesting to note that the timing of when standing timber would be cut under this fourth rationale is the opposite of when it would be cut under the second and third rationales. As a business, timber would be cut when prices are strong (heavy demand) and would be allowed to stand when prices are weak (slack demand). As noted above, the second and third rationales involve cutting more timber when prices are weak and buying more timber (cutting less) when prices are strong.

As a general observation, it could be argued that National's cutting practices reflected the cash flow and earnings smoothing rationales to a large extent. The stated objectives of National's Timberlands operations were "to minimize the cost of wood supplied to company mills, to maximize the value obtained from timber harvested, to cost-effectively maximize the growth on company controlled lands, and to assure that an adequate supply of wood fiber will be available at a favorable cost far into the future".

FORESTRY

Forest users have long recognized that a forest can yield more than twice as much volume when efficiently and professionally managed. National used a wide range of activities to increase productivity on its lands. These included developing and planting genetically superior seedlings, thinning of stands to concentrate growth on the best trees, site preparation of the land before planting to eliminate competition from grasses and shrubs, pest and fire control, and fertilization of some lands deficient in essential nutrients. National conducted both a genetics improvement program and research into such areas as cloning and tissue cultures in order to continually improve the trees planted on its lands each year.

Timberlands management, as practiced by National and most other forest products firms, was similar to farming any other crop, with the major difference being the length of time between planting and harvest. These commercial forestry practices were decried by some as "unnatural" in that the result was far from being the typical "wild" forest. At harvest time, hunters and wildlife lovers complained that their sporting fields, enjoyed for decades, were being "ruined".

Of course, one can also argue that cutting of mature trees is good for the forest because very old trees (like very old people) are much more susceptible to disease and pests that can then spread to younger trees as well. Essentially, forest management represents good forestry as well as good business, unless one believes that "benign neglect" is the right way to treat the forests.

The whole issue of "managing" corporate-owned forests, as well as government-owned forests, is as much emotional and political as it is financial. There are very few aspects on which it is really clear that the public interest diverges from the interests of the forest products companies. Even as apparently one-sided an issue as forest fires can be viewed two ways. The Forest Service until recently has regarded infestation and disease as 'nature's way' but has not thought of fire similarly. Efforts to control forest fire have led to more intensive fires when they do occur. This has resulted in fires that completely devastate national forests and private ones as well, if they are in the way. In the typical fire in a healthy forest some trees will not be destroyed. For example, a healthy Ponderosa Pine has such a great resistance to fire that when the fire burns itself out, the Ponderosa Pine forms the core of the natural reforestation process. This is one reason the Ponderosa is so prevalent in the fire prone regions of the west and mountain states. But, when a forest is 'protected' from fire and become overly mature, even the Ponderosa will burn. This creates fires with much higher temperatures which will destroy even healthy trees. The Forest Service has recently begun to allow some fires to burn which, they now believe, will lead to more healthy and natural forests overall. But, can you really imagine Smokey the Bear saying, "Help stamp out some forest fires"?!!

Even claims in Maine about protecting the "wild" Allegash river from "desecration" conveniently ignore the fact that the Allegash basin was clear-cut by timer companies in the 1940s and 1950s. What stands there now as a "wilderness" has regrown naturally from bare stumps in about forty years.

National Paper is very interested in the way the national forests are managed since a large percentage of its supply of fiber comes from contract cuttings on national forest land. Overall, it just isn't clear what their future policies will be. Depending on what you read, the government may cut less timber, more timber, or just about the same amount as now.

National has nurseries in six states with capacity sufficient to fill virtually all the company's seedling needs, about 75 million in 1984—or about five seedlings for every tree that was harvested.

THE FORESTRY INDUSTRY

The early forest products industry in the United States consisted primarily of mill operations that provided lumber and millwork for commerce and construction. In the late 19th century most forest products companies practiced "cut and run" forestry. That is, they bought timber land in the lake states and the west, cut the best timber, and then allowed the land to revert to public ownership by failing to pay taxes. As the "timber barons" saw it, there was plenty of timber "out West" and there was little advantage in planting trees and waiting for them to mature. By 1900, with the forests of the northeast and the lake states stripped of the best virgin timber, the lumber industry shifted into the south and the pacific northwest. In 1910 lumber production reached a peak of 40 billion board feet -- a level that has been approached again only in recent years.

As the forests were cleared and the population

increased, pressure mounted to curtail wasteful practices in the industry. The federal government responded by enacting the Organic Act of 1897 which carved forest reserves out of western federal lands. In 1905, these reserves became the basis for the National Forests system. Among other things, the Act of 1897 introduced "sustained yield" management based on the principle that the amount of timber harvested should not exceed the amount of timber grown. European countries had developed similar forestry practices a century before. It is worth noting that controlled cutting has always been a part of the national forests concept. It is really only the relative amount of cutting that generates so much controversy.

Long term commitments to land ownership and good forestry were not widely adopted by private or corporate landowners until after World War II because the returns to owners were not proportionate to the costs and risks involved in nurturing and holding timber over the long maturation period. Section 177(K) of the Internal Revenue Code of 1939 and its descendant, Section 631 of the Internal Revenue Code of 1954, were devised to provide a strong incentive to encourage practices that would ensure a permanent sufficient supply of timber. In essence, these sections of the IRS Code allowed capital gains treatment for harvested timber and ordinary deductions for all operating costs as they are incurred, while only the direct costs of reforestation were capitalized. That is, after planting, all the annual expenses of forest management were expensed currently for tax purposes.

One result of these laws was that timber growing became a competitive investment opportunity. But not everyone takes advantage of the opportunity. In 1985, it was estimated that whereas 95% of corporately-owned timberland was artificially regenerated, 85% of privately-owned timberland was allowed to regenerate naturally. Of course, when selective cutting of mature trees from a forest is practiced, rather that clear cutting the entire area, it is much less clear that planned replanting is necessary. Foresters "clear cut" because it isn't economically feasible to "hunt and pick" for certain trees once the loggers and trucks and equipment are on the site. But, "selective cutting" is much less labor and capital intensive.

Mr. Mark Smith, Vice President-Controller of Forest Products commented on several aspects of the Timberlands Division:

> "The 1986 Tax Act is one more reason to question the long-term viability of the timberlands organization as it exists today. The lowering of tax rates and the elimination of

special capital gains rates both serve to raise the after tax cost of producing fee wood.

"The question of how much land to own has always been difficult, with some companies relying on fee timberland almost completely and others buying all of their wood from outside sources. Reasons that we previously accepted for holding timberlands are now being questioned. Recently, some of the best financial performers in the paper industry are firms with little or no land. There is some question, however, whether their performance will be sustained. During the last few years, stumpage prices have been low relative to 1975 and there has been an abundant supply of wood. If prices begin to approach the 1975 levels again (Exhibit 2), wood costs will clearly have a damping effect on the financial performance of those who buy all their wood.

"On the other hand, vast untapped timber resources exist outside of the United States, particularly in South America. In Brazil, where we have a mill and a 100,000 acre forest, we find that the Eucalyptus tree will regenerate 3 harvests from the same stump in a twenty-five year period. That is 3 times the growth rate from a fast-growing North American tree like the Loblolly Pine. The economics of that situation are pretty obvious. This probably represents downward pressure on future domestic prices."

Mr. Rich Gates, General Manager, Northeast Region, commented on the question, "Should National be in the forestry business?"

"I suppose the purist would say, 'If you have a better investment for your capital dollars, then sell Timberlands and invest the money elsewhere.'. This is all well and good, but what do you do with 4.6 million acres of land? You don't want to sell it at a loss. What's more, by selling the land and timber base, you may be selling one of the reasons why that alternative capital investment looks so good.

"Let me explain. If we wanted to divest of all the Timberlands today, we would likely receive about $700 million versus book value of $1 billion. The market for forest land in 1987 is pretty depressed. That amount of money could just about buy another paper mill. Assuming we do just that, how do we go about supplying this new mill at prices National is used to paying?

"The way I see it, three things could happen.

1) We could sell our lands to a competitor who can use all the excess wood in their own mills (effectively locking us out of a major source of wood).

2) We could sell to an investor with long term objectives and no need for immediate cash, or

3) We could sell to an investor with an interest in forest land and an immediate need for cash.

"If 1 or 2 occurs we can expect to pay more for our wood. If the increase were 30% and raw material accounts for 20% of all costs, then our finished product costs would increase 6%. Certainly this would have a negative influence on our profitability.

"Timberlands now supplies low-cost wood to our mills. Our land ownership position also tends to depress local market price. How? When the cost of outside wood increases, we cut more of our own wood and buy less which tends to drive the outside price back down again. Do we need 4.6 million acres of land? Maybe not, but let's be careful about where we divest. There are 'hidden' benefits in timberland ownership that are not apparent in the marketplace until they are gone. The task of justifying Timberlands ownership is a difficult one, I know. The direct profits of Timberlands operations, mineral leases and recreational leases are easily quantifiable, but they are only a portion of the benefits derived from Timberlands ownership. How do we quantify the benefit of price stability to our mills? What value should we assign to the stable supply of raw material? What's the risk of temporary shutdowns caused by seasonal shifts in the open market wood supply, and what is the resultant cost? What is an acceptable risk?

FINANCIAL CONSIDERATIONS

The economic returns from the timber business are extremely difficult to measure because they involve cash flows spread over very long periods of years and widely differing beliefs about the future. One component in the calculation is the trend in prices for the land upon which the timber grows. Over the period from 1950 to

EXHIBIT 2
TIMBER PRICES

Part A: **Timber Prices in Region 6 of U.S. National Forests**
          [1960-Quarter 1 through 1982-Quarter 4]
          [Quarters 1 through 92]

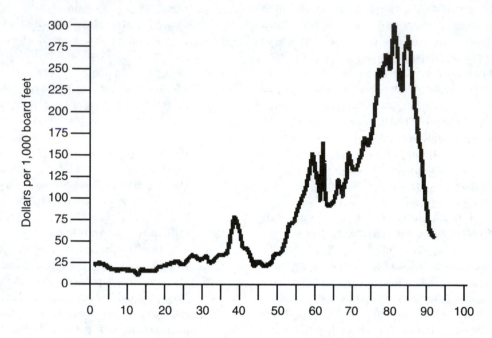

Source: *Forest Science* 31, No. 2 (1985), p. 407.

Part B: Over a much longer time period, and stated in real prices, the picture looks like this:

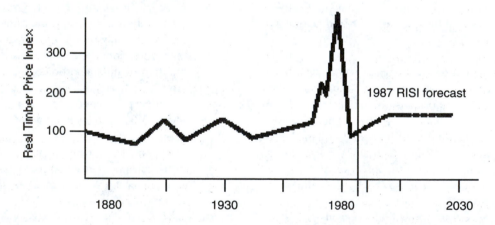

In short, real prices were at the same level in 1986 that they were in 1886. The huge increase from 1973 to 1980 was followed by an even bigger decrease from 1980 to 1985.

1983 timberland prices, excluding timber, grew at a compound 9% rate in a 34 state survey. Prices were generally depressed from 1982 through 1986. Future price trends are the subject of much highly diverse speculation. Fortune reported in June, 1985 that American Can was struggling to get rid of 500,000 acres which is valued at $220 million ($440./acre). American Can believed that pension funds were likely to invest $1 billion in timberlands over the next five years. Pension World confirmed the interest in timberlands in a March, 1986 story which cited a John Hancock study showing timber investment returns of 10.5% compounded between 1958 and 1984 (versus common stocks at 9.6%). Business Week, in February, 1985, cited a U.S. Forest Service estimate that timberland would increase in value 2.1% a year faster than inflation over the next forty-five years. In 1985 Pension World cited Equitable Insurance as believing timberland to be as great a current investment opportunity as commercial real estate had been in the 1970's.

On the other hand, 7 to 10 million acres of timberland was "on the market" in 1987 with very few large-scale buyers. "Prime" tracts were selling for 30 to 50% below "appraised value." A widely cited study by the University of Georgia School of Forestry showed that southern pine pulpwood had actually declined in real value between 1952 and 1982. DRI forecasts in 1985 indicated flat real timberland prices over the following 20 years, but these forecasts were widely criticized in the industry. A Mead Corporation study described in Pulp and Paper in July, 1985 indicated internal rates of return on timber investments ranging only between 10% and 14% which, at best, barely meet the cost of capital. The Mead study was also bearish on timber investment because of extreme uncertainty about future global supply/demand patterns, the relative illiquidity of the investments, and the reduced attractiveness of such projects under the new tax proposals (which are now in effect).

Forbes (December, 1985) saw well-managed long-term investments in timber earning 4 to 6% above inflation, but Fortune (June, 1985) cited security analysts who felt that timberland was substantially overpriced, even at the relatively depressed levels ($250 to $350 per acre) based on recent past history. One interesting piece of evidence often cited is the purchase by Sir James Goldsmith of Crown Zellerbach in 1985. He promptly sold the paper mills to James River, keeping only the timberland and some miscellaneous assets. The acquisition of 1.7 million acres (and cutting rights to another .3 million acres) by such an internationally acclaimed investor seems to be a major vote of confidence

for the timberland business. However, of the $570 million he invested, Goldsmith recouped $400 million from selling the non-timber holdings. He thus acquired the timberland for only about $100 per acre. In April of 1985, CZ had estimated that the timberland was worth $500 per acre. Buying it for $100 per acre is more easily viewed as a steal than a commitment to the business.

Mr. John Baxter, Vice President of Timberlands Operations commented on the past financial performance of Timberlands and his view of the future:

"During the decade immediately preceding 1985, Timberlands was a major contributor to profits and cash flow. It contributed nearly $1 billion in cash flow from a 3 million acre land base. This equated to a $333 return per acre from a land base whose invested capital value averaged about $140/acre. We returned well over twice the land's book value in cash flow during the decade. This amounted to average annual return of 24% on invested capital.

"But we in Timberlands are not naive. We recognize that we cannot justify a corporate commitment to forestry that is based on past performance. We need to review our land management programs as business enterprises and aggressively seek ways to improve our financial performance. Based on market values, the revenues from timberlands in 1975 was $215 million. Based on current thinking, we see many opportunities to improve the financial performance of our land management program. We see Timberlands as a solid investment, showing good returns for the foreseeable future.

In considering the Timberlands question, Mr. Matt Clemens, Chairman and CEO, observed:

"We are looking at several complex issues that interact in ways that make rational, systematic analysis very difficult. First, we want to become the leading white paper company in the world. Given that this is where National wants to be, what should be our position regarding Timberlands? Have we really been involved in forestry just because of the tax breaks? If we were to simply harvest what we have already planted and sell the land after harvest we would eventually become totally dependent on outside sources for our most important raw material. Would it be available in fifty years? At what prices? Should we sell our

EXHIBIT 3

For 1 Acre of Timberland

	Texas	Maine[2]	Washington
Growing Cycle	30 years	50 years	50 years
Current site preparation cost	$ 62.	$ 12.	$ 95.
Planting Cost	44.	0.	130.
Forest management cost/year[1]	5.	2.	9.
Ad valorem tax/year	3.	1.	2.
Total cost in year 0 (not deductible until sale)	106.	12.	225.
Total annual cost over the growing cycle (fully tax deductible)	8.	3.	11.
Current Revenue Yield (weighted average of pulpwood and sawtimber yield)	924.	195.	4,150.
Estimated market value of the land, ex trees	200.	100.	300.

[1] Annual forest management expenses include road construction and maintenance, silviculture, fire control, boundary maintenance, inventory costs and division overhead.

[2] Maine timberland is allowed to regenerate naturally. Thus, planting cost is zero

timberlands? If we do and if the government later revises taxes to restore the incentives for forest lands, it may not be possible to recreate this level of resources—the forests, the silvicultural researchers, the skilled foresters—again.

"How should I evaluate these tradeoffs with regard to National's current responsibility to it stockholders and its responsibility to future managers and future generations of Americans? While I plan to hold this job for a while longer, I know that the operational effects of a decision in this area will not be noticed for years or even decades after I'm gone."

The basic economics of the forestry business in 1987 are illustrated in Exhibit 3 which summarizes selected facts from 3 regions of the country in which National has major timber holdings.

ASSIGNMENT QUESTIONS

1) Using the information in Exhibit 3, evaluate the prospective profitability over the growing cycle of planting one acre of trees in Texas, Maine, and Washington. The time value of money is obviously one issue here since the cash flows are spread over many years. Present your analysis in real terms in order to eliminate one major assumption (future inflation rates). You may also assume that land values for timberland (ex trees) will move in direct proportion to timber or "stumpage" prices. Use a tax rate of 35%.

Do you believe it is more useful to make assumptions about real price escalation and solve for an expected rate of return or to assume a break-even real hurdle rate and solve for the implicit price escalation necessary to yield that return?

2) What do you believe should be National's timberlands strategy in 1987? Why?

Petersen Pottery*

This case is set in rural West Virginia in 1980 in the $450 million per year "vitreous clay fixtures" industry. There are 70 firms in the industry and Petersen is somewhere in the middle. The case deals with the need for formal cost control systems.

Just outside of Elkins, West Virginia, high in the Appalachian Mountains, Clive Petersen had been making ceramic bathroom fixtures (sinks, toilets, and bathtubs) since 1960. Petersen fixtures had become known over the years for their distinctive custom features, their high quality, and their long life. Petersen Pottery had grown from a two-man operation in 1960 to the present group of 20 master potters located in two large old warehouses, converted from World War II storage depots. By 1980 Clive's business had expanded to the point where he felt he must institute some type of formal, systematic controls over his costs. His banker was more and more concerned about the lack of any kind of modern cost accounting system as the loan balances kept growing to fund Clive's expansion and seasonal operations.

The manufacture of ceramic "sanitary ware" consists of two processes: "green" molding and glazing, each of which involves a four day kiln cycle. Raw clay is first packed into "plaster of paris" molds where it is allowed to dry before it is baked in a kiln to harden. In the second stage, the fixture is coated with a glaze mixture to give it its color and characteristic smooth finish. The fixture is then baked again (fired) to harden and fix the glaze to the clay. The kiln time is as follows:

	Green Molding Cycle	Glazing Cycle
Drying	1 day	1 day
Firing	1 day	1 day
Cooling	2 days	2 days

The finished product is then shipped to various wholesale outlets around the East Central States region. The molding and firing of ceramics, although not highly complex, requires an experienced potter to assure the quality of the product. Excessive heat or excessive time in the kiln can ruin a fixture. The mixing and application of the glaze also requires a significant amount of skill. However, too much time cannot be spent on the molding and glazing processes because delays can cause bottlenecks in the whole production process.

---

* The case was written by Thomas Graham under the supervision of Professor John K. Shank at the Ohio State University in 1980.

The need for better cost control, coupled with a need for better control over production scheduling to meet the increases in demand, led Clive Petersen to adopt a standard cost system. After extended discussion with his most experienced master potters, Clive and his new cost accountant arrived at the following cost standards for a toilet, one of the high volume products:

Materials
Raw Clay	25 lb @ $.95/lb	$23.75
Glazing Mix	5 lb @ $.75/lb	3.75

Direct Labor
Molding	1 hr @ $15/hr[1]	15.00
Glazing	.5 hr @ $15/hr[1]	7.50

Manufacturing Overhead Costs: Absorbed
@ $5 per Fixture		5.00[2]
	Total per Fixture	$55.00

[1] Petersen paid wages of about twice the average for "stone and clay workers" because he wanted only top quality products.

[2] Normal volume per month for overhead allocation purposes was assumed to be 1,200 toilets. The estimated monthly manufacturing overhead allocation to this product was $1.94 per unit plus $3,672 of fixed cost.

ANALYSIS OF OPERATIONS

After 6 months of operations using the new cost system Petersen was disturbed over the lack of attention paid to the standards. He felt that the potters were just too set in their ways to pay any attention to the "confusing" new system. As one of the potters observed, "I have been making these fixtures a lot longer than these new ideas had been around, and I don't see how a bunch of numbers that some hot-shot accountant puts together are going to help me make any better toilets." The result was that although the standards existed, they were seldom met.

In reviewing the June production results, the following actual costs were noted in connection with manufacturing 1145 toilets:

Materials Purchased
Clay	30,000 lb @ $.92/lb
Glaze	6,000 lb @ $.78/lb

Materials Used
Clay	28,900 lb
Glaze	5,900 lb

Direct Labor
Molding	1,200 hr @ $15.25/hr
Glazing	600 hr @ $15.00/hr

Overhead Assigned to Toilets: $6,100

The sales manager was unhappy that production was 45 units below plan. The cost accountant was unhappy about continuing unfavorable variances. Before proceeding with further analysis, Petersen met with his most experienced master potter, Jim Sedgefield, to discuss the variances from the standards. He was seriously considering implementing a new and much faster "pressure casting" mold system to replace the existing manual system. When Sedgefield arrived, Clive explained the problem: "Jim, you agreed when we set them up that the standards are reasonable and yet you never meet them. It looks like we will have unfavorable variances again this month as well as more missed shipping dates." Sedgefield was not impressed. "Well Clive," he said, "I never have understood this system at all. Why don't you ask that fast-talking accountant to explain the variances? He seems to know what these numbers mean. All I know is, we seemed to spend all month fussing with that new brand of clay you said was going to be cheaper for us. Do you want me to make lots of toilets or good toilets?"

QUESTIONS

1. First enter the cost activity for the month of June in the blank T-accounts in Exhibit 1. There are 8 accounting entries for you to make.

2. Analyze the variances for the month using whatever format you like.

3. What conclusions are suggested regarding cost performance for the month?

4. What suggestions do you have for Mr. Petersen regarding his new standard cost system?

EXHIBIT 1
The Toilets Product Line

R/M - Clay	WIP	Finished Goods

R/M - Glaze

Manufacturing Overhead Assigned	Cost of Goods Sold (including all variances)	Accts. Payable & Accrued Expenses

ENTRIES

1. Record the purchase of clay and glaze
2. Record the transfer of clay and glaze into production (WIP)
3. Record labor expense as part of WIP inventory
4. Record the assignment of manufacturing overhead to the product line
5. Record the "absorption" of manufacturing overhead into WIP inventory
6. Record the transfer of 1145 units from WIP to Finished Goods
7. Record the Cost of Goods Sold for 1145 units shipped
8. Record all cost variances for the month

Assume, additionally, that of the $6,100 manufacturing overhead assigned to toilets, $2,300 was Variable Overhead and $3,800 was Fixed Overhead.

A Note on Computing Manufacturing Cost Variances

(For use with Petersen Pottery case)

I. "PRIME" COSTS

The term "prime" costs refers to those costs which can be directly identified with one unit of product. Another term for "prime" cost is "direct" cost or "variable" cost. You will often hear the terms "direct" material cost or "direct" labor cost. Traditionally, labor has been considered a prime cost by most companies. "Indirect" material and "indirect" labor costs are considered to be part of manufacturing overhead or "burden" rather than part of prime cost. Example of these four cost categories are shown below:

Cost Category	Cost Classification	Example
Direct Labor	Prime Cost	Cost for a worker's time spent assembling a product
Indirect Labor	Overhead Cost	Cost for a worker's time spent repairing manufacturing equipment
Direct Material	Prime Cost	Cost of steel used in manufacturing an automobile
Indirect Material	Overhead Cost	Cost of supplies used in maintaining manufacturing equipment

Today, many companies treat manufacturing labor cost more as fixed than as volume dependent. In this case, the only "prime" or "direct" cost is raw material.

The standard for any element of prime cost involves two components: a price component and a quantity component. The standard cost is the standard quantity to be used multiplied by the standard price per unit of measure. For example, if an electric motor contains four bushings and each bushing should cost $.25, then the standard cost for bushings is $1.00 (standard quantity of 4 X the standard price per unit of $.25). Variances are usually computed for each of the two components. The formulas for calculating the variances are as follows:

This note was prepared as a basis for class discussion by Professor John K. Shank of the Amos Tuck School.

Price variance (PV)= (AP - SP) X AQ
Quantity variance (QV)= (AQ - SQ) X SP
Total variance (TV)= PV + QV

where   SP = standard price
         AP = actual price
         SQ = standard quantity
         AQ = actual quantity

Since the total variance is the difference between the standard cost allowance (SP X SQ) and the actual cost incurred (AP X AQ), you should be able to verify for yourself that the price and quantity variance in the above formulas do sum to the total variance.

We can illustrate these calculations with the following example which assumes that both material and labor cost are volume dependent.

	Calculation
Standard per Unit	
Material	2 pounds per unit at $1.00 per pound = $2.00 per unit
Labor	3 hours per unit at $4.00 per hour = $12.00 per unit
Production	10 units. Therefore, the standard cost allowance is $20 for material and $120 for labor.
Actual Costs	
Material	Used 25 pounds which were purchased at a cost of $.80 per pound, for a cost of $20.
Labor	Used 25 hours at an average rate of $5.00 per hour, for a cost of $125.
Prime Cost Variances	
Material	Price variance: ($1.00 - $.80) X 25 lb = $5 Favorable
	Quantity variance: (20 - 25) X $1.00/lb = $5 Unfavorable
	Total variance: $5F + $5U = 0 = $20 - $20
Labor	Price variance: ($4 - $5) X 25 hr = $25 Unfavorable
	Quantity variance: (30 - 25) X $4/hr = $20 Favorable
	Total variance: $25U + $20F= $5U = $120 - $125

We suggest that you not worry about whether to put standard or actual first in the formulas or about trying to keep track of whether a negative result is favorable or unfavorable. Instead, just think about whether the direction of the variance is good or bad and forget about algebraic signs.

A Complication- "The Joint" Variance. If you look closely at the variance formulas above, you will see that quantity variance is computed using *standard* prices while the price variance is computed using *actual* quantities. This is logically inconsistent, but it makes sense to most people. Most people feel that price fluctuations should not be considered when measuring the variance due to quantity fluctuations—vary only one component at a time. However, most people also feel that the price variance should be measured over the actual quantities for which the price difference obtains, not the standard quantities. Some people do not like this logical inconsistency. They prefer to vary only one component at a time in both the price and quantity variance calculations. They then set up a third variance (joint variance) caused by the joint fluctuation in both prices and quantities. Under this approach the formulas are as follows:

PV = (AP - SP) X SQ
QV = (AQ - SQ) X SP
JV = (AP - SP) X (AQ - SQ)
TV = PV + QV + JV

This can be illustrated graphically as follows, assuming both price and quantity variations are unfavorable:

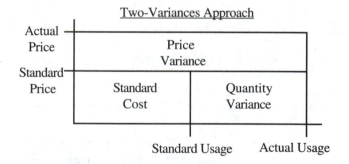

Two-Variances Approach

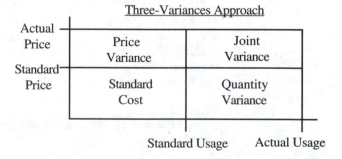

Three-Variances Approach

It is impossible to give a commonsense interpretation to the joint variance when one of the two components varies favorably and the other varies unfavorably. Furthermore, most authors believe that purchasing agents should be assessed for price variations on quantities actually purchased but that production managers should be assessed for quantity differences scaled with standard prices (ignoring price fluctuations). For these reasons, they favor the simpler, two variance approach.

The two variance equality set up in this note (PV + QV = TV) is often violated in practice in regard to material variances. That is, many firms prefer to compute the price variance over quantities *purchased* and the quantity variance over quantities *used*. Since purchase and usage quantities often differ in any given period, the two variances cannot be aggregated algebraically. They can, however, still be combined for cost reporting purposes to get a picture of purchasing and usage variances together.

Suppose, for example, that in our earlier illustration material purchases totaled 30 pounds at $.80 even though only 25 pounds were used in production. The material variance calculation could then be as follows:

Price variance: ($1.00 - $.80) X 30 lb = $6 Favorable
Quantity variance: (20 - 25) X $1.00/lb = $5 Unfavorable
Total variance: $6F + $5U = $1F ≠ $20 - $20

A labor price variance is often called a "labor rate" variance and a labor quantity variance is often called a "labor efficiency" variance. A material quantity variance is often called a "material usage" variance and a material price variance is often called a "purchase price" variance.

II.   OVERHEAD COSTS

Conventional Overhead Budgets. Budgets for prime costs hinge on unit-level standard costs. Once standard prime costs per unit are determined, the budget for any given period is just the standard cost per unit times the number of units produced. A simple approach like this works because prime costs are variable costs. The cost allowance or budget thus varies directly as production volume varies.

Because manufacturing overhead costs typically do not vary directly with volume, it is a more difficult task to determine allowable overhead at any given level of production.

Fixed Budgets. One approach to overhead budgeting ignores the volume dependence issue entirely. This approach is called *fixed* overhead budgeting. Under a fixed-budget approach, management determines the amount of overhead which should be incurred at the normal or most likely production level. This expense total becomes the budget against which cost performance is measured, regardless of the level of production output actually achieved. To the extent that manufacturing overhead costs do vary with production, the fixed-budget approach does not yield meaningful variance data when actual output varies from planned output. There is no conceptual support for a fixed-budget approach to manufacturing overhead, but many companies still use it.

Flexible Budgets. The more conceptually sound approach to determining overhead standards in conventional cost accounting is called *flexible* budgeting. A flexible manufacturing overhead budget specifies allowable cost at each possible output level. Once a period is over and the actual production volume is known, the "flexed" cost allowance is determined by reference to the flexible budget for that level of output. This is a direct parallel to the way a budget for direct material is determined. If all manufacturing overhead is either pure "variable" or pure "fixed," a flexible budget is just a formula of the following type:

$$\text{Budget allowance} = a + bx$$

where a = fixed overhead costs for the period
b = variable overhead costs per unit
x = units produced during the period

An example of a simplified flexible budget is shown below:

Capacity Utilization:[1]	40% ...	80% ...	100% ...	
Units Produced	4,000	8,000	10,000	
Allowed Overhead				Cost Behavior
Depreciation	$1,000	$1,000	$1,000	Pure non-variable or "fixed"
Supervision	500	1,000	1,500	"Step" cost[2]
Supplies	400	800	1,000	Pure variable at $.10 per unit
Power	600	800	900	Semivariable ($400 + $.05 per unit)
Total	$2,500	$3,600	$4,400	

1 It is assumed that volume would never fall below 40% of capacity or above 100%
2 A "step" cost is one which doesn't vary directly with production but does increase in lump-sum jumps when volume rises substantially. An example would be adding a second foreman when volume rose to the level that a second shift was needed.

Flexible Budget Formula

Up to 80% of capacity: $2,400 + $.15 per unit
Above 80% utilization: $2,900 + $.15 per unit

Overhead Absorption

Under GAAP or IRS rules, manufacturing overhead is considered to be part of product costs. It is therefore necessary to find some way of charging or "absorbing" manufacturing overhead into inventory. However, the simple approach of charging actual manufacturing overhead each period directly to work-in-process (WIP) inventory is usually <u>not</u> considered to be an acceptable approach for two reasons:

1. Variances are not considered to "add value" to the inventory. Thus, overhead variances are not considered to be product costs. Thus, only *allowable* overhead is to be "inventoried."

2. Volume considerations also affect the decision of how much overhead to absorb in inventory. Suppose, for example, that depreciation is $1,000 per period. Also suppose that 1 unit is produced in period 1 and 1,000 units are produced in period 2. It doesn't seem "fair" to most accountants to say that in period one, the one unit carries a cost of $1,000 for depreciation ($1,000 depreciation ÷ 1 unit) and in period two, each unit only $1 ($1,000 depreciation ÷ 1,000 unit). A unit can't really be "more valuable" just because fewer were produced that month.

"Fair" allocation of depreciation to inventory seems to require a concept of "normal" volume. The $1,000 depreciation expense is incurred as a "reasonable" charge on the assumption that some reasonable or normal number of units will be produced on the equipment. It is this normal volume level over which the planned overhead should be spread, so the argument goes.

For these two reasons, conventional practice for charging manufacturing overhead into inventory is to use a "normal absorption rate." This rate is computed as planned overhead cost at normal production volume (per the flexible budget) divided by that normal volume. In the example above, the normal volume is 8,000 units (80% of capacity). At this level of output, budgeted overhead is $3,600. The "normal absorption rate" is thus $3,600/8,000, or $.45 per unit.

In single-product firms, output can be expressed in units of product. In multiproduct firms, however, it is necessary to set some other measure of capacity utilization, such as labor hours, labor dollars, or machine hours. The choice of a volume measure in a particular business should be based on which variable best measures the level of capacity utilization for that business.

Of course, the notion that <u>any one</u> measure of activity can capture the essence of capacity utilization across manufacturing departments ignores the richness which activity-based costing tries to capture.

The accounting works as follows. A T-account is established in the books of account called "factory overhead" or "burden" or something equivalent. Actual manufacturing overhead expenses are charged (debited) to this T-account. Overhead is absorbed into inventory by crediting the "factory overhead" account and debiting the work-in-process inventory in an amount equal to the absorption rate times the actual volume attained. In our example, if actual volume was 6,000 units, $2,700 of overhead would be charged to WIP (6,000 X $.45).

This absorption process will only "clear" the factory overhead account if two conditions are both met.

1. *If actual volume equals planned volume.* Manufacturing overhead cost does not vary directly with production. The absorption rate, however, is a pure variable rate. Thus, absorbed overhead will only equal planned overhead at one particular volume level—that level used in computing the absorption rate.

2. *If actual overhead expenses equal planned expenses per the flexible budget.* Since only budgeted overhead is absorbed, any differences between budgeted costs and actual costs will not be "cleared" from the factory overhead T-account.

At the end of any accounting period, there is usually a residual balance in the factory overhead account resulting from failure to meet one or both of these two conditions. This end-of-period residual in the factory overhead T-account is sometimes called the "book" overhead variance because it is what shows up in the books of account. It is also sometimes called the total overhead variance.

Normal accounting practice is to charge this variance to cost of goods sold for the month as a period expense.

Analyzing the Total Overhead Variance

Using the same example from above with actual production of 7,000 units, we can produce the following cost table:

Cost Item	Flexible Budget Allowance at Actual Volume of 7,000 Units	Actual Expense at Actual Volume	Spending Variance
Depreciation	$1,000	$1,100	$100U
Supervision	1,000	1,050	50U
Supplies	700	690	10F
Power	750	770	20U
Total	$3,450	$3,610	$160U

Manufacturing Overhead Absorbed into Inventory
    7000 X $.45 = $3,150

As shown in the table, the difference between actual overhead incurred and the flexible budget at this level of output is called the overhead "spending" variance. It measures cost control performance under the assumption that the flexible budget is a useful cost benchmark.

The total variance which shows up in the T-account is equal to the difference between actual overhead (the debits) and absorbed overhead at actual volume (the credit). In this example, the total variance is $460U (3610 - 3150).

The variance which is useful in measuring cost control effectiveness (the spending variance) is equal to the difference between actual overhead and allowed overhead at actual volume. For the example, this is $160U. In order to present an analysis which "balances," cost accountants need to have some name for the difference between the total variance and the spending variance. Using a little algebra, we can see that the quantity for which we need a name, "the plug," is allowed OH - absorbed OH:

Actual Minus Allowed		Allowed Minus Absorbed		Actual Minus Absorbed
Spending Variance	+	"Plug"	=	Total Variance
$160U	+	+ $300 U	=	= $460U

Regarding the plug, we have already observed that allowed OH will only equal absorbed OH when the firm operates at normal volume. Why? Because budgeted overhead does not vary directly as production varies, but absorbed overhead is purely variable, by convention. The absorption rate is set to just absorb into inventory the planned overhead when the firm actually operates at its normal volume. The idea here is that the normal absorption rate is the normal amount of manufacturing overhead each unit should carry.

Standard (absorbed) overhead cost per unit, for purposes of valuing inventories, is thus equal to a proportional share of normal overhead when production volume is at normal levels. The plug variance (allowed OH - absorbed OH) results from the difference between planned and actual production volume. It is usually called the "production volume variance." The dollar amount of this production volume variance has no particular management significance whatsoever. The dollar amount is just the plug required to reconcile a managerially significant number (the spending variance) to a number which shows up in the income statement (the total variance). The production volume variance *does* result from variation between planned and actual production volume. In this sense, the name is appropriate. However, the amount is not managerially useful—the amount is just a plug. For our example, the amount is $300U as shown above.

Going one step further, we can talk about what comprises the "plug". It does not include any variable overhead because items which are directly variable with production are treated identically in the absorption rate ($.15 per unit) and in the flexible budget ($.15 per unit). They thus cancel out in computing the difference between allowed and absorbed cost. In our illustration, for example, the absorption rate of $.45 per unit includes $.15 of variable cost and the flexible budget also includes $.15 per unit of variable cost ($.10 for supplies and $.05 for power). At actual volume of 7,000 units, therefore, both the allowed OH of $3,450 and the absorbed OH of $3,150 include $1,050 of variable cost. This $1,050 thus does not contribute anything to the difference between $3,450 and $3,150.

The difference is the fixed-cost portion of the absorption rate ($.30) times the unfavorable volume fluctuation of 1,000 units, or $300U. The $.30 fixed cost portion of the absorption rate is equal to the $2,400 of planned fixed overhead at normal volume divided by the volume measure of 8,000 units. When operating at the 7,000 unit level, we are allowed $2,400 of fixed manufacturing overhead, but we only absorb $2,100 (7,000 x $.3).

III.   MANAGERIAL USE OF VARIANCES

It is very widely assumed in "cost accounting circles" that variances calculated according to the techniques explained here in Parts I and II represent useful management information. We will summarize here the particular slant on this point of view from four of the "top 20" MBA programs as reflected in textbooks written by faculty members there.

A.   Stanford Business School (Professor Charles Horngren)

"Standard costs are the building blocks of a budgeting and feedback system. A standard cost is a carefully predetermined cost that should be attained."

"In practice, direct materials and direct labor are often said to be controlled with the help of standard costs."

"Perfect standards are expressions of the absolute minimum costs possible under the best conceivable conditions. No provision is made for waste, spoilage, machine breakdowns, and the like. Those who favor this approach maintain that the resulting unfavorable variances will constantly remind managers of the perpetual need for improvement in all phases of operations. Perfect standards are not widely used, however, because they have an adverse effect on employee motivation."

"Currently attainable standards are costs that can be achieved by a specified level of effort. Allowances are made for normal spoilage, waste, and nonproductive time. There are at least two popular interpretations of the meaning of 'currently attainable' standards. The first interpretation has standards set just tightly enough so that employees regard their fulfillment as highly probable if normal effort and diligence are exercised. That is, variances should be negligible. A second interpretation of currently attainable standards is that standards are set tightly. That is, employees regard their fulfillment as possible, though unlikely."

"Managers responsible for variances should be required to explain them. In addition, managers who have control over the causes of the variances should be held accountable for avoiding unfavorable variances or correcting the factors causing them. The primary function of variances is explanation. The main goal is to understand what is affecting costs and revenues so that managers can make better decisions in the future."

"Variances do not, by themselves show why the budget (standard) was not achieved. But they raise questions, provide clues, and direct attention."

"Because there are so many interdependences among activities, a variance should not lead a manager to jump to conclusions. By themselves, such variances merely raise questions and provide clues. They are attention directors, not answer givers."

B.   Colgate - Darden Business School (Professors Brandt Allen and William Rotch)

"There are three important ways in which standard costing systems assist management:

1.   The automatic built-in provision of variances helps identify areas that need management's attention.

2.   The development of a data base of standard costs and quantities supports pricing decisions and helps the overall planning process.

3.   The use of standard product costs simplifies inventory accounting."

C.   The Vanderbilt Business School (Professor Germain Boer)

"A standard, as defined by the Oxford English Dictionary, is a definite level of excellence or a definite degree of quality, viewed as a prescribed object of endeavor or a measure of what is adequate for some purpose. A standard, as used in management accounting, is a predetermined cost."

"The primary purpose of standards is to measure the difference between what costs are and what costs should be for the purpose of controlling costs. In a more general sense, the benefits of standards can be classified as follows:

1.   Better control over costs and thus income through the identification of variances between actual and standard costs.

2.   More informative income statements which can illustrate the profit impact of variances by showing excess costs as waste and cost savings as gains.

3.   Ease and expedition of cost accounting since all inventories can be valued at standard.

4.   Basic data are provided for planning and special studies.

5.   Other benefits include:

    a.   The planning required to set-up standards.
    b.   Coordination and cooperation is enhanced by and within all areas.
    c.   Standards set total and individual goals."

"Standards should be based on a scientific study of the quantities of material and units of labor which should be used to produce the product; that is, they should be engineered standards. The setting of standards is the responsibility of the technical staff of a plant, such as industrial engineers, design engineers, and chemists. Unless the supervisor agrees that a standard is fair, their reaction to variances will be defensive rather than corrective. After the standard quantities are set, they are normally submitted to the accountants for conversion into standard costs."

"Two types of standards have been found acceptable for cost control purposes: (1) the attainable standard, and (2) the perfect standard. The former can be used for cost control and for the development of standard costs. The latter is used only for cost control and may supplement the use of attainable standards. The basic consideration in selecting either or both types is how well they will serve the purposes of cost control."

"Attainable direct materials standards are based on the type and quantity of material which should be used to produce a finished product of specified quality. Allowance is made for normal losses in initial processing, and considering this, the yield in quantity of finished or semi-finished product is determined."

"When standard costs are used, allowances are set for spoilage at each operation."

"Under a standard cost system, a standard percentage of total production is set as the quantity of seconds expected to be produced."

"From practical experience, it is evident that perfect operation can never be attained. Thus, perfect standards should be taken as the direction in which attainable standards should move."

D.   **Cornell Business School (Professor Ronald Hilton)**

"Standards should not be determined by the managerial accountant alone. People generally will be more committed to meeting standards if they are allowed to participate in setting them."

"Some managers believe that perfect standards motivate employees to achieve the lowest cost possible. They claim that since the standard is theoretically attainable, employees will have an incentive to come as close as possible to achieving it.

    Other managers and many behavioral scientists disagree. They feel that perfect standards discourage employees, since they are so unlikely to be attained. Moreover, setting unrealistically difficult standards may encourage employees to sacrifice product quality to achieve lower costs. By skimping on raw-material quality or the attention given manual production tasks, employees may be able to lower the production cost. However, this lower cost may come at the expense of a higher rate of defective units. Thus, the firm ultimately may incur higher costs than necessary as defective products are returned by customers or scrapped upon inspection."

"Practical standards allow for such occurrences as occasional machine breakdowns and normal amounts of raw-material waste. Attaining a practical standard keeps employees on their toes, without demanding miracles. Most behavioral theorists believe that practical standards encourage more positive and productive employee attitudes then do perfect standards."

"Standard costs and variance analysis are useful in diagnosing organizational performance. These tools help managers to discern 'the story behind the story' - the details of operations that underlie reported cost and profit numbers. Standard costs, budgets, and variances are also used to evaluate the performance of individuals and departments. The performance of individuals, relative to standards or budgets, often is used to help determine salary increases, bonuses, and promotions. When standards and variances affect employee reward structures, they can profoundly influence behavior."

"A standard-costing system offers six clear advantages if used properly:

1.   Standard costs provide a basis for sensible cost comparisons. It would make no sense to compare budgeted costs at one (planned) activity level with actual costs incurred at a different (actual) activity level. Standard costs enable the managerial accountant to compute the standard allowed cost, given actual output, which then serves as a sensible benchmark to compare with the actual cost.

2.   Computation of standard costs and cost variances enables managers to employ management by exception. This approach conserves valuable management time.

3.   Variances provide a means of performance evaluation and rewards for employees.

4.   Since the variances are used in performance evaluation, they provide motivation for employees to adhere to standards.

5.   Use of standard costs in product costing results in more stable product costs than if actual production costs were used. Actual costs often fluctuate erratically, whereas standard costs are changed only periodically.

6.   A standard-costing system is usually less expensive than an actual costing system.

IV. A FINAL THOUGHT

It is problematic today whether this point of view from section III—standard costs and variances are useful to management—represents best thinking in the 1990s or merely a 1990s recapitulation of best thinking in the 1960s. Exploring this dilemma is beyond the scope of this note.

Reichard Maschinen, GmbH*

This case is set in Western Europe in 1974, just after the Arab oil shocks of 1972 and 1973. National borders were still very important business barriers. But, the concept of open trade borders (EC-1992) was beginning to grow.

In June of 1974, Mr. Kurtz, managing director of the Grinding Machines Division (GMD) of Reichard Machines, was considering how he should handle a meeting that afternoon that would involve his sales manager, his controller, and his product engineering manager. The meeting concerned the introduction by a Belgian competitor, Bruggeman Grinders, SA, of plastic rings to take the place of steel rings which were a standard component in many grinding machines, including many of the machines made and sold by GMD.

The new plastic rings, which had only been introduced in April, not only appeared to have a much longer life than the steel rings, but also apparently were much less expensive to manufacture. Mr. Kurtz' problem in responding to the new ring was complicated by the fact that he had 25,000 steel rings in inventory and 26 tons of special alloy steel purchased recently for the sole purpose of making more rings. He knew that this raw steel could not even be sold as scrap because of the special alloys in it. He had been required to buy a full year's supply in order to convince a steel mill to make the special product. Overall, he was holding about $93,000 worth of inventory related to steel rings (see Exhibit 1).

For almost 100 years, Reichard had manufactured industrial machines which it sold throughout Europe and North America. It enjoyed a reputation for high quality, technology leadership, and excellent customer service. There were dozens of companies of all sizes who competed, one way or another, in industrial machines in Europe. Reichard was one of the leaders in several segments. Each division operated as a fairly autonomous profit center. Corporate management, headquartered in Frankfurt, operated mainly as a holding company.

The Grinding Machine Division (GMD) had about a ten percent marketshare in Europe, its principal market area. GMD's one plant was located in Cologne and employed 400 production workers. Its different models were priced between $4500 and $7000, averaging about $6000. The machines were used in metal working plants in many industries. Their useful life was about ten years with normal maintenance.

---

* This case is adapted by Professor John Shank of the Amos Tuck School from an earlier case published by IMEDE (now IMD in Lausanne, Switzerland) and revised by Professor M. Edgar Barrett of the American International Graduate School.

Replacement parts in aggregate accounted for more than half of GMD's turnover. As is common for industrial machinery, margins on machine sales are often reduced in anticipation of higher margins on replacement parts over the life of the machine. This creates the opportunity for price discounting by parts suppliers on those replacement parts which are interchangeable across models and across manufacturers. The steel rings were one of the standard component items which were interchangeable.

In recent years Japanese manufacturers had entered Reichard's markets with lower priced spare parts. Other companies had entered with lower quality and lower priced machines and parts. Kurtz felt sure that competition would continue to intensify in the future. But, he was fully committed to Reichard's strategy of high quality, innovation and excellent service, at a price.

The steel rings manufactured by GMD had a useful life of about two months under normal machine use. A worn-out ring could be replaced in a minute or two. Different machine models required from two to six rings, but the average was four rings per machine. Usually, rings were replaced one at a time, as they were worn-out.

The sales manager, Mr. Goerner had learned of the new plastic ring almost immediately after its appearance and had asked when GMD would be able to supply them, particularly for sale to customers in Belgium where Bruggeman was the strongest competitor. In mid-May Mr. Hainz, the development engineer, estimated that the factory could be ready to produce plastic rings by mid- September. The factory already had a plastics injection molding department. The additional molds and tooling necessary could be produced for about $10,000, but would have to be specially designed which would take a few months.

At this point Mr. Hainz had raised the question about the investment in steel ring inventories which would not be used up by the end of September. Mr. Goerner said that if the new ring could be produced at a substantially lower cost than steel, the inventory problem was irrelevant. The steel inventory should be sold for whatever could be obtained or even thrown away if it could not be sold.

Mr. Goerner stated that Bruggeman was selling the plastic ring for about $340. per hundred. This was $15. per hundred higher than the price of GMD's steel ring even though the manufacturing cost of the plastic was much less. Goerner wanted the company to prepare to manufacture the new ring as soon as possible. Hainz suggested that until the steel inventories were exhausted, they could be sold only in those markets where plastic rings were not offered by competitors. No one expected that the new plastic rings would be produced by any company other than Bruggeman for some time. This meant that no more than 10% of GMD's markets would be effected.

In late May, Mr. Metz of the headquarter group in Frankfurt visited Cologne. During a review of GMD's problems, the plastic ring case was discussed. Although the ring was a very small part of the finished machines, Mr. Metz was interested in the problem because the holding company wanted all divisions to establish comparable policies for the production and pricing of all such parts. Mr. Metz pointed out to Mr. Kurtz that replacement parts pricing and availability was a critical component of Reichard's business strategy. Metz saw no problem with GMD getting ready to produce plastic rings, although he was skeptical of the market acceptance of such a product. But, he added, "I would certainly expect you to recover your investment in steel inventory." Mr. Kurtz understood that he would need a very good story if he decided to scrap any of the steel rings or raw material.

A few days after Mr. Metz' visit, both Mr. Hainz and Mr. Goerner came in to see Mr. Kurtz. The former came because he felt that the plastic ring would completely destroy demand for the steel ring. New tests had indicated that plastic had at least four times the wearing properties. However, because the price of the competitive ring was very high, he felt that the decision to sell the plastic ring only in Bruggeman's market area was a good one. "In this way we would probably be able to continue supplying the steel ring until stocks, at least of processed parts, were used up."

Goerner said he was still strongly against selling any steel rings after the new plastic ones became available. If the higher quality plastic rings were only being sold in some areas, customers would soon find out. The result would affect the sale of machines, the selling price of which was many times that of the rings. He produced figures to show that even if the selling price of both rings were the same at $325 per hundred, the additional profit from plastic rings, which would cost $66.60 per hundred as contrasted with $263.85 per hundred for steel rings, would more than cover the "so-called" investment in the steel inventory in little more than a year at present volume levels.

Mr. Kurtz did not commit himself to a decision, but agreed to have another discussion in a week. In anticipation of the meeting, Kurtz obtained the following cost information from his controller comparing plastic and steel rings:

| | Per 100 Rings | |
	Plastic	Steel
Material	$4.20	$76.65
Direct Labor	15.60	46.80
Overhead*		
Manufacturing	31.20	93.60
Selling & Admin.	15.60	46.80
Total	$66.60	$263.85

* Overhead was allocated to all products on the basis of direct labor dollars. Manufacturing overhead was allocated at 200% of direct labor, and selling and administration overhead at 100%. The controller estimated that the only variable overhead costs for ring production would be the payroll taxes and benefits related to direct labor (approximately 80% of labor cost).

Mr. Kurtz learned that the raw steel inventory on hand was sufficient to produce approximately 34,500 more rings (See Exhibit 1). Assuming that sales continued at the current rate of 690 rings per week, some 15,000 finished rings would be left on hand by mid-September without any further production taking place. It then occurred to him that during the next two or three months the plant would not be operating at capacity. The company had a policy of employing its excess labor during slack periods at about 70% of regular wages on various make-work projects rather than laying workers off. He wondered if it would be a good idea to commit additional resources now to the steel rings by converting the raw steel inventory into rings during this period and use some of this slack labor productively. If workers produced rings, they would be paid full wage rates.

ASSIGNMENT

1) What is the "differential" or "incremental" cost to produce 100 plastic rings?

2) What is the "incremental" cost, per 100 rings, to produce the next 34,500 steel rings?

3) What is the "differential" cost of the 25,450 steel rings which are already in inventory at the end of May?

4) Which is more profitable, the steel rings or the plastic rings? Be prepared to show the calculations which support your answer.

5) What actions do you recommend to Mr. Kurtz regarding

- manufacture of plastic rings
- further manufacture of steel rings
- pricing of steel and plastic rings
- availability of steel and plastic rings over the next 1 to 2 years
- longer-run availability and pricing of steel and plastic rings

6) Assess the likely impact of your recommendations, both quantitatively and qualitatively.

EXHIBIT 1

MEMORANDUM

To:	Mr. Kurtz, Managing Director
FROM:	Mr. Politzer, Controller
RE:	Steel Inventory for Rings
DATE:	31.5.74

	Units	$
Finished Rings in Inventory	25,450	$67,149 (*)
Raw Steel in Inventory	34,500	26,400
(*) 254.5 x $263.85	59,950	$93,549

1) If we convert the raw steel to rings, the total of 59,950 would last about 87 weeks at our current sales rate of about 690 rings per week.

2) If we do not produce any more steel rings, we will have about 15,000 rings in inventory in September when we would be ready to begin producing and selling plastic rings.

3) We have exhausted all possible sources for selling this raw steel in bulk. Because of its special chemistry, it has no value to anyone else.

4) During our normal summer slowdown period (July and August), the factory could convert all the raw steel to finished rings, if you wish.

Ringo Rag Company*

The setting for this case is Columbus, Ohio in the early 1950s. The numbers in the case have not been updated because there is no way to do so without changing one or more of the interrelationships which make the case so useful from a pedagogical standpoint. In tackling the case, keep in mind that when it was "current," an hourly wage of $1.10 was reasonable and a new Thunderbird sold for $3,232. In terms of the managerial issues involved, it is still an excellent case for the 1990s.

The Ringo Rag Company purchases scrap cotton fabric which is then converted into handy cleaning rags in usable sizes, after it is cleaned and graded. Main customers for these rags are garages, service stations, factories, and machine shops. The company buys its rags from three sources: textile converters, commercial laundries, and junk dealers.

The production process for the company is not complicated. First, rags purchased from junk dealers are washed and dried in special heavy duty machines. The cleaned rags and those purchased from laundries, which are already washed, move next to the grading department. Here, each rag is inspected and graded according to its absorption ability as either A, B, or C quality, with A as the best grade. Textile converters sell their "spoils" (rags) clean and already graded. Next, the rags are cut into squares of about 1 to 1 1/2 feet. At the same time, any attached items such as buttons, metal ornaments, or snaps are removed. Rags purchased from textile converters do not have anything attached to them. Pieces of material which are too small for further cutting or contain holes or are not usable for any other reason are burned. The cut rags are then packaged in 5, 10, 20, and 50 pound cartons.

Selling prices are as follows (quoted FOB warehouse):

| | Carton Size | | | |
Quality	5 lb	10 lb	20 lb	50 lb
C	$.70	$1.30	$2.40	$5.00
B	.75	1.40	2.60	5.50
A	.90	1.70	3.20	7.00

---

* This case is adapted by Professor John Shank of The Amos Tuck School, with permission, from an earlier version prepared by Professor Felix Kollaritsch of The Ohio State University.

Raw material costs vary by source. Textile converters charge $6.00, $5.00, and $4.00 per cwt (hundred weight) for grades A, B, and C, respectively. Twenty percent of the weight purchased is lost as waste during the cutting process. This is referred to as "loss factor." Last month, the following quantities were purchased from textile converters:

Grade A	43,750 lb
Grade B	25,000 lb
Grade C	6,250 lb

Although each purchase was a little different, the company usually had to agree to take some quantity of C grade fabric when it bought A grade fabric.

Laundries charge $3.00 per cwt. Past experience indicates a 33.33% loss factor. The yield ratio of material from the laundries is typically about 1/4 grade A, 1/2 grade B, and 1/4 grade C. Last month, Ringo purchased 60,000 pounds of material from laundries.

The highest loss factor is incurred from material purchased from junk dealers, where it amounts to 50%. The junk dealers' price for material is $1.00 per cwt. Last month, the company purchased 50,000 pounds from this source. This ungraded material usually yields about 1/5 grade A, 2/5 grade B, and 2/5 grade C rags. For the rags purchased from junk dealers and laundries, about half of the overall loss occurs in grading and about half in cutting.

The company employs twenty-five women, each of whom is paid $1.10 per hour. Last month's time cards indicate that their time was spent as follows:

Grading	1,000 hrs
Cutting	3,000 hrs.
Packing	600 hrs.
Total	4,600 hrs.

Last month's production and sales (cleaned, cut, and boxed), in pounds, was:

		Sold	
	Produced	Pounds	$
Grade A	50,000	50,000	7,750
Grade B	50,000	50,000	6,500
Grade C	25,000	25,000	3,125
Total	125,000	125,000	17,375

All sales are local, and orders are received by phone or mail.

Last month's production activities, sources of materials, prices, costs, and yields are representative of normal operations. Sales usually follow production very closely, with very little seasonal fluctuation.

Two foremen are employed by the company, each paid $7,500 per year. Both are nephews of Mr. Ringo. One-fourth of their time is spent loading and unloading the washers and dryers. Another quarter of their time is spent moving packed boxes to the loading zone of the building for shipment. The balance of their time is spent supervising and checking the women.

The two washer and dryer sets owned by the company are depreciated over 5 years on a straight-line basis. Each set has a capacity of 100 pounds per load and can cycle about 16 loads during a working day.

Expenses other than raw material and labor for a typical year are as follows:

Depreciation	$3,060	($760 washer and dryer; $300 cutting machines and tables; $2,000 for two cars[a]).
Natural Gas	600	(Used for the dryers)
Electricity	480	(3/4 is attributable to the washers and dryers, 1/4 to cutting)
Rent	3,200	(Leased building[b])
Detergent (for the washers)	1,000	
Bookkeeper/ Secretary	4,100	
Gasoline and Oil (for cars)	400	(about $.01 per mile)
Travel (Lodging and Meals)	6,000	(Half for purchasing, half for selling)
Packing cartons	7,200	(5 and 10 lb. boxes at $.07 each, and 20 and 50 lb. boxes at $.10 each)
Miscellaneous Expenses	1,200	

[a]One car is used in selling, the other in purchasing.
[b]The building is used as follows: 1/4 for storing unprocessed rags (average about 1 month's purchases), 1/4 for storing boxed rags (about one month's sales), 1/4 for cutting, and 1/8 each for grading and cleaning. One room used as an office is not counted in the building usage.

The company is organized as a partnership between Mr. James Ringo, who acts as purchasing agent and president, and Mr. John Wall who handles all sales. Before forming their partnership 6 years ago, Mr. Ringo was purchasing manager for a paper mill which produced fine rag-content papers. Mr. Wall had been responsible for waste products sales for a large clothing manufacturer.

This case was written as part of a student project to provide cost analysis and business advice for the company. Mr. Ringo said he agreed to the project because he had no formal cost accounting records at all. He said he and Mr. Wall ran the business pretty much on their intuition and they often wondered whether there might be more profitable ways to do things.

For example, Mr. Wall had asked him once why he bothered to sort the junk rags at all since almost half of them are C grade anyway. He didn't really have a good answer, and the question had led him to wonder whether he shouldn't perhaps drop the junk source altogether when the washer/dryers wore out in a few years. He liked the idea of having several sources for raw material so he could shop around to keep his purchase prices low, but he couldn't prove to himself whether he was buying the right mix.

He and Mr. Wall had built up a good set of steady customers over the years with good service and good quality at competitive prices. But they had no idea which products were most profitable.

ASSIGNMENT

Your first task is to prepare a cost analysis for each of the 5 different purchased items. We suggest you start as follows:

1. Calculate average revenue per pound, by grade.

2. Calculate weighted average revenue per pound for each source.

3. Calculate raw material cost per pound sold, for each source.

4. Calculate direct labor cost per pound sold for:
   a. grading
   b. cutting | consider yields carefully

5. Calculate packing cost (labor and material) per pound sold.

6. Calculate variable overhead per pound sold for the junk source.

7. Assign fixed overhead costs to each purchasing source.

   first, assign costs to functions
   then calculate cost per pound produced at that function
   then convert to yielded pounds sold

8. Items 1 to 5 represent profit contribution by source.

9. Items 1 to 6 represent full cost profit by source.

Now, what does this have to do with the management issues? Specifically:

1. Can you calculate short run and long run profitability by purchasing source? Is this a useful calculation?

2. Can you calculate profitability by grade? Is this information useful?

3. What is your recommendation regarding selling all cleaned, cut and packaged junk rags as C grade, without sorting?

4. What other recommendations do you have for Mr. Ringo?

5. As an overall assessment, is this business in serious need of your help, or not?

Sheridan Carpet Company*

This case is set in the automotive carpeting business in 1983. The issue is cost analysis for pricing.

Sheridan Carpet Company produced high-grade carpeting materials for use in automobiles and recreational vans. Sheridan's products were sold to finishers, who cut and bound the material so as to fit perfectly in the passenger compartment or cargo area (e.g., automobile trunk) of a specific model automobile or van. Some of these finishers were captive operations of major automobile assembly divisions, particularly those that assembled the "top of the line" cars that included high-grade carpeting. Other finishers concentrated on the replacement and van customizing markets.

Late in 1982, the marketing manager and chief accountant of Sheridan met to decide on the list price for carpet number 104. It was industry practice to announce prices just prior to the January-June and July-December "seasons." Over the years, companies in the industry had adhered to their announced prices throughout a six-month season unless significant unexpected changes in costs occurred. Sales of carpet 104 were not affected by seasonal factors during the two six-month seasons.

Sheridan was the largest company in its segment of the automobile carpet industry. Its 1981 sales had been over $40 million. Sheridan's salespersons were on a salary basis, and each one sold the entire product line. Most of Sheridan's competitors were smaller than Sheridan. Accordingly, they usually awaited Sheridan's price announcement before setting their own selling prices.

Carpet 104 had an especially dense nap. As a result, making it required a special machine, and it was produced in a department whose equipment could not be used to produce Sheridan's other carpets. Effective January 1, 1982, Sheridan had raised its price on this carpet from $3.90 to $5.20 per square yard. This had been done in order to bring 104's margin up to that of the other carpets in the line. Although Sheridan was financially sound, it expected a large funds need in the next few years for equipment replacement and plant expansion. The 1982 price increase was one of several decisions made in order to provide funds for these plans.

EXHIBIT 1
CARPET 104: PRICES AND PRODUCTION, 1980-1982

Selling Season*	Production Volume (square yards)		Price (per square yard)	
	Industry Total	Sheridan Carpet	Most Competitors	Sheridan Carpet
1980-1	549,000	192,000	$5.20	$5.20
1980-2	517,500	181,000	5.20	5.20
1981-1	387,000	135,500	3.90	3.90
1981-2	427,500	149,500	3.90	3.90
1982-1	450,000	135,000	3.90	5.20
1982-2	562,500	112,500	3.90	5.20

*198x-1 means the first 6 months of 198x; 198x-2 means the second six months of 198x.

---

* Reprinted from Accounting: Text and Cases, Anthony & Reece, 7th ed, 1983, by permission of Prof. James S. Reece.

Sheridan's competitors, however, had held their 1982 prices at $3.90 on carpets competitive with 104. As shown in Exhibit 1, which includes estimates of industry volume on these carpets, Sheridan's price increase had apparently resulted in a loss of market share. The marketing manager, Mel Walters, estimated that the industry would sell about 630,000 square yards of these carpets in the first half of 1983. Walters was sure Sheridan could sell 150,000 yards if it dropped the price of 104 back to $3.90. But if Sheridan held its price at $5.20, Walters feared a further erosion in Sheridan's share. However, because some customers felt that 104 was superior to competitive products, Walters felt that Sheridan could sell at least 65,000 yards at the $5.20 price.

During their discussion, Walters and the chief accountant, Terry Rosen, identified two other aspects of the pricing decision. Rosen wondered whether competitors would announce a further price decrease if Sheridan dropped back to $3.90. Walters felt it was unlikely that competitors would price below $3.90, because none of them was more efficient than Sheridan, and there were rumors that several of them were in poor financial condition. Rosen's other concern was whether a decision relating to carpet 104 would have any impact on the sales of Sheridan's other carpets. Walters was convinced that since 104 was a specialized item, there was no interdependence between its sales and those of other carpets in the line.

Exhibit 2 contains cost estimates that Rosen has prepared for various volumes of 104. These estimates represented Rosen's best guesses as to costs during the first six months of 1983, based on past cost experience and anticipated inflation.

QUESTIONS

1. Assuming no intermediate prices are to be considered, should Sheridan price 104 at $3.90 or $5.20?

2. If Sheridan's competitors hold their prices at $3.90, how many square yards of 104 would Sheridan need to sell at a price of $5.20 in order to earn the same profit as selling 150,000 square yards at a price of $3.90?

3. What additional information would you wish to have before making this pricing decision? (Despite the absence of this information, still answer Question 1!)

4. With hindsight, was the decision to raise the price in January of 1982 a good one?

EXHIBIT 2
ESTIMATED COST OF CARPET 104 AT VARIOUS PRODUCTION VOLUMES
First Six Months of 1983

Costs/sq. yd.	Volume (square yards)					
	65,000	87,500	110,000	150,000	185,000	220,000
Raw materials	$0.520	$0.520	$0.520	$0.520	$0.520	$0.520
Materials spoilage	0.052	0.051	0.049	0.049	0.051	0.052
Direct labor	1.026	0.989	0.979	0.962	0.975	0.997
Department overhead:						
Direct*	0.142	0.136	0.131	0.130	0.130	0.130
Indirect (A)	1.200	0.891	0.709	0.520	0.422	0.355
General overhead (B)	0.308	0.297	0.294	0.289	0.293	0.299
Factory cost	3.248	2.884	2.682	2.470	2.391	2.353
Selling and administrative (C)	2.111	1.875	1.743	1.606	1.554	1.529
Total cost	$5.359	$4.759	$4.425	$4.076	$3.945	$3.882

*Materials handlers, supplies, repairs, power, fringe benefits.
(A) Supervision, equipment depreciation, heat and light.
(B) 30 percent of direct labor.
(C) 65 percent of factory cost.

Societé Bonlieu*

This case is set in a carpentry job shop in Grenoble, France in 1956 in the midst of the post-WWII construction boom. The issues it addresses are timeless.

Mr. Bonlieu, owner of a small carpentry business, was concerned about his accounting system. He felt he was in danger of losing sales of desks, which made up nearly half of his business, because his prices were too high. Yet, according to his accounting figures, his margin on these desks was very low. At the same time, competitors were accusing him of selling staircases, another of his products, below cost. Yet his margin on staircases was apparently good.

Mr. Bonlieu was a sub-contractor for furniture dealers and manufacturers, who supplied him with the lumber for each order. In October, 1956, the plant consisted of a lumber warehouse, a kiln (drying oven), a drafting room, a machine shop, and an assembly shop. He had acquired the drying oven two years elarier to enable him to offer his customers the option of supplying him with "green" wood if they preferred.

The accounting system then in use was a simple "job order" system. Direct labor was charged on the basis of actual labor costs incurred on each job in the drafting, machine and assembly shops. Supplies, such as screws and varnish, were similarly charged to each job on the basis of actual consumption. All other expenses—"overhead"—was allocated to jobs as a percentage of the direct labor cost charged to the job. Selling expense was charged in proportion to the sales value of each job.

In the quarter ended September, 1956, five jobs had been started, completed, and delivered. No other jobs had been worked on. Although this mix of jobs was not unusual, the actual mix changed substantially, quarter by quarter. Costs for the quarter are shown in Exhibit 1. The assignment of costs to jobs is shown in Exhibit 2.

One thing which struck Mr. Bonlieu about the cost calculations was the magnitude of overhead costs in relation to labor costs. Great care was taken in recording and assigning labor, yet overhead expenses, which were much larger in total, were allocated with very basic and simple rules. He suspected that this caused distortions in the costs charged to various jobs and was the explanation for the apparent discrepancies in his prices. Accordingly, he sought the advice of a consultant.

The consultant's report advised setting up eight cost centers -- five production centers (warehouse, drying oven, drafting shop, machine shop, and assembly shop), two overhead centers (administration and indirect labor), and a selling expense center.

Where possible, costs would be assigned directly to the center in which they were incurred. Thus coal costs were charged entirely to the oven, power entirely to the machine shop, and car expense entirely to selling. Building expenses were to be allocated on the basis of floor space used, as follows: 20% to the warehouse, 30% to the drying oven, 10% to drafting, 15% to machining, and 25% to assembly. Office expense was to be allocated on the basis of wage and salary costs.

---

* This case is adapted by Professor John Shank of The Amos Tuck School, with permission, from an earlier version copyrighted in 1957 by IMEDE in Lausanne, Switzerland (now IMD).

Depreciation of equipment was to be charged on the basis of the cost center in which the equipment was used. Thus the oven was to carry ffr. 300,000, and the machine shop ffr. 430,000 for each quarter. Interest expense was to be allocated to the items which had been purchased with the borrowed funds. The machine shop was responsible for ffr. 8,600,000 of the debt, the drying oven for ffr. 4,800,000, and the delivery truck for ffr. 600,000.

After all costs had been assigned to cost centers, the administrative and indirect labor centers were to be closed out to the five production centers and to sales expense. Administrative expense was to be allocated 25% to selling expense, and the remaining 75% to the production departments on the basis of direct labor. Indirect labor was to be allocated to the five production departments, also on the basis of direct labor. The warehouseman and the oven attendant were to be re-classified as direct labor.

The next step was to assign costs in the remaining 6 cost centers to jobs on the basis of "activity measures" in each center, as follows:

Cost Center	Activity Measures
Warehouse	m^3 of lumber used
Oven	m^3 of lumber dried
Drafting	Direct labor hours
Machinery	Direct labor hours
Assembly	Direct labor hours
Selling	Sales value

Exhibit 3 is a worksheet for assigning costs for the third quarter of 1956 on the above basis to generate the cost center rates which this accounting system uses.

In order to apply these rates to specific jobs, Mr. Bonlieu gathered the information shown in Exhibit 4.

ASSIGNMENT

1. Complete Exhibit 3 according to the consultant's proposal. Make sure you understand the logic and the calculations required. Appendix A is a completed version of the Exhibit to facilitate your preparation.

2. Use the costs per activity unit from the bottom of Exhibit 3 and the activity quantities from Exhibit 4 to work out the costs and profits of Orders 28 and 32, according to the new accounting system.

3. Is the new system "better"? Should Mr. Bonlieu adopt the new accounting system?

4. Should Mr. Bonlieu change his prices because of the results obtained in Question 2?

5. Mr. Bonlieu has the opportunity to sell 12 more staircases at the same unit price as in Order 28. (He has sufficient capacity.) Should he accept the order?

6. What other advice do you have for Mr. Bonlieu? (Hint: What is Mr. Bonlieu's business strategy and what does that have to do with the case? How is he doing, financially?)

Exhibit 1
Cost Data for the Quarter Ending
September 30, 1956
(in French Francs)

Direct Labor

Drafting room	270,000	
Machine shop	740,000	
Assembly shop	256,000	
Subtotal	1,266,000	

Other Wages & Salaries

Foreman & indirect workers	450,000	
Warehouseman	90,000	
Oven attendant	90,000	
Administrative & management personnel	978,000	
Delivery driver	126,000	
	1,734,000	

Total Wages & Salaries		3,000,000

Other Expense

Supplies	144,000
Coal for the oven	80,000
Power	36,000
Sales commissions	154,000
Truck expense (depreciation, garage)	50,000
Building expense (rent, insurance and taxes)	330,000
Office expense (postage, telephone, etc.)	198,000
Interest on equipment loans (ffr. 14,000,000 at 6% per annum)	210,000
Depreciation of equipment	730,000
Total	4,932,000

Recap:

Supplies	144,000	Overhead Rate:	
Direct Labor	1,266,000	3192/1266 = 252%	
Selling	330,000	Selling Cost Rate:	
All other	3,192,000	330/5472 = 6.03%	
	4,932,000		

Exhibit 2

Cost Data for Quarter Ending September, 1956
(000s French Francs)

	Order 27 50 Windows	Order 28 4 Staircases	Order 32 172 Desks	Order 35 130m² Floors	Order 36 20,000 Wood soles¹	TOTAL
Drafting at ffr. 180/hr.	16.2	18.0	100.8	9.0	126.0	270
Machining at ffr. 185/hr.	64.7	101.8	370.0	18.5	185.0	740
Assembly at ffr. 160/hr.	64.0	48.0	112.0	32.0	--	256
Total Labor	144.9	167.8	582.8	59.5	311.0	1,266
Overhead (at 252% of Labor)	365.3	423.2	1,469.4	150.0	784.1	3,192
Supplies	60.0	48.0	30.0	6.0	--	144
Subtotal	570.2	639.0	2,082.2	215.5	1,095.1	4,602
Selling expense (at 6.03% of Sales)	40.1	61.9	136.3	14.9	76.8	330
Total Cost	610.3	700.9	2,218.5	230.4	1,171.9	4,932
Selling Price	665.0	1,026.0	2,261.0	247.0	1,273.0	5,472
Profit	54.7	325.1	42.5	16.6	101.1	540
% Profit Margin	8.2%	31.7%	1.8%	7.0%	7.9%	9.8%

1 Wood "soles" are the pieces at the bottom of door frames and window frames. They are often made from pieces of scrap wood left from other orders. A typical wood sole is about 1m long by 2.5 cm thick by 7.5 cm wide.

Exhibit 3

Assignment of Costs to Cost Centers
(000s of French Francs)

	Cost to Allocate	Administrt. Expense	Indirect Labor	Warehouse	Oven	Drafting	Machinery	Assembly	Selling
Wages & salaries	3,000								
Coal	80								
Power	36								
Commissions	154	—	—	—	—	—	—	—	—
Building expense	330	—	—	—	—	—	—	—	—
Office expense	198	—	—	—	—	—	—	—	
Depreciation - equipment	730	—	—	—	—	—	—	—	—
Truck expense	50	—	—	—					—
Interest expense	210	—	—	—					—
Total	4,788								
Administrative expense		(							
Indirect labor		(	(—						—
Total assigned									
Activity measures				m3	m3	DL.hrs	DL.hrs	DL.hrs.	Sales in Francs
Activity units				140	140	1,500	4,000	1,600	5,472,000
Cost per activity unit (000s ffr.)									

Exhibit 4

Supplementary Cost Data
Resource Usage Across the September Quarter Job Mix

Cost Centers	Activity Units	Order No. 27 50 Windows	Order No. 28 4 Staircases	Order No. 32 170 Desks	Order No. 35 130m² Floors	Order No. 36 20,000 Woodsoles	TOTAL
Warehouse	m³	10	80	25	5	20	140
Oven	m³	10	80	25	5	20	140
Drafting	DL.hrs.	90	100	560	50	700	1,500
Machining	DL.hrs.	350	550	2,000	100	1000	4,000
Assembly	DL.hrs.	400	300	700	200	--	1,600
Selling	Actual Sales ffr.	665,000	1,026,000	2,261,000	247,000	1,273,000	5,472,000
Supplies	Actual use ffr.	60,000	48,000	30,000	6,000	--	144,000

APPENDIX A
A Completed Version of Case Exhibit 3
Assignment of Costs to Cost Centers
(000s of French Francs)

	Cost to Allocate	Administr. Expense	Indirect Labor	Warehouse	Oven	Drafting	Machinery	Assembly	Selling
Wages & salaries	3,000	978	450	90	90	270	740	256	126
Coal	80	--	--	--	80	--	--	--	--
Power	36	--	--	--	--	--	36	--	--
Commissions	154	--	--	--	--	--	--	--	154
Building expense	330	--	--	66	99	33	49	83	--
Office expense	198	65	30	6	6	18	48	17	8
Depreciation - equipment	730	--	--	--	300	--	430	--	--
Truck expense	50	--	--	--	--	--	--	--	50
Interest on expense	210	--	--	--	72	--	129	--	9
Total	4,788	1,043	480	162	647	321	1,432	356	347
Administrative expense		(1,043)		49	49	147	400	137	261
Indirect labor			(480)	30	30	90	245	85	--
Total assigned				241	726	558	2,077	578	608
Activity measures				m3	m3	DL.hrs	DL.hrs	DL.hrs	Sales in Francs
Activity units				140	140	1,500	4,000	1,600	5,472,000
Cost per activity unit (000s ffr.)				1.72	5.18	0.372	0.519	0.361	0.111

Tashtego*

Should the motor vessel Tashtego be used as a freight tender between Dar-es-Salaam and Zanzibar in East Africa or as a tapioca ship between Balik Papan and Singapore in the East Indies? Or, is this too narrow a view of the management issue involved?

Macedonian Shipping (MS) typically purchased one or two ships each year. In 1963 MS bought only the Tashtego. She was launched in October. The ship was named for the Wampanoag Indian from Martha's Vineyard who was second harpooner on the whaling ship Pequod in Melville's novel, Moby Dick. In contrast to the other 27 vessels of the fleet which were all of about 12,500 tons burden, the Tashtego was a small ship of only 4,500 tons (the burden of a freighter is the weight of freight of standard bulk it can carry). It had been acquired to allow Macedonian Shipping to compete on the tapioca trade between Balik Papan in South Borneo and Singapore. There was essentially unlimited tapioca for export out of Balik Papan, but the harbor channel was such that only small vessels like the Tashtego could get in. Tashtego was making 50 round trips a year on this route. The operating cost per dollar of revenue for a small vessel, fully laden, was higher than would be the case for a large ship. But the larger ships were not able to navigate the channel. Operating costs for the two sizes of vessel owned by Macedonian are shown in Exhibit 1.

Less than a year after MS put the Tashtego into service, the port authority of Balik Papan obtained a grant to deepen the harbor channel. Ships of up to 15,000 tons would be able to use the port after the deepening project, which was expected to be completed in September or October of 1965. It would then be possible for the larger vessels of the MS line to serve Balik Papan. The greater carrying capacity of the larger ships should, it was thought, more than compensate for the higher total operating costs of such a vessel. The larger vessels would have to call at Balik Papan at least as frequently as Tashtego in order to fulfill shippers' requirements. If the big ships called at Balik Papan, they would have to stop twice at Singapore, once before Balik Papan and once after. This was because (1) the tapioca had to be transshipped at Singapore, (2) the large vessels were usually too full of cargo on the eastward run to get the tapioca in as well before calling at Singapore, and (3) the cargo to be moved from Singapore to Balik Papan had to be loaded. Whether the company dedicated one large ship to this route or used different ships as necessary as they passed Singapore was not deemed critical to the analysis.

---

* This case is adapted by Professor John Shank of the Amos Tuck School from an earlier version (which is now out of print) written by Professors David Hawkins and John Yeager of the Harvard Business School.

The round trip between Singapore and Balik Papan by the best navigable route was 960 sea miles. At the normal sailing speed of the larger vessels in these waters—16 knots—they required approximately 2 1/2 steaming days. This compares with slightly less than 3 1/2 steaming days for Tashtego.

The larger vessels could carry 6,850 tons of tapioca on each voyage from Balik Papan to Singapore versus 3,950 tons for Tashtego. It was thought that the bookings of manufactured goods that were currently being taken from Singapore to Balik Papan by Tashtego would be the same for the larger vessels. This quantity was based on demand, not capacity. Tashtego was carrying 3,150 tons of manufactured goods on a typical voyage from Singapore to Balik Papan, at an average revenue of $2.70 per ton.

The current freight rate for tapioca was $5.10 per ton for the trip from Balik Papan to Singapore. There appeared to be a stable or increasing demand for the commodity. While the freight rate might go up in the future, it was reasonable to assume that it would not go down.

The turn around time (the period between the ship's arrival at a port and departure from it) at Balik Papan was relatively slow. Because of the inadequacy of the cranage facilities, it would take 3 days to turn one of the large vessels versus 2 1/2 days to turn Tashtego. This difference was caused by the greater amount of cargo to be moved in the larger vessels.

Because of the extensive modern facilities at Singapore, all ships of the size being considered could be turned around in 1 day, regardless of the amounts being loaded or discharged.

ALTERNATIVE USE OF TASHTEGO

Peter Georgopoulis, President of Macedonian, felt he needed to find a new use for Tashtego. The best alternative seemed to be using it as a freight tender between Dar-es-Salaam (in East Africa) and the island of Zanzibar. At present, the large vessels of the line called at both of these ports, incurring port charges as detailed in Exhibit 2. The Macedonian ships used lighters in place of docking in all the ports listed here because it was less expensive and often quicker for the small amounts of cargo involved. The cargo, which consisted of dates and ground nuts from Dar-es-Salaam, and coconuts, copra, and special timbers from Zanzibar, was usually carried to the United States. The freight normally collected on each trip at the two ports amounted to about 1350 tons in Dar-es-Salaam and 2500 tons in Zanzibar. The large vessels were calling 80 times a year at the two ports.

If Tashtego were to be used on this alternative route, it would shuttle the cargo from one of the two ports to the other, so that the large vessel need make only one stop in the area on a given run, thereby saving time and portage dues. The incremental costs which would be incurred by Tashtego at the two ports are summarized in Exhibit 3.

The sailing time between the two ports was very short, and this distance (72 miles) was such that only 1 day (2 days round trip) was involved no matter which vessel is being used. The higher speed of the larger vessels had no noticeable effect over such a short trip. It was thought that an overall savings of 3 days per voyage would be attained by the large vessels (one port call (2 days in either port) and a day of steaming in transit) if Tashtego were used on the Zanzibar/Dar-es-Salaam run. If Tashtego were to be used as a "shuttle," it would be necessary for scheduling purposes to have the larger ships call at the same port each time. Exhibit 4 evaluates which port to eliminate for the large vessels.

Mr. Georgopoulis was anxious to arrive at a decision about whether or not to move Tashtego. An opportunity had arisen to move the ship from Singapore to Zanzibar with a cargo which would cover the cost of moving the ship. As this was a very unusual cargo, it was not thought likely that a similar opportunity would arise before autumn.

He was anxious to keep all the ships as active as possible. The company had a very good reputation among shippers and had therefore been able to fill its ships all the time. In fact, Macedonian was one of very few fully booked shipping lines in the business.

The most recent income statement of the company is shown in Exhibit 5. The year ended December 31, 1963 was considered a typical year for the company.

REQUIRED

The issue in this case is very exotic—should the motor vessel Tashtego be used on the tapioca run between Singapore and Balik Papan in East Asia or as a freight tender between Zanzibar and Dar-es-Salaam in East Africa? This decision hinges on a cost analysis as to which option is more profitable. One issue we will discuss in class is what constitutes a "variable" cost when some costs vary per ton, some per day, some per mile, and some per stop. Other issues we will discuss include the importance of defining the alternatives precisely, the concept of profit contribution per unit of capacity, and the role of cost analysis in helping management to ask the right questions.

In order to help you work through this difficult but also valuable case, the following specific questions should be answered in order. These questions help you develop, piece by piece, an overall analysis of the decision. Try to imagine tackling the case with no specific questions as a guide!

1. How much profit contribution can be earned by carrying 1 ton of tapioca from Balik Papan to Singapore, dock to dock, considering revenue and cargo costs? How much can be earned by carrying 1 ton of general merchandise from Singapore to Balik Papan?

2. Given the contribution/ton figures arrived at in question 1, what is the total contribution which can be earned on one round trip by Tashtego between Singapore and Balik Papan and return? By one of the large vessels?

3. Independent of the amount and type of cargo carried, what are the incremental trip costs of sending Tashtego on a round trip between Singapore and Balik Papan? One of the large vessels?

4. Considering revenue, trip costs, and cargo costs what is the total contribution *per round trip* for each of the vessel types? What is the total contribution *per year* for each of the vessel types?

5. What is the overall profit impact if Tashtego is moved and large vessels are used on the tapioca run? (Hint: Pull your answer to question 4 together with the information in Exhibits 3 and 4.)

6. What actions should Mr. Georgopoulis take? Why? (Hints: 1) What is Macedonian's average profit contribution per shipping day for 1963? 2) Was buying Tashtego to use as a tapioca ship a good investment decision, based on information available at that time?)

EXHIBIT 1
Annual Operating Costs of Vessels

| | Costs Typical for Size of Vessel | |
Item	4,500 Tons	12,500 Tons
Payroll	$143,594	$210,877
Depreciation (straight line, 15 yr. life)	222,956	363,226
Repairs	40,000	47,500
Stores and Provisions	32,657	39,283
Insurance	36,030	46,750
Miscellaneous	12,975	22,525
Total Annual Cost*	$488,212	$730,163
On average, there were 345 operating days in a year, so the cost per operating day was	$1,415	$2,116
In addition, bunkering costs (fuel costs) were incurred amounting to	$0.73 per mile	$1.27 per mile

*In general, these costs were committed one year at a time if a vessel was in use. The costs did not vary depending on cargo or route.

Typically, 2/3 of the cost of a ship could be financed over its depreciable life at rates averaging 5% in 1963.

EXHIBIT 2
Cost of Port calls

Cost Item	Varies with:	Unit	Balik Papan	Singapore	Zanzibar	Dar-es Salaam
Trip Costs						
Portage dues	Tonnage of burden	$/day in port/ ton burden	0.14	0.20	0.13	0.31
Lighthouse	Per trip	$/visit	73.0	126.0	--	62.0
Special Assessment	Per stop	$/visit	--[a]			
Cargo Costs						
Lighterage[b]	Freight moved	$ ton of freight moved	0.25	0.16	0.14	0.15
Stevedoring	Freight moved	$/ton of freight moved	0.56	0.32	0.32	0.32
Cranage	Freight moved	$/ton of freight	--[c]	0.14	0.13	0.13

[a] All ships exceeding 8,000 tons burden were to be assessed $2,000 for each port call (in addition to portage dues). This assessment was intended to contribute to the investment in and maintenance of the new deep channel that these ships required.

[b] Lighterage expense is the cost of having small barges called "lighters" come alongside the vessel anchored in the harbor to facilitate loading and unloading of cargo.

[c] There is no cranage charge at Balik Papan because the freight is manhandled. This considerably increases the charge for stevedoring relative to other ports.

EXHIBIT 3
Costs of Using the Tashtego in East Africa

	Dar-es-Salaam	Zanzibar	Total
1. Trip Costs			
Portage	$1,395[a]	$1.170[b]	
Lighthouse	62	--	
	$1,457 +	$1,170	$ 2,627
Sea Bunkering (.73/mile x 144 mile round trip) =			105
		Total	2,732/trip
Times 69 trips[c]			$188,508/year

2. Additional Cargo Costs on the Dar-es-Salaam Cargo[d]

Total tons/year = (1,350/trip x 80 trips) = 108,000 tons
Unloading costs @ Zanzibar (.14 + .32 + .13) = .59 | 1.18 x 108K tons = $127,440/year
Reloading costs @ Zanzibar (.14 + .32 + .13) = .59 |

Total = $315,948/year

[a] 4,500 tons x .31/day/ton x 1 day = $1,395

[b] 4,500 tons x .13/day/ton x 2 days = $1,170

[c] 345 days (from Exhibit 1)/5 days per trip (2 in Zanzibar + 2 at sea + 1 in Dar-es-Salaam). It is assumed in the case that the decline in customer service in Dar-es-Salaam involved in cutting back from 80 pickups per year to 69 is not a binding consideration.

[d] The same tonnage must be loaded at Dar-es-Salaam per year as now, so the only additional charges are for unloading this Dar-es-Salaam cargo in Zanzibar and for reloading it in Zanzibar onto a large vessel.

EXHIBIT 4
Why the Large Vessels Should Eliminate the Stop at Dar-es-Salaam

Inspection of Exhibit 2 shows that Zanzibar has far cheaper portage dues than Dar-es-Salaam, is at least as cheap in all other cost categories, and has no lighthouse charge. Therefore, at first glance it appears that the Dar-es-Salaam port call should be eliminated for the large vessels. We must be careful, however, because cargo at the eliminated port will have to be doubled handled. If Dar-es-Salaam generates more cargo, *total* cost might be lower if Zanzibar were eliminated. But Zanzibar generates more cargo (2,500 tons per call vs. 1,350 tons). Therefore, without detailed calculation, we can conclude that the large vessels should call at Zanzibar.

Cost savings by having large vessels avoid Dar-es Salaam:

Portage dues (2 day port call)	$7,750[a]
Lighthouse fee	62
	7,812
Bunkerage	91[b]
Total per trip[c]	$7,903
Times 80 trips	$632,240 per year

[a] 12,500 tons x $.31/day/ton x 2 days = $7,750
[b] $1.27/mile x 72 miles = $91
[c] No stevedoring, lighterage or cranage will be saved as the cargo will still have to be loaded onto a ship at Dar-es-Salaam eventually.

EXHIBIT 5
MACEDONIAN SHIPPING COMPANY
Income Statement
for the Year Ended December 31, 1963

Voyage Revenues for the Year	$49,661,000
Voyage Expenses*	33,480,000
Gross Margin	16,181,000
Shore Support and Administrative Expenses	10,234,000
Net Income before Taxes	5,947,000
Income Tax Expense (52%)	3,088,000
Net Income	$2,859,000

*Ship costs, trip costs, and cargo costs.

Trubrite Dyes*

This case is set in 1983 and deals with dyestuffs for textile manufacturing, a well known example of an American industry that is well past its prime. The subject is product line profitability.

Once known in world markets for product dominance, manufacturing innovations, cost and price leadership, and substantial profits, US textile manufacturing by 1983 was growing at less than 1% per year, was only marginally profitable and was operating substantially below capacity. Foreign competition continued to erode the markets for US-produced textile products. Nevertheless, the industry was still huge, accounting for 700,000 jobs and $51 billion in sales in 1983. Monarch Chemical was a leading firm in dyestuffs sold to domestic textile manufacturers.

Monarch, a broad-based chemicals manufacturer, had considered divestiture of its entire dyestuffs business as recently as 1980 because of the obsolescent technologies used, the vast industry overcapacity, the severe price competition, the limited profitability, the possibility of latent toxicology problems, and the fact that Monarch did not have sufficient strength in any segment of the industry. Long run viability required the development either of a product leadership position or a cost leadership position in selected segments as a basis for building sales volumes large enough to generate an acceptable return on the invested capital. Rather than divest the U.S. business, Monarch made the commitment in 1981 to become the low cost producer in selected segments to permit capturing leading sales volume positions. Two major positive features of the dyestuffs business are that the product is essential in textile manufacturing (no substitutes) and is a small factor in final product cost (only a few cents per square yard of fabric). The goal for dyestuffs was cash generation for investment in other, more dynamic, businesses. This case concerns the firm's programs to achieve acceptable profitability in one segment of the dyestuffs business which is still experiencing at least modest growth, Trubrite fabric dyes.

Trubrite dyes. In 1976 Monarch had introduced a new system of fabric dyeing in the product niches it served. The new system used a dramatically different chemical formulation which was patentable. Other firms had collaborated with Monarch in parts of the research and thus were included in some of the patents. This new system was given the brand name "Trubrite" by Monarch. The Trubrite dyes not only exhibited much better color "fastness," but were also technologically superior in terms of "diffusion" rate, "migration" rate, "adsorption" rate, and "solubility," all very important features to textiles manufacturers.

---

* This case was written by Professor John Shank of the Amos Tuck School with the cooperation of a major multinational firm which prefers to remain anonymous. All the information in the case has been disguised.

All shades of fabric color are achieved by blending appropriate proportions of the three primary color dyes; red, blue and yellow. The new Trubrite dye system worked best when all three Trubrite dyes were used together. This presented a dramatic opportunity to sell manufacturers all of the dyestuff required for all three blending colors instead of selling each color separately as had been the practice in the past. Because Trubrite was such a major technological innovation, it achieved widespread market acceptance even though Monarch priced the Trubrite three color system at more than twice the prices for competing dyes. As a result, the achieved margins for the new dyes were very high initially.

All manufacturing of Trubrite dyes was done in one plant which was among the largest dyestuffs manufacturing facilities in the US. This plant had been built in 1956 as a joint venture of three chemical firms, Monarch, Trojan and Ajax.

Yellow Trubrite Dye. Over the late 1970s, Yellow Trubrite (Yellow TB) dye accounted for a steady 65 percent of total sales of yellow dye to customers in this niche. All three of the joint venture partners, Monarch, Ajax and Trojan, shared rights to the Yellow TB dye. Thus, all three were selling an identical product produced at the same factory and purchased at the same price. Monarch had about one-half of this business originally. However, by the end of 1980, price cutting by both Ajax and Trojan had reduced Monarch's penetration to about 25 percent of the business and the downward trend was continuing.

In mid-1981, Monarch undertook a special "blitz" sales campaign, offering customers who would sign up immediately for a one year contract a price of $5.50 per pound versus its previous price of $6.50 (competitors were at about $6.00). Monarch gained a 68 percent share of the business with this ploy which took the competitors completely by surprise. A few months later Monarch announced that it had bought out Ajax and Trojan from the joint venture manufacturing plant. This plant then was solely-owned and was Monarch's only dyestuffs plant. Ajax gave up on the yellow fabric dyes business soon thereafter.

After the one year contracts expired, Trojan moved aggressively to regain the business it had lost. In 1982, Trojan began to manufacture yellow fabric dye at its own facility, a newly constructed plant in which, presumably, they also were trying to achieve cost leadership via large volumes. By 1983, the yellow fabric dye business had become primarily a two competitor race with Trojan and Monarch both using price very aggressively and each possessing about fifty percent of the business. Data on price, volumes and profitability for this segment between 1976 and 1983 are summarized in Exhibit 1 below.

Blue Trubrite Dye. The market for blue fabric dye is split depending on whether or not sensitivity to light is important. For that portion of the business for which this feature is not important, Monarch is not a factor. For the major and growing portion of the business for which light sensitivity is important, the major competitors have been Monarch, Ajax and Spartan. Between 1976 and 1981, Monarch and Ajax shared the

EXHIBIT 1
Yellow Dye

	Industry Volume (000 lbs)	Monarch Volume (000 lbs)	Monarch Share (%)	Monarch Selling Price (per lb)	Monarch Variable Cost (per lb)
1976	225	113	50	$ 7.14	3.00
1977	310	154	50	7.58	2.72
1978	500	251	50	8.00	2.80
1979	880	353	40	7.48	2.62
1980	1850	554	30	6.96	3.20
1981	2214	443*/920	20*/42	6.30*/5.50	3.48
1982	2065	1164	56	4.40	3.70
1983	2637	1285	49	4.24	3.30

* The numbers above the diagonal for 1981 represent the projected figures for the year if price had not been cut at mid-year. The numbers below the diagonal are the actual numbers for the year reflecting the price cuts at mid-year. In the fourth quarter of 1981, penetration actually achieved a 68% figure.

rights to Blue TB and thus were selling exactly the same product manufactured at the same (joint venture) plant. Trojan, the third partner in this plant, had not chosen to compete in the blue dyes business because of patent access complications. The Spartan product (Blue 79) is similar to Blue TB, but somewhat lower in quality. Also, its patent protection is not as secure. Blue 79 is somewhat cheaper to produce (about 10% less than Blue TB).

Through 1980, Blue TB captured about half the business and Blue 79 about half. Monarch and Ajax were roughly comparable on price for Blue TB ($19.00 per lb.) and Spartan was about $1.00 below for Blue 79 ($18.00 per lb.) When Monarch acquired Ajax' share of the joint venture factory in 1981, Monarch was confident that Ajax was dropping out of the Blue TB business. Monarch decided to follow a strategy of meeting Spartan's prices in the marketplace head-on, trying to push technical superiority to achieve 60 percent penetration. In late 1981 Monarch cut price to $18.00 per lb. to meet the Blue 79 price. Spartan nudged price a little below $18.00 and the two way struggle seemed to be underway, but still at a profitable price level. Then the roof fell in!

Ajax, which had lost out to Monarch in the yellow dye business in 1981, did not drop out of the blue dye business when it sold its share of the joint venture manufacturing plant. Instead, it took advantage of the softer patent protection on Blue 79 to begin manufacturing it at another plant. To take away Blue 79 business from Spartan, Ajax used very aggressive price cuts. They cut the price to $14.50 per pound in late 1981, but Spartan matched them. At this point, Monarch held Blue TB at $18.00. By 1983, Ajax had cut Blue 79 all the way to $9.00 per lb. and Spartan had followed.

Monarch had cut Blue TB to $16.40 per lb. by 1983. From a 49% penetration in 1981, Trubrite Blue had dropped all the way to 22% in 1983. Blue TB sales volume was stable and even growing somewhat, but the much lower price for Blue 79 had generated dramatic sales growth in which Monarch was not sharing. At these lower prices, users who don't require the light sensitivity feature began switching to the light sensitive segment anyway. Everyone likes this feature even though it is not critical in all applications. At a low enough price, even those who don't require it will buy it. Data on price, volumes and profitability for this segment for 1981-1983 are summarized in Exhibit 2 below.

Red Trubrite Dye. Trubrite is the clearly superior red product for fabric dyeing. The patents are owned separately by Monarch so neither Trojan nor Ajax had ever had access to red dye manufacturing at the joint venture plant. Up through 1982, Red TB was the high price, high quality, high margin, leading product in this business segment.

The main difficulty with Red TB stems from a change in dyeing technology which has been underway since the late 1970s. By 1983, only about 30% of fabric in the relevant niche was still being dyed by batch processing. Continuous spray dyeing machines were used for 70% of the applications. It was believed in the industry that batch dyeing would remain the preferred method for perhaps 25% of the fabric sold. The continuous spray dyeing machines operate at much lower temperatures. They substitute pressurized spraying for "cooking" as the way to fully impregnate the fabric with the dye. At these lower temperatures, the technical superiority of the Trubrite Red dye is not achieved. Not only are competing products such as Red 66 dye technically comparable in the "cold spray" continuous dyeing machines, they also were priced much lower ($6.60 per lb. in October of 1983 versus $16.70 for Red TB). Even more troublesome was a new Red dye (Red XL) introduced by Spartan in 1983 which seemed to be

EXHIBIT 2
Blue Dye
(Light Sensitive Segment only)

	Industry Volume (000 lbs)	Monarch Volume (000 lbs)	Monarch Share (%)	Monarch Selling Price (per lb)	Ajax Selling Price (per lb)	Monarch Variable Cost (per lb)
1981	907	449	49%	$ 18.00	$ 14.50	$ 6.04
1982	1322	476	36%	16.60	11.00	6.06
1983	2586	573	22%	16.40	9.00	7.22

not just equal but actually technically superior to Red TB in some lower temperature continuous spray dyeing applications. Spartan appeared to be willing to stay close to Monarch's "price umbrella", as they had for blue dyes. They introduced this new Red XL at a $16.00 price per pound. This was still $.70 below the price of Red TB, however.

Trubrite Red was still the leading product for both batch and continuous dyeing applications in late 1983 with more than 40 percent penetration. In fact, Monarch had successfully defended patent infringement suits against both Ajax and Spartan for Red TB, indicating the superiority of this product. However, its penetration was beginning to erode for the continuous applications. A new technology using high temperature spray dyeing (gaining the joint benefits of heat and pressure) was emerging in 1983. This process could reassert the technical superiority of Red TB, were it to gain acceptance. Monarch, in fact, was experimenting with a hot spray dyeing process in its research labs. Equipment manufacturers were also touting new hot spray processes. It thus was not clear that Red TB was in a state of decline. However, implementing a strategy of high volume to achieve cost leadership suggested that pricing for Red TB needed to be carefully evaluated. Complicating this picture was the fact that lower prices did not necessarily move the short run price-volume-profitability trade off in the direction of higher distributable cash generation for a product. Price, volume and profitability data for red fabric dyes for 1981-83 are summarized in Exhibit 3 below.

Trubrite Manufacturing Costs. Another factor to consider in pricing the Trubrite dyes was manufacturing cost performance. In 1983 Monarch's only dyestuffs plant (though fully utilized) was very inefficient by modern standards. Most of the equipment was more than 20 years old. Even though it was generally well maintained, the basic production process had not changed since 1956, and was out of date. During 1983, however, a major consolidation, renovation and modernization program was initiated which was designed to improve yields substantially, to double the output per equipment hour, to cut labor costs dramatically, and to reduce inventory levels significantly. Overall, this program involved a time-phased expenditure of $35 million to generate $14 million per year in savings by 1985. It was felt that this program would give Monarch a cost leadership edge for approximately 4 to 7 years, and perhaps for 8 to 10 years if competitors did not react quickly and could not match the inherent advantages from the large size of Monarch's plant. Still, it had to be acknowledged that the plant was never going to overcome the cost problems typical of any multi-purpose chemicals factory. In 1983 the plant produced and sold 400 different compounds using 100 different basic chemicals drawn from 25 different chemical reaction types. Also, costing individual products was made very difficult by the fact that 2/3 of manufacturing cost (excluding raw material)

EXHIBIT 3
Red Dye

	Industry Volume (000 lbs)	Monarch Volume (000 lbs)	Monarch Share (%)	Monarch Selling Price	Red 66 Selling Price	Red XL Selling Price	Monarch Variable Cost
1981	2053	732	36%	17.50	$ 8.00	$ --	$ 5.22
1982	1914	867	45%	16.60	7.80	--	5.78
1983	2409	1036	43%	16.70	6.60	16.00	6.14

EXHIBIT 4
Trubrite Products Costs (dollars per lb.)

	YELLOW		BLUE		RED	
	V/C	T/C	V/C	T/C	V/C	T/C
1981	$ 3.48	$ 5.28	$ 6.04	$17.02	$ 5.22	$ 8.96
1982	3.70	5.72	6.06	14.52	5.78	9.20
1983	3.30	4.94	7.22	10.00	6.14	8.40

was joint across the entire product line.

Cost data for the three major Trubrite dyes for 1981-83 are summarized in Exhibit 4 below. Variable product cost data (V/C) were already shown in earlier Exhibits. The total cost data (T/C) add on a share of fixed manufacturing expenses allocated to products based on the percentage of attainable capacity dedicated to each product, measured by equipment hours. Attainable capacity was relevant because the manufacturing plant was operating at full capacity in 1983. However, substantial excess capacity had existed as recently as 1981 and could be present again in 1985, after the modernization program was complete.

Other ways of allocating fixed manufacturing expenses to products could produce different product cost figures. The range of such potential variation is suggested by the fact that Trubrite dyes produced twice as much of the profit contribution at the factory in 1983 as the equipment hours utilized would indicate. An old and very tough question is whether overhead should be allocated based on unit volumes, sales dollars or profitability, if at all. It is common (although not necessarily appropriate) to charge heavier overhead to the "winners."

An overall summary of financial results for the dyestuffs business for Monarch for 1983 is shown in Exhibit 5.

ASSIGNMENT QUESTIONS

1. Was the Trubrite dyes product line "successful' in 1983? What measure of success do you consider to be most appropriate?

2. Does this product line meet the "Performance Factor" standard set by Monarch? (See Exhibit 5)

3. How do you reconcile the use of a performance standard based on return on assets with the strategic objective of this business which is "distributable cash generation"? Can you suggest better "management control measures" for Trubrite dyes?

4. Do you believe that pricing is appropriate for the three dyes as of 1984? Consider each dye separately, as well as the overall pricing strategy. Calculate the expected profit impact of any pricing changes you believe appropriate.

5. Evaluate the overall strategic position of the Trubrite dyes in 1984. What strategic issues seem critical at this time?

EXHIBIT 5
Monarch Dyestuffs Financial Summary—1983
($000,000)

Operations:

Sales	$326.0*	
Variable Product Cost	(162.0)	
Variable Expenses (Sales Commission)	(7.6)	
Contribution Margin	156.4	
Fixed Manufacturing Expense	(119.4)	[Plant level mfg. overhead]
Manufacturing Profit	39.0	
Plant-level Selling and Admin. Expense	(18.8)	
Special "startup" Expenses on the Plant Modernization Project	(9.4)	
Allocated Corporate Services	10.0	[$6M of corporate OH less $16M of mfg. cost charged to other divisions]
Plant Level Contribution Before Taxes	$18.8	

Investment (Assets):

Average Accounts Receivable	$30.6
Average Inventories	$106.0
Average Gross Fixed Assets Valued at Current Replacement Value:	
Manufacturing	$205.2
Other	$11.0

Return on Assets (ROA):

Profit Before Taxes ÷ Average Current Assets plus 1/2 of Average Gross Fixed Assets (at current value)
=   18.8/(30.6 + 106.0 + (216.2 ÷ 2))
=   18.8/244.8
=   7.7%

Performance Factor:

=   Percentage Return on Investment versus the 15% Standard
=   7.7/15 = .51

The Plant is only 1/2 as profitable in 1983 as Monarch expects.

---

*Sales exclude the value of domestic production transferred to Monarch affiliates overseas. Sales include export sales and also include sales of some products purchased from outside suppliers. Sales value of domestic production at the plant for 1983 was about $355 million.

Tuck Industries, Inc.*

This case is set in a "mini-conglomerate" in the last years of the "soarin' sixties" when many people still believed that conglomerate mergers added value for shareholders.

"I don't understand. I've got a great new product proposal that can't help but make money, and top management rejects it. No matter whether we price high or low on the new item, we expect to make $130,000, pre-tax. That would contribute eleven cents per share to our earnings after taxes, which is more than the nine cent increase the president touted in last year's annual report. It just doesn't make sense for the president to be talking growth while his subordinates are rejecting profitable projects like this one."

> Nancy Seward, Product Development Manager
> Consumer Products Division
> Tuck Industries

Tuck Industries was created in the 1960s through a series of mergers and acquisitions. Sales revenue grew from $25 million in 1963 to $74 million in 1968. Comparative financial statements for 1967 and 1968 are shown in Exhibits 1 and 2.

Exhibit 1
Comparative Income Statements
(Millions)

	Year Ended December 31	
	1967	*1968*
Sales	$70.7	$74.2
Cost of goods and services sold	54.1	56.3
Gross margin	16.6	17.9
Corporate expenses		
Selling and marketing expenses	8.5	9.0
Corporate and general expenses	2.0	1.8
Interest	0.6	1.0
Total	11.1	11.8
Income before taxes	5.5	6.1
Income tax expense (52%)	2.9	3.2
Net income	$2.6	$2.9
Earnings per share (500,000 and 550,000 shares outstanding, respectively)	$5.27	$5.36

---

*This case is adapted by Professor John Shank of the Amos Tuck School from an earlier version written by Professor James Reece of the University of Michigan.

Exhibit 2
Comparative Balance Sheets
(Millions)

	As of December 31	
Assets	*1967*	*1968*
Cash and temporary investments	$1.4	$1.4
Accounts receivable*	13.7	15.6
Inventories*	22.2	25.5
Plant and equipment:		
Original cost	37.3	45.7
Accumulated depreciation	12.7	16.0
Net	24.6	29.7
Investment in corporate securities	2.1	3.2
Total	$64.0	$75.4
Liabilities and Owners' Equity		
Accounts payable and accruals	$10.9	$13.4
Deferred income taxes	.6	1.0
Long-term debt	12.6	17.0
Total Liabilities	24.1	31.4
Common stock	17.4	19.5
Retained earnings	22.5	24.5
Total Owners' Equity	39.9	44.0
Total	$64.0	$75.4

*

Current Assets, by Division				
1967	Consumer	Industrial	Professional	Total
A/R	5.7	3.0	5.0	13.7
Inventory	12.3	9.9	--	22.2
1968				
A/R	6.2	3.4	6.0	15.6
Inventory	14.1	11.4	--	25.5

Tuck had three divisions, Consumer Products, Industrial Products, and Professional Services, each of which accounted for about one third of total sales. Consumer Products, the oldest of the three divisions, designed, manufactured, and distributed a line of branded kitchen houseware items. It was a very marketing intensive business in which Tuck competed against much larger firms. The Industrial Products division built one-of-a-kind machine tools to customer specifications. It was a large "job shop", with the typical job taking several months to complete. This business competed on a bid basis with other job shops. It had upgraded production facilities substantially in 1968 to compete on higher value jobs. The Professional Services division, the newest of the three, had been added to Tuck in 1966 by acquiring a firm that provided consulting engineering services. This division was growing at a 20% rate since acquisition because of its capability to perform "environmental impact" studies, as required by new federal EPA requirements, on many real estate development projects. This division was investing about 10% of revenue in selling and marketing to try to stimulate even more growth.

Because of the differing nature of their activities, each division was treated as an essentially independent company. There were only a few corporate-level managers and staff people, whose job was to coordinate the activities of the three divisions. One aspect of this coordination was that all proposals requiring capital investment in excess of $250,000 had to be reviewed by the corporate vice president of finance, Mark Hosbein. It was Hosbein who had recently rejected Nancy Seward's new product proposal for which the financial statistics are shown in Exhibit 3.

Exhibit 3
Financial Data For the New Product Proposal in the Consumer Products Division

1. Projected Investment[1]
   Accounts receivable (based on current credit policy for the division) 150,000
   Inventories (variable costs only) 300,000
   Plant and equipment[2] .... <u>550,000</u>
       Total $1,000,000

2. Cost Data:
   Variable cost per unit $3.00
   Incremental division fixed costs (per year)[3] $170,000

[1] Assumes a sales level of 100,000 units.
[2] Annual capacity of 120,000 units.
[3] Includes straight-line depreciation over a 10 year life on new plant and equipment, with a $50,000 salvage value.

3. Price/Market Estimates (per year):

Unit Price	Unit Sales	$ Sales	Profit Before Taxes	Project Margin	Break-even Volume (units)
$6.00	100,000	600,000	$130,000	22%	56,667
8.00	60,000	480,000	130,000	27%	34,000

4. Projected Return:

EPS

PAT	$62,400
Shares Outstanding	550,000
Increase in EPS	$62,400/550,000 = 11¢

Gross Return

$$\text{EBIT} = \frac{130,000}{1,000,000} = 13\%$$
$$\text{Assets}$$

Prior to 1967, each division had been treated as a profit center, with an annual profit budget negotiated between the president and the division general manager. In 1966 Tuck's president, Fred Richards, had become concerned about the impact of asset utilization on the company's profitability. At the urging of Mark Hosbein, Richards had decided to begin treating each division as an investment center, in order to relate profit to the assets used to generate it.

Monthly reports still focused strictly on financial results. But, starting in 1967, each division was evaluated based on "gross return on assets," which was defined to be division EBIT divided by total assets. EBIT for a division was calculated by taking the division's gross margin (which was specifically identified at division level) and then subtracting the division's share of corporate expenses (allocated on the basis of divisional revenues).

Similarly, Tuck's total assets were subdivided among the three divisions. Since each division operated physically separate facilities, it was easy to attribute most assets, including inventory and receivables, specifically. Corporate assets, including the centrally controlled cash account, were allocated to the divisions on the basis of divisional revenues. All fixed assets were recorded at book value (original cost less accumulated straight-line depreciation). Thus the sum of the divisional assets for 1968 was equal to the $75.4 million shown on the corporate balance sheet. Compensation for the general manager and other senior managers in each division was partially tied to gross ROA targets for the division and for the firm as a whole.

For 1968, Hosbein felt that a company like Tuck should have a gross return on assets of at least 12 percent, especially given the interest rates the corporation was paying on its recent borrowings. He had instructed all three division managers that they were expected to earn a gross return of at least 12 percent in 1968. In order to help pull the return up to

| | | | | ASSETS | | | | | |
| | | | | Specific | | | | | |
	Sales	EBIT	Current	Gross Fixed -	Deprec.	= Net Fixed	Allocated	Total	Gross ROA
Consumer	$24.8	$3.6	$20.3	$21.2	$(9.7)	$11.5	$1.6	$33.4	10.8%
Industrial	24.7	2.4	14.8	24.5	(6.3)	18.2	1.5	34.5	7.0%
Professional Services	24.7	1.1	6.0	-----	-----	-----	1.5	7.5	14.7%
Total	$74.2	$7.1	$41.1	$45.7	$(16.0)	$29.7	$4.6	$75.4	9.4%

this level, Hosbein decided that new investment proposals would have to show a "gross return" of at least 15 percent in order to be approved.

In late 1968, Richards put pressure on the general manager of the Industrial Products division to improve ROA, suggesting that this division was not "carrying its share of the load." The division manager had bristled at this comment, saying the division could easily show a higher return "if we had older equipment like Consumer Products does." The president had responded that he did not understand the relevance of the division manager's remark, adding "I don't see any particular reason why the return on an old asset should be higher than that on a new asset."

The 1968 results both disappointed and puzzled Fred Richards. Gross ROA was only 9.4%. The Professional Services division comfortably exceeded the 12 percent gross return target. Consumer Products' gross return was at least "reasonable" at 10.8 percent whereas Industrial Products' showed a dismal 7.0 percent. These calculations are broken down in the above table.

In an informal conversation in mid-1969, Fred Richards expressed his frustrations to Mark Hosbein:

"You know, Mark, I've been a marketer most of my career; but, I always thought I understood financial measures. I've kept the reporting scheme simple, focusing just on profitability because that's how the shareholders judge us, and that's about the only measure common to all three businesses. But in the past year, I've begun to wonder whether our basic measurement system is on target.

"ROA seems like a key measure for us, but none of the division managers seem to take it that seriously. Moreover, there seems to be a lot more tension among our managers since we started tracking ROA. The general manager of Professional Services seems to be doing a good job, and she's happy as a lark about the praise I've given her. But when I urged her to try to get the gross return above 15% for this year, she laughed and said the measure was meaningless to her. And the general manager of Industrial Products looks daggers at me every time we meet. He says I can have either high returns now or a viable business for the long run, but not both. He says he doesn't think I know which I want. And last week, when I was eating lunch with the division manager for Consumer Products, the product development manager came over to our table and really burned my ears over a new product proposal of hers you had rejected. She said since Industrial Products got 95% of the capital spending in 1968, she thought it was unfair not to give Consumer Products more of a chance now.

"To top it off, our banker, who is also our stock registrar, called last week to say that there was some suspicious accumulation of our shares in accounts known to be linked to Billy Bob Justice, the notorious corporate raider. I know our EPS growth has been disappointing, but I can't figure out why a raider would be interested in us. Do you think we need to reevaluate our businesses and how we look at them?"

ASSIGNMENT

1. Based on the information in the case, what is your best estimate of the "gross ROA" for each of the three divisions for 1968? What inferences do you draw?

2. What inferences do you draw from a cash flow statement for 1968? Is a breakdown by divisions useful?

3. What inferences do you draw from the comparative balance sheets and income statements for 1967 and 1968?

4. What is your assessment of the new product proposal from Consumer Products? Was Hosbein wrong to reject it?

5. Why do you suppose a "corporate raider" has taken an interest in Tuck Industries? Be specific as to what Billy Bob sees and what he might do about it.

6. What approach would you suggest for assessing the performance of the three divisions on an on-going basis? Be specific for each division.

7. What other advice do you have for Mr. Richards?

Unitron Corporation*

This case is set in 1974 in a Boston-based "hi-tech" firm which was a pioneer in the "solid state" electronic components that were the basis for "third generation" computers and were the early prototypes for modern integrated circuits. The basic issue is the classic "joint cost" dilemma.

In 1974, Unitron Corporation was only 20 years old, but it had already succeeded in positioning itself as a respected producer of high-quality electronic components. Included among the firm's product lines were rectifiers, thyristors, zeners, diodes, and other high-voltage assemblies. These products represent fundamental electronic components in such fields as minicomputers, process controllers, defense systems, and communications equipment. With sales of $30 million, Unitron was clearly much smaller than the component industry's "Big Three" of Texas Instruments, Fairchild, and Motorola. However, by concentrating on high performance in selected high-quality segments of the market, Unitron had developed into the market leader in many specialty components. This gave the firm a competitive advantage that permitted them to maintain a price-leadership position within these segments.

Rectifiers were a significant product group for Unitron. A rectifier's function is to allow electrical current to pass in one direction while preventing movement in the reverse direction. Its action therefore is similar to that of a valve in fluid mechanics. Exhibit 1 shows the steps in producing a completed rectifier unit which is about 1/2 the size of a cigarette. The value of this product to the final user is primarily determined by two characteristics; the rapidity of response in blocking current reversals and the "surge capacity" or maximum voltage level the rectifier can withstand. Unfortunately, for all manufacturers including Unitron, there is no known method of controlling production procedures to obtain exact electrical characteristics. Each production batch differs from other batches processed under ostensibly the same conditions. Furthermore, within each batch, the individual units do not have precisely the same characteristics. Over many production runs, the distribution of unit characteristics closely resembles a standard "bell curve."

The production process starts by placing a "batch of 50 silicon wafers (purchased from outside suppliers) in a furnace heated to 1,200°C and containing specially prepared metallic gas impurities. By altering the concentration of the impurities, different electrical characteristics can be induced in the wafers. However, an improvement in one characteristic is often accompanied by a decline in another. Also, in spite of strict monitoring of the furnace conditions, small differences in temperature and gas distribution do occur and these variations alter the final products.

---

* This case was prepared by Professor John Shank of the Amos Tuck School. It is adapted from an earlier version written by John Shank, Neil Churchill and Bill Rauwerdink, at Harvard Business School, with the co-operation of Unitrode Corporation, but not based on actual decisions faced by that company.

243

Upon leaving the furnace, each wafer is cut into about 2,000 silicon chips, each approximately the size of a ball-pointpen tip. Exhibit 1 illustrates the production sequence then followed. First a chip is fused between two metal cylinders making a "sandwich." In Step 2 this "chip sandwich" is enveloped in a glass sleeve. In Step 3 this sleeve is heated while in place, forming a molecular bond with the silicon chip. Silver or copper wires are then attached in Step 4. In Step 5, the finished product is painted according to a color code.

The wafers and chips are tested at each step during production for physical and electrical defects. About 60% of the 100,000 chips in a batch reach the end of Step 3. Of that percentage, only one-third or less are eventually sold as part of the regular product line. Another 5,000 units at the lower end of the distribution have limited marketability and are not repairable. Although Unitron did not consider these items to be part of the regular product line, they were offered for sale as "seconds" for use as components in relatively inexpensive and usually disposable items such as toys or small home appliances. No marketing effort was devoted to these "by-product" units. The overall manufacturing process in summarized in Exhibit 2.

Production cost data relating to the rectifier series is reproduced below:

Product Cost Data for 400 Series Rectifiers

			Annual Costs
Batch Costs			
Direct Materials	$2,500		
Direct Labor	1,600		
Variable Overhead	2,300		
Total	$6,400	x 20[1]	$128,000
Nonvariable Rectifier			
Manufacturing Costs[2]			32,000
General Factory Overhead			
Costs[2]			40,000
Total Manufacturing Cost			$200,000

1 Production of 400 Series rectifiers was running at about 20 batches per year.
2 Allocated to 400 Series rectifiers based on direct labor cost.

ACCOUNTING - THE JOINT COST PROBLEM

Whenever production costs are not directly assignable to specific units, cost accounting systems rely on allocation rules to assign the costs to the units. Direct material cost, for example, is usually directly identifiable with individual units. But, equipment depreciation must somehow be allocated to the units produced on that equipment. A "fully allocated cost per unit" is deemed necessary by most companies for purposes of valuing inventory and to create a cost base for use in managerial decision making.

The manufacturing of the silicon "sandwich" by Unitron creates components with differing electrical characteristics and therefore differing sales value, but the manufacturing costs are "joint" with respect to the batch. In other words, there is no way to specifically match any of the costs with any of the individual components produced in one batch. All that can be said is that certain costs are incurred to produce a batch which contains rectifiers with varying electrical characteristics.

There are two common techniques used for allocating such joint costs. The first method is to divide all joint costs by the total number of salable units produced during the process. This method is often called the "average" or "physical unit" approach. It normally yields a different gross margin percentage for each end product since the allocated costs per unit are equal regardless of the sales value per unit.

A second widely used joint cost-allocation method is called the "relative sales value" approach. It assigns costs to units based on each unit's pro-rata share of the total market value of all units produced. For example, if products A, B, and C cost $800 to produce, jointly, and have sales values of $500, $300, and $200, respectively, the allocation of costs to produce B is 30% (300/1000) of $800, or $240. When this method is used, the gross margin percentage for all products is always the same. Exhibit 3 shows some common examples of the joint cost problem and a more detailed example of the two main methods of accounting for joint costs.

THE BUSINESS PROBLEMS

Exhibit 4 lists sales prices and present inventory levels for the 400 series rectifiers, along with projected annual sales and production. The breakdown of products per batch remains fairly constant from batch to batch.

Helen Barnes, a recent MBA graduate, was just beginning a 6 month training assignment as assistant to Unitron's sales manager, Jim Jacoby. He called her attention one morning to an order for 6,000 units of series 401 rectifiers which had just been received. While many of the product lines were not inventoried, rectifiers normally were. However, very few of the 401 units were currently available in inventory. To satisfy the customer's needs, the order had to be filled with units that met or exceeded the specifications of the product ordered. The customer was perfectly willing to accept rectifiers whose performance characteristics exceeded the minimum specified levels; however, the customer was not willing to pay for the extra quality.

Jim Jacoby asked Helen which would be better for Unitron:

1. to fill out the order with 402 rectifiers,
2. to trigger a production run in order to be able to fill the order with 401s,
3. to turn down the order because of the "out of stock" condition.

If additional production were authorized, inventory levels of other units would obviously go up. Jacoby was concerned about this because his performance was evaluated partly in terms of the profits generated by the rectifier lines after deducting a charge for inventory carrying cost. Besides the chance of inventoried rectifiers becoming obsolete in the marketplace, the higher level of inventory would tie up more cash. Jacoby was charged carrying costs of 2% a month on all inventory. He liked to keep inventory at no more than one month's sales, because he thought a turnover ratio of 12 times was a good compromise between stockout risk and excess investment.

After discussing this order, Jacoby also asked Barnes for her opinion about an offer which had recently been received from a local toy company to purchase 4,000 of the Series 400 "seconds" units each month at a price of $.15 per unit. The toy company was willing to sign a firm contract calling for 48,000 units during the next year. Jacoby said the production manager was against accepting this business at what he called a "giveaway price." He had said that $.15 wouldn't even cover the out-of-pocket expenses of $.32 per unit and that no one in their right mind would tie themselves down to a long-run contract at a price which didn't even cover the variable costs. Jacoby, however, was bothered by the growing accumulation of inventory of the seconds, even though they were carried at zero inventory value (see Exhibit 4). He asked Helen whether she agreed with the production manager that he was being naive to think of the $.15 as pure profit just because of the zero inventory value assigned to these units by the cost accounting department.

Another problem Jacoby was considering involved a one-time Defense Department request for bids on 100,000 units of the 404 Series rectifiers. The request asked for a "cost plus" bid, but Jim was not sure what "cost " was. He felt sure the government was expecting bids at something less than Unitron's list price of $.80 per unit. Probably, $.75 was close to what the government was expecting to pay, per unit. Delivery was to be scheduled over eighteen months, at about 5500 units per month.

Unitron did not want to be too heavily dependent on government business and had worked hard to bring the mix of business up to 75% commercial/ 25% government in 1974. But this bid was for work on a prestigious new defense system which could be good for Unitron's reputation, if costs and prices could be worked out.

ASSIGNMENT

1. In a period which began with zero inventories, how should Unitron assign the production output (400,000 units) of 20 batches to the sales orders (400,000 units)? The idea here is to construct a "produced as/sold as" matrix.

2. Compute the per unit costs for rectifiers in the 400 series under an average costing system and under a relative sales value system.

3. A. What would be the revenue, cost, and profit if the order for 6000 401's were accepted for immediate shipment:

    — under a physical unit costing system
    — under a relative sales value costing system.

   B. What should Helen Barnes recommend to Jim Jacoby regarding this order? Why?

4. What should she recommend regarding the offer from the toy company?

5. Which method of allocating joint costs should Unitron use? Which method yields better data for decision-making? Consider the behavioral implications of the two different approaches.

6. A government purchasing agent has just inquired again about the "cost plus" purchase contract for 100,000 404's. The contracting official had stated that a 10% profit margin would probably be allowable, if the price were "right" ($.75, or so). How much is the "cost"? What are your thoughts about price and manufacturing strategy for this possible contract? Assuming excess manufacturing capacity is available, would you recommend bidding on this contract? If so, at what price?

EXHIBIT 1

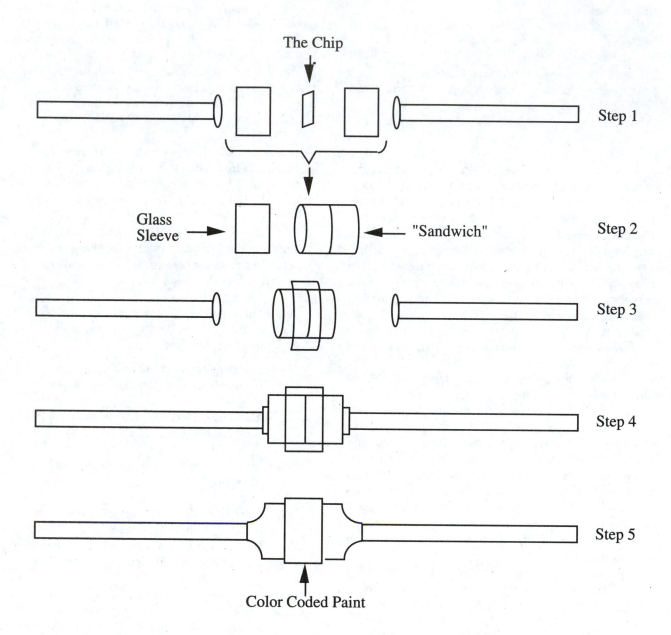

The Chip

Glass Sleeve → "Sandwich"

Step 1
Step 2
Step 3
Step 4
Step 5

Color Coded Paint

EXHIBIT 2

The Manufacturing Process

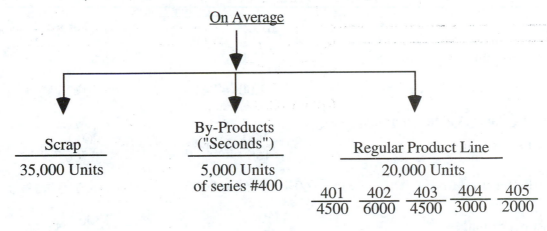

Purchased Raw Material
(50 Silicon Wafers)

Bake at 1200° C with Special Gasses

Cut into 100,000 Very Small Chips

Manufacture a "Chip Sandwich"
(Lose 40,000 Chips in Manufcturing)

Test 60,000 Chips for Electrical Characteristics

(There is a Random Distribution of Product Specifications)

On Average

Scrap	By-Products ("Seconds")	Regular Product Line				
35,000 Units	5,000 Units of series #400	20,000 Units				
		401	402	403	404	405
		4500	6000	4500	3000	2000

EXHIBIT 3

The <u>Joint Cost</u> Problem

<u>All</u> manufacturing (or service) costs apply jointly to all of the products (services). There is no way to specifically identify costs with each specific product (service).

Examples

Oil Refinery	(Gasoline/ Diesel/ Heating oil/ Jet Fuel)
Railroads or Airlines	(Passengers/ Freight/ Mail)
Postal Service	(Home mail/ Bulk mail/ Packages)
Slaughterhouse	(Steak/ Roasts/ Hamburger)
Mining	(High grade ore/ Low grade ore)
Batch Process Electronic Components	

Two Major Accounting Methods

1. Physical Unit Approach
2. Relative Sales Value Approach

A Simple Example (Butchering a Cow)

<u>Joint Costs:</u>			
	The Cow	$580	
	Labor Cost	$160	(8 hours x $20/hour)
	Depreciation on the butcher knife & table	$10	
	Total Cost	$750	

Meat Produced =	300 pounds of hamburger (which sells for $2.00/lb.)
	200 pounds of steak (which sells for $4.50/lb.)
	500 pounds ($1500 sales value)

<u>Physical Unit Approach</u>

Cost = $750
Meat produced = 500 pounds

	Cost Per Pound	
	<u>Steak</u>	<u>Hamburger</u>
Cost/pound (for all meat)	$1.50	$1.50
Profit/pound (% of Sales)	$3.00 (67%)	.50 (25%)

<u>Relative Sales Value Approach</u>

	Steak	Hamburger
% of sales value	$\frac{900}{1500} = 60\%$	$\frac{600}{1500} = 40\%$
Cost allocation	60% x $750 = $450	40% x 750 = $300
Cost per pound	$\frac{$450}{200} = 2.25	$\frac{$300}{300} = 1.00
Profit per pound (% of Sales)	2.25 (50%)	1.00 (50%)

EXHIBIT 4
Series 400 Rectifiers

Product	Blockage	Maximum Voltage (volts)	Annual Sales Orders (units)	Sales Price/Unit	Current Inventory (units)	Annual Production (units)
401	.25-.74	300	100,000	$ .40	3,000	90,000
402	.75-1.24	400	140,000	.60	10,000	120,000
403	1.25-1.74	500	100,000	.70	9,000	90,000
404	1.75-2.24	600	40,000	.80	8,000	60,000
405	2.25-2.75	700	20,000	1.00	5,000	40,000
			400,000		35,000	400,000

A typical batch also yields 5,000 of the lower-quality "by-product" units which Unitron offered for sales as "seconds." Demand for the "seconds" fluctuated widely and was very price-sensitive. Unitron offered these units at a price of $.25 each, but sales had been very slow during the past year. An inventory of 65,000 units had accumulated. By-products like these units were not considered to be part of the regular product line, and were not assigned an inventory value. Whatever revenue they generated was considered miscellaneous income and was offset against cost of goods sold for financial statement purposes.

Wellington Chemicals Division*

This case is set in 1965 in a division of a major UK-based chemicals firm. The issue is make versus buy for packaging containers. The container is technologically advanced and is an important element of the value of the end product to the customer.

The Wellington Chemicals Division manufactures and sells a range of "hard to hold" chemical products throughout Great Britain. Since these products require careful packing and storing, the company has always made a feature of the special properties of the containers it uses. In fact, a major element of Wellington's marketing strategy is its container. The containers are large steel drums with a unique patented lining made from a specialty chemical known as GHL. The firm operates a department especially to maintain its containers in good condition and to make new ones to replace those that are past repair.

Mr. Walsh, the division general manager, has for some time suspected that the firm might save money, and get equally good service, by buying its containers from an outside source. After careful inquiries, he approached a firm specializing in container production, Packages, Ltd., and asked for a quotation. At the same time, he asked Mr. Dyer, his chief accountant, to provide him with an up-to-date statement of the cost of operating the container department.

Within a few days, the quotation from Packages, Ltd. came in. The firm was prepared to supply all the new containers required—at that time running at the rate of 3,000 per year—for L125,000 per year, the contract to run for a guaranteed term of five years and thereafter to be renewable from year to year. If the required number of containers increased, the contract price would be increased proportionally. Additionally, and irrespective of whether the above contract was concluded or not, Packages, Ltd. would undertake to carry out purely maintenance work on containers, short of replacement, for a sum of L37,500 per year, on the same contract terms.

Mr. Walsh compared these figures with the cost figures prepared by Mr. Dyer, covering a year's operation of the container department of Wellington Chemicals Division, which were as follows:

Materials (mostly steel and GHL)		L 70,000
Labor		
Foreman		5,000
Workers		45,000
Department Overheads		
Manager's Salary	L 8,000	
Rent on Container Dept. Facility	4,500	
Depreciation of Machinery	15,000	
Maintenance of Machinery	3,600	
Other Expenses	15,750	
		46,850
		L 166,850
Proportion of General Administrative Overheads		22,500
Total Cost of Department for One Year		L 189,350

---

* This case is adapted from an earlier case called Liquid Chemical Company written by Professor David Solomons of the Wharton School.

Walsh's conclusion was that no time should be lost in closing the department and in entering into the contracts offered by Packages, Ltd. However, he felt bound to give the manager of the department, Mr. Duffy, an opportunity to question this conclusion before he acted on it. He therefore called him in and put the facts before him, at the same time making clear that Mr. Duffy's own position was not in jeopardy—even if his department were closed, there was another managerial position shortly becoming vacant to which he could be moved without loss of pay or prospects.

Mr. Duffy looked thoughtful throughout their conversation and asked for time to think the matter over. The next morning, he asked to speak with Mr. Walsh again and said he thought there were a number of considerations that ought to be borne in mind before his department was closed.

"For instance," he said, "what will you do with the drum making machinery? It cost L120,000 four years ago, but you'd be lucky if you got L20,000 for it now, even though it's good for another four years at least. And then there's the stock of GHL we bought a year ago. We bought a five year supply in order to be able to buy directly from the manufacturer and we paid L100,000. Dyer's figure of L70,000 for materials probably includes about L20,000 for GHL. But it'll be tricky stuff to handle if we don't use it up. We bought it for L500 a ton, and you couldn't buy it today for less than L600. But you wouldn't have more than L400 a ton left if you sold it, after you'd covered all the handling expenses."

Walsh thought that Dyer ought to be present during this discussion. He called him in and put Duffy's points to him. "I don't much like all this conjecture," Dyer said. "I think my figures are pretty conclusive. Besides, if we are going to have all this talk about 'what will happen if,' don't forget the problem of space we're faced with. We're paying L8,500 a year in hire purchase fees for a warehouse a few kilometers away from our plant. If we closed Duffy's department, we'd have all the space we need without that warehouse."

"That's a good point," said Walsh, "though I must say I'm a bit worried about the workers if we close the department. I don't think we can find room for any of them elsewhere in the firm. I could see whether Packages, Inc. can take any of them. But some of then are getting on. There's Walters and Hines, for example. They've been with us since they left school 40 years ago. I'd feel bout to give them pensions—L1,500 a year each, say."

Duffy showed some relief at this. "But I still don't like Dyer's figures," he said. "What about this L22,500 for general administrative overhead? You surely don't expect to sack anyone in the general office if I'm closed, do you?" "Probably not," said Dyer, "but someone has to pay for these costs. We can't ignore them when we look at an individual department, because if we do that with each department in turn, we shall finish up by convincing ourselves that directors, accountants, typists, stationery, and the like don't have to be paid for. And they do, believe me."

"Well, I think we've thrashed this out pretty fully," said Walsh, "but I've been turning over in my mind the possibility of perhaps keeping on the maintenance work ourselves. What are your views, Duffy?

"I don't know," said Duffy, "but it's worth looking into. We shouldn't need any machinery for that, and I could hand supervision over to the foreman. You'd save L3,000 a year there, say. You'd only need about one-fifth of the workers, but your could keep on the oldest. You wouldn't save any space, so I suppose the hire purchase fees would be the same. I shouldn't think the other expenses would be more than L6,500 a year." "What about materials?" asked Walsh. "We use about 10 percent of the GHL on maintenance," Duffy replied, "and not much else."

"Well, I've told Packages, Ltd. that I'd let them know my decision within a week," said Walsh. "I'll let you know what I decide to do before I write to them."

ASSIGNMENT

One common approach in analyzing a situation like this is to prepare a comprehensive, multi-year cash flows schedule for the various options. This requires careful attention to differential cash flows, a relevant time frame, inflation, taxation, and time value of money. If you choose this approach, be careful in carrying it through comprehensively and in considering what inferences it will support.

If you choose some other cost analysis approach, be sure you are clear as to why you are not doing a multi-year cash flow analysis.

What conclusions do you draw from your cost analysis? What recommendation would you make to Mr. Walsh? Why?